Undergraduate Topics in Computer Science

'Undergraduate Topics in Computer Science' (UTiCS) delivers high-quality instructional content for undergraduates studying in all areas of computing and information science. From core foundational and theoretical material to final-year topics and applications, UTiCS books take a fresh, concise, and modern approach and are ideal for self-study or for a one- or two-semester course. The texts are authored by established experts in their fields, reviewed by an international advisory board, and contain numerous examples and problems, many of which include fully worked solutions.

The UTiCS concept centers on high-quality, ideally and generally quite concise books in softback format. For advanced undergraduate textbooks that are likely to be longer and more expository, Springer continues to offer the highly regarded *Texts in Computer Science* series, to which we refer potential authors.

Gerard O'Regan

Guide to Software Project Management

 Springer

Gerard O'Regan
Mallow, Ireland

ISSN 1863-7310   ISSN 2197-1781 (electronic)
Undergraduate Topics in Computer Science
ISBN 978-3-031-80577-6   ISBN 978-3-031-80578-3 (eBook)
https://doi.org/10.1007/978-3-031-80578-3

This Springer imprint is published by the registered company Springer Nature Switzerland AG
The registered company address is: Gewerbestrasse 11, 6330 Cham, Switzerland

In memory of Prof./Dr. Mícheál Mac An Airchinnigh Requiescat in pace

Preface

Overview

The objective of this book is to provide a concise introduction to software project management in a professional and ethical software engineering environment to students and practitioners. The key principles of project management are discussed, and the goal is to give the reader an appreciation of the fundamentals of the field, as well as guidance on how to apply the theory in an ethical software engineering environment.

Organization and Features

Chapter 1 presents a broad overview of software engineering, and discusses various software lifecycles and the phases in traditional software development. We discuss requirements gathering and specification, software design, implementation, testing and maintenance. The lightweight Agile methodology is discussed and it is mainstream in software engineering.

Chapter 2 discusses professional responsibility in software engineering, and we discuss the code of ethics of various bodies such as the British Computer Society, Institute of Electrical and Electronic Engineers and the Association of Computing Machinery. Chapter 3 discusses ethical software engineering and we discuss notable failures such as the space shuttle disaster and the defective Therac-25 radiotherapy machine.

Chapter 4 discusses legal, ethical and professional responsibilities of project managers. Project managers have a professional responsibility in their work and are accountable for the actions that they take or fail to take. They are required to behave ethically with their clients, and to be aware of their legal and ethical responsibilities during the project.

Chapter 5 provides an overview of software project management, and we discuss project estimation, project planning and scheduling, project monitoring and control, risk management, managing communication and change, and managing project quality. We conclude with a discussion of well-known project management methodologies such as Prince 2 and Project Management Professional.

Chapter 6 discusses software project planning, and we discuss activities such as project initiation, effort estimation, project planning and scheduling, and risk identification. We discuss the preparation and evaluation of the business case to determine if the project makes business sense, and the composition of the project board.

Chapter 7 discusses risk management, and we discuss activities such as risk identification, risk analysing and evaluation, identifying responses to the risk, selecting and implementing a response, and managing risks throughout the project lifecycle. We conclude with a case study on risk management in dealing with the COVID-19 pandemic.

Chapter 8 discusses software quality management for projects, and it is essential that the software be of high quality, as well as being safe, reliable and fit for purpose. We discuss software inspections, testing, audits, quality reviews and lessons learned, as well as process maturity frameworks such as the CMMI and ISO 9000. We discuss various problem-solving tools to support quality management, including fishbone diagrams, histograms, pareto charts, and trend charts.

Chapter 9 discusses project monitoring and control, which involves monitoring project execution against the plan, and taking corrective action when progress deviates from expectations. It involves monitoring the project activities and checking that they are completed on schedule and with the required quality, and re-planning where appropriate.

Chapter 10 is concerned with software outsourcing and we discuss the selection and management of a software supplier. We consider how candidate suppliers may be identified, formally evaluated against selection criteria, and how the appropriate supplier is selected. We discuss how the selected supplier is managed during the project, and consider legal and ethical aspects of outsourcing.

Chapter 11 is concerned with the activities during project closure, which includes the successful completion of the customer acceptance testing and the handover of the software to the customer. It involves the preparation of the lessons learned report and the end project report.

Chapter 12 discusses software configuration management and discusses the fundamental concept of a baseline. Configuration management is concerned with identifying those deliverables that are subject to change control, and controlling changes to them.

Chapter 13 discusses project management in the Agile world, where Agile is a popular lightweight approach to software development. Agile provides opportunities to assess the direction of a project throughout the development lifecycle, and ongoing changes to requirements are considered normal in the Agile world.

Chapter 14 is concerned with project metrics and we discuss the balanced score card which assists in identifying appropriate metrics for the organization. The Goal, Question, Metrics (GQM) approach is discussed, and this allows appropriate metrics related to the organization goals to be defined. A selection of sample metrics for project management is presented.

Chapter 15 discusses various tools to support project management. We discuss the Cocomo estimating approach developed by Barry Boehm in the late 1970s. We discuss the ProjectLibre tool that is an alternative to Microsoft Project. We also discuss Project Manager, Jira and Planview.

Chapter 16 discusses continuous improvement of project management. It begins with a discussion of a software process, and we discuss the benefits that may be gained from a software process improvement initiative. We discuss several models that support software process improvement such as the Capability Maturity Model Integration (CMMI) and ISO 9000. We discuss best practice in project management from methodologies such as Prince2, Project Management Professional (PMP) and the CMMI.

Chapter 17 is the concluding chapter in which we summarize the journey that we have travelled in this book.

Audience

The main audience of this book are computer science students who are interested in learning about professional and ethical software project management, and in learning on how to build high quality and reliable software on time and on budget. It will also be of interest to industrialists including project managers, software engineers, quality professionals and software managers, as well as the motivated general reader.

Mallow, Ireland   Gerard O'Regan

Acknowledgments

I am deeply indebted to family and friends who supported my efforts in this endeavour, and my thanks, as always, to the team at Springer. I would like to pay a special tribute to my late friend and Ph.D. advisor, Prof./Dr. Micheál Mac an Airchinnigh of Trinity College Dublin, who introduced me to the world of formal methods and the Irish school of VDM, and for sharing many happy times during the Trinity years. Mícheál had great wit and charisma and a wonderful sense of humour. He was a great orator and I recall a very entertaining after dinner speech at a Formal Methods Europe conference at Odense, Denmark many years ago where he joked "Why am I Aristotelian? Well, my wife is and I can't be Platonic with her." *Requiescat in pace.*

Cork, Ireland   Gerard O'Regan

Contents

Abbreviations

AC	Actual Cost
ACM	Association Computing Machinery
AECL	Atomic Energy of Canada Limited
BCS	British Computer Society
BSC	Balanced Score Card
BSI	British Standards Institute
CBA/IPI	CMM Based Appraisal/Internal Process Improvement
CCB	Change Control Board
CEI	Computer Ethics Institute
CMM®	Capability Maturity Model
CMMI®	Capability Maturity Model Integration
COCOMO	Constructive Cost Model
COPQ	Cost of Poor Quality
COTS	Customized Off the Shelf
CPAL	Common Public Attribution License
CPI	Cost Performance Index
CR	Change Request
CSR	Corporate Social Responsibility
CV	Cost Variance
DoS	Denial of Service
DPIA	Data Privacy Impact Assessment
DSA	Digital Services Act
DSDM	Dynamic Systems Development Method
ESA	European Space Agency
ESI	European Software Institute
EULA	End User License Agreement
EV	Earned Value
EVA	Earned Value Analysis
EVA	Economic Value Added
FDA	Food and Drug Administration
FMEA	Failure Mode and Effects Analysis
FOSS	Free Open Source Software

FSF	Free Software Foundation
FSM	Functional Size Measurement
GDPR	General Data Packet Regulation
GNU	GNU's Not Unix
GPL	General Public License
GQM	Goal, Question, Metric
GUI	Graphical User Interface
IBM	International Business Machines
IEC	International Electro Technical Commission
IEEE	Institute of Electrical and Electronic Engineers
IFPUG	International Function Point User Group
IRR	Internal Rate of Return
ISACA	Information Systems Audit and Control Association
ISEB	Information System Examination Board
ISO	International Standards Organization
ISP	Internet Service Provider
ISTQB	International Software Testing Qualifications Board
IT	Information Technology
JAD	Joint Application Development
KLOC	Thousand Lines of Code
LCL	Lower Control Limit
LOC	Lines of Code
MTBF	Mean Time Between Failure
MTTR	Mean Time to Repair
NASA	National Aeronautics and Space Administration
NATO	North Atlantic Treaty Organization
NHS	National Health Service
NPV	Net Present Value
PCE	Phase Containment Effectiveness
PDCA	Plan, Do, Check, Act
PM	Project Manager
PMBOK	Project Management Book of Knowledge
PMI	Project Management Institute
PMO	Project Management Office
PMP	Project Management Professional
PPM	Project Portfolio Management
Prince	Projects in a Controlled Environment
PSP	Personal Software Process
PV	Planned Value
PVCS	Polytron Version Control System
QCC	Quality Control Circle
RAD	Rapid Application Development
RAG	Red, Amber, Green
RAID	Risk, Assumption, Issue, Dependency
RFP	Request for Proposal

ROI	Return on Investment
RUP	Rational Unified Process
SCAMPI	Standard CMMI Appraisal Method for Process Improvement
SCM	Software Configuration Management
SEI	Software Engineering Institute
SG	Specific Goal
SLA	Service Level Agreement
SLOC	Source Lines of Code
SOW	Statement of Work
SP	Specific Practice
SPC	Statistical Process Control
SPI	Schedule Performance Index
SPI	Software Process Improvement
SPICE	Software Process Improvement Capability dEtermination
SQA	Software Quality Assurance
SRB	Solid Rocket Booster
SV	Schedule Variance
TDD	Test Driven Development
TDI	Turbo-Charged Direct Injection
TQM	Total Quality Management
TSP	Team Software Process
UAT	User Acceptance Testing
UCL	Upper Control Limit
UK	United Kingdom
UML	Unified Modelling Language
URS	User Requirements Specification
VDM	Vienna Development Method
VSS	Visual Source Safe
WBS	Work Breakdown Structure
XP	Extreme Programming
Y2K	Year 2000
ZD	Zero Defects

List of Figures

List of Tables

Fundamentals of Software Engineering

1

Key Topics

Standish chaos report
Software lifecycles
Waterfall model
Spiral model
Rational unified process
Agile development
Software inspections
Software testing
Project management

1.1   Introduction

The approach to software development in the 1950s and 1960s has been described as the *"Mongolian Hordes Approach"* by Fred Brooks [1].[1] The "method" or lack of method was applied to projects that were running late, and it involved adding many inexperienced programmers to the project, with the expectation that this would allow the project schedule to be recovered. However, this approach was deeply flawed as it led to programmers with inadequate knowledge of the project attempting to solve problems, and they inevitably required significant time from the other project team members.

---

[1] The "Mongolian Hordes" management myth is the belief that adding more programmers to a software project that is running late will allow catch-up. In fact, as Brooks says, adding people to a late software project makes it even later.

G. O'Regan, *Guide to Software Project Management*, Undergraduate Topics in
Computer Science, https://doi.org/10.1007/978-3-031-80578-3_1

This resulted in the project being delivered even later, as well as subsequent problems with quality (i.e., the approach of throwing people at a problem does not work). The philosophy of software development back in the 1950/60s was characterized by

The completed code will always be full of defects.

The coding should be finished quickly to correct these defects.

Design as you code approach.

This philosophy accepted defeat in software development, and suggested that irrespective of a solid engineering approach, that the completed software would always contain lots of defects, and that it therefore made sense to code as quickly as possible, and to then identify the defects that were present, and to correct them as quickly as possible to solve a problem.

In the late 1960s it was clear that the existing approaches to software development were deeply flawed, and that there was an urgent need for change. The NATO Science Committee organized two famous conferences to discuss critical issues in software development [2]. The first conference was held at Garmisch, Germany, in 1968, and it was followed by a second conference in Rome in 1969. Over 50 people from 11 countries attended the Garmisch conference, including Edsger Dijkstra, who did important theoretical work on formal specification and verification. The NATO conferences highlighted problems that existed in the software sector in the late 1960s, and the term *"software crisis"* was coined to refer to these. There were problems with budget and schedule overruns, as well as problems with the quality and reliability of the delivered software.

The conference led to the birth of *software engineering* as a discipline in its own right, and the realization that programming is quite distinct from science and mathematics. Programmers are like engineers in that they build software products, and they therefore need education in traditional engineering as well as in the latest technologies. The education of a classical engineer includes product design and mathematics. However, often computer science education places an emphasis on the latest technologies, rather than on the important engineering foundations of designing and building high-quality products.

Programmers therefore need to learn the key engineering skills to enable them to build products that are safe for the public to use. This includes a solid foundation on design and on the mathematics required for building safe software products. Mathematics plays a key role in classical engineering, and in some situations, it may also assist software engineers in the delivery of high-quality software products. Several mathematical approaches to assist software engineers are described in [3].

There are parallels between the software crisis in the late 1960s, and serious problems with bridge construction in the nineteenth century. Several bridges collapsed, or were delivered late or over-budget, since people involved in their design and construction did not have the required engineering knowledge. This

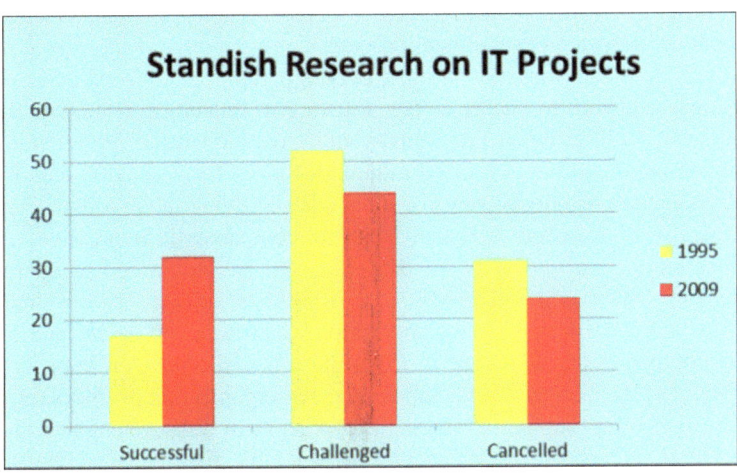

Fig. 1.1 Standish report—results of 1995 and 2009 survey

led poorly designed and constructed bridges that collapsed with loss of life, as well as endangering the lives of the public.

This led to legislation requiring engineers to be licensed by the Professional Engineering Association prior to practicing as engineers. This organization specified a core body of knowledge that the engineer is required to possess, and the licensing body verifies that the engineer has the required qualifications and experience. This helps to ensure that only personnel competent to design and build products actually do so. Engineers have a professional responsibility to ensure that the products are properly built and are safe for the public to use.

The Standish group has conducted research (Fig. 1.1) on the extent of problems with IT projects since the mid-1990s. These studies were conducted in the United States, but there is no reason to believe that European or Asian companies perform any better. The results indicate serious problems with on-time delivery of projects, and projects being cancelled prior to completion.[2] However, the comparison between 1995 and 2009 suggests that there have been some improvements with a greater percentage of projects being delivered successfully, and a reduction in the percentage of projects being cancelled.

Fred Brooks argues that software is inherently complex, and that there is no *silver bullet* that will resolve all the problems associated with software development such as schedule or budget overruns [1, 4]. Poor software quality can lead to defects in the software that may adversely impact the customer, and even lead

---

[2] These are IT projects covering diverse sectors, including banking, telecommunications, etc., rather than pure software companies. Software companies following maturity frameworks such as the CMMI generally achieve more consistent results.

to loss of life. It is therefore essential that sufficient emphasis is placed on quality throughout the software development process.

The Y2K problem was caused by a two-digit representation of dates, and it required major rework to enable legacy software to function for the new millennium. Clearly, well-designed programs would have hidden the representation of the date, which would have required minimal changes for year 2000 compliance. Instead, companies spent vast sums of money in rectifying the problem.

The quality of software produced by some companies is impressive.[3] These companies employ mature software processes and are committed to continuous improvement. There is a lot of industrial interest in software process maturity models for software organizations, and various approaches to assess and mature software companies are described in [5].[4] These models focus on improving the effectiveness of the management, engineering, and organization practices related to software engineering, and in introducing best practice in software engineering. The use of mature software processes enables high-quality software to be consistently produced.

1.2   What is Software Engineering?

Software engineering involves the multi-person construction of multi-version programs. The IEEE 610.12 definition of Software Engineering is

> *Software engineering is the application of a systematic, disciplined, quantifiable approach to the development, operation, and maintenance of software; that is, the application of engineering to software, and the study of such approaches.*

Software engineering includes

1. Methodologies to design, develop, and test software to meet customers' needs.
2. Software is engineered. That is, the software products are properly designed, developed, and tested in accordance with engineering principles.
3. Quality and safety are properly addressed.
4. Mathematics may be employed to assist with the design and verification of software products. The level of mathematics employed will depend on the *safety-critical* nature of the product. Systematic peer reviews and rigorous

---

[3] I recall projects at Motorola that regularly achieved 5.6σ level of quality in a L4 CMM environment (i.e., approx. 20 defects per million lines of code. This represents very high quality).

[4] Approaches such as the CMMI focus mainly on the management and organizational practices required in software engineering. The emphasis is on defining software processes that are fit for purpose (the models provide useful information on practices to consider in the implementation) and consistently following them. The process maturity models focus on what needs to be done rather how it should be done, and this gives the organization the freedom to choose the appropriate implementation to meet its needs.

testing will often be sufficient to build quality into the software, with heavy *mathematical techniques reserved for safety and security critical software.*

5. Sound project management and quality management practices are employed.
6. Support and maintenance of the software are properly addressed.

Software engineering is not just programming. It requires the engineer to state precisely the requirements that the software product is to satisfy, and then to produce designs that will meet these requirements. The project needs to be planned and delivered on time and budget. The requirements must provide a precise description of the problem to be solved: i.e., *it should be evident from the requirements what is and what is not required.*

The requirements need to be rigorously reviewed to ensure that they are stated clearly and unambiguously and reflect the customer's needs. The next step is then to create the design that will solve the problem, and it is essential to validate the correctness of the design. Next, the software code to implement the design is written, and peer reviews and software testing are employed to verify and validate the correctness of the software.

The verification and validation of the design is rigorously performed for safety-critical systems, and it is sometimes appropriate to employ mathematical techniques for these systems. However, it will often be sufficient to employ peer reviews or software inspections as these methodologies provide a high degree of rigour. This may include approaches such as Fagan inspections [6], Gilb inspections [7], or Prince 2's approach to quality reviews [8].

The term "*engineer*" is a title that is awarded on merit in classical engineering, and is generally applied only to people who have attained the necessary education and competence to be called engineers, and who base their practice on classical engineering principles. The title places responsibilities on its holder to behave professionally and ethically. Often in computer science the term "*software engineer*" is employed loosely to refer to anyone who builds things, rather than to an individual with a core set of knowledge, experience, and competence.

Several computer scientists (such as Parnas[5]) have argued that computer scientists should be educated as engineers to enable them to apply appropriate scientific principles to their work. They argue that computer scientists should receive a solid foundation in mathematics and design to have the professional competence in building high-quality products that are safe for the public to use. The use of mathematics is an integral part of the engineer's work in other engineering disciplines, and so the *software engineer* should be able to use mathematics to assist in the modelling or understanding of the behaviour or properties of the proposed software system.

---

[5] Parnas has made important contributions to computer science. He advocates a solid engineering approach with the extensive use of classical mathematical techniques in software development. He also introduced information hiding in the 1970s, which is now a part of object-oriented design.

Software engineers need education[6] on specification, design, turning designs into programs, software inspections, and testing. The education should enable the software engineer to produce well-structured programs that are fit for purpose.

Parnas has argued that software engineers have responsibilities as professional engineers.[7] They are responsible for designing and implementing high-quality and reliable software that is safe to use. They are also accountable for their decisions and actions,[8] and have a responsibility to object to decisions that violate professional standards. Engineers are required to behave professionally and ethically with their clients. The membership of the professional engineering body requires the member to adhere to the code of ethics[9] of the profession. Engineers in other professions are licensed, and Parnas argues that a similar licensing approach be adopted for professional software engineers.[10] Software engineers are required to follow best practice in software engineering and the defined software processes.[11]

Many software companies invest heavily in training, as the education and knowledge of its staff are essential to delivering high-quality products and services. Employees receive professional training related to the roles that they are performing, such as project management, software design and development, software testing, and service management. The fact that the employees are professionally

---

[6] Software Companies that are following approaches such as the CMM or ISO 9001 consider the education and qualification of staff prior to assigning staff to performing specific tasks. The appropriate qualifications and experience for the specific role are considered prior to appointing a person to carry out the role. Many companies are committed to the education and continuous development of their staff.

[7] The concept of accountability dates back to the Hammurabi Code c. 1750 B.C. The code included a law that stated if a house collapsed and killed the owner then the builder would be executed.

[8] However, it is unlikely that an individual programmer would be subject to litigation in the case of a flaw in a program causing damage or loss of life. A comprehensive disclaimer of responsibility for problems rather than a guarantee of quality accompany most software products. Software engineering is a team-based activity involving many engineers in various parts of the project, and it would be potentially difficult for an outside party to prove that the cause of a particular problem is due to the professional negligence of a particular software engineer, as there are many others involved in the process. Companies are more likely to be subject to litigation, as a company is legally responsible for the actions of their employees in the workplace, and a company is a wealthier entity than one of its employees. The legal aspects of licensing software may protect software companies from litigation. However, greater legal protection can be built into the contract between the supplier and the customer for bespoke-software development.

[9] Many software companies have a defined code of ethics that employees are expected to adhere. Larger companies will wish to project a good corporate image and to be respected worldwide.

[10] The British Computer Society (BCS) has introduced a qualification system for computer science professionals that it used to show that professionals are properly qualified. The most important of these is the BCS Information Systems Examination Board (ISEB) which allows IT professionals to be qualified in service management, project management, software testing, and so on.

[11] Software companies that are following the CMMI or ISO 9001 standards will employ audits to verify that the processes and procedures have been followed. Auditors report their findings to management and the findings are addressed appropriately by the project team and affected individuals.

qualified increases confidence in the ability of the company to deliver high-quality products and services and achieve positive results.

1.3   Challenges in Software Engineering

The challenge in software engineering is to deliver high-quality software on time and on budget to customers. The research done by the Standish Group was discussed earlier in this chapter, and the results of their 1998 research (Fig. 1.2) on project cost overruns in the US indicated that 33% of projects are between 21 and 50% over estimate, 18% are between 51 and 100% over estimate, and 11% of projects are between 101 and 200% over estimate.

The accurate estimation of project cost, effort, and schedule is a challenge in software engineering. Therefore, project managers need to determine how good their estimation process actually is and to make appropriate improvements. The use of software metrics is an objective way to do this, and improvements in estimation will be evident from a reduced variance between estimated and actual effort (see Chap. 14). The project manager will report the actual versus estimated effort and schedule during the project.

Risk management is an important part of project management, and the objective is to identify potential risks early and throughout the project, and to manage them appropriately. The probability of each risk occurring, and its impact is determined, and the risks are managed during project execution.

Software quality needs to be properly planned to enable the project to deliver a quality product. Flaws with poor quality software may lead to a negative perception of the company and may potentially lead to damage to the customer relationship with a subsequent loss of market share.

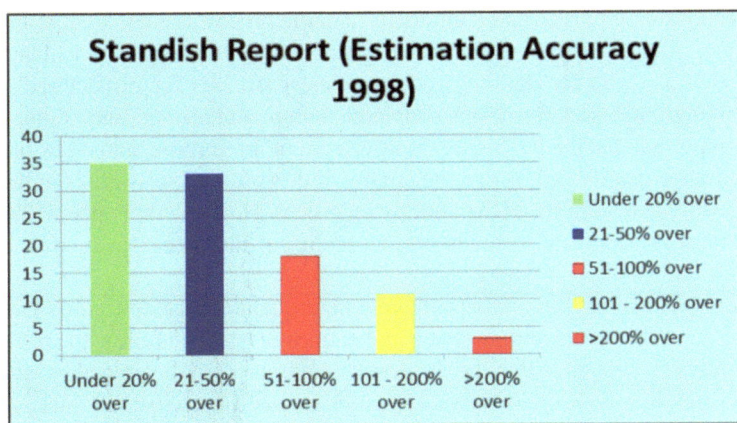

Fig. 1.2 Standish 1998 report—estimation accuracy

There is a strong economic case to building quality into the software, as less time is spent in re-working defective software. The cost of poor quality (COPQ) should be measured, and targets set for its reductions. It is important that lessons are learned during the project and acted upon in future projects. This helps to promote a culture of continuous improvement.

Several high-profile software failures are discussed in [5]. These include the millennium bug (Y2K) problem, the floating-point bug in the Intel microprocessor, the European Space Agency Ariane-5 disaster, and so on. These failures led to embarrassment for the organizations, as well as the associated cost of replacement and correction.

The millennium bug was due to the use of two digits to represent dates rather than four digits. The solution involved finding and analysing all codes that had a Y2K impact, planning and making the necessary changes, and verifying the correctness of the changes. The worldwide cost of correcting the millennium bug is estimated to have been in billions of dollars.

The Intel Corporation was slow to acknowledge the floating-point problem in its Pentium microprocessor, and in providing adequate information on its impact to its customers. It incurred a large financial cost in replacing microprocessors for its customers. The Ariane-5 failure caused major embarrassment and damage to the credibility of the European Space Agency (ESA). Its maiden flight ended in failure on 4 June 1996, after a flight time of just 40 s.

These failures indicate that quality needs to be carefully considered when designing and developing software. The effect of software failure may be large costs to correct the software, loss of credibility of the company, or even loss of life.

1.4   Software Processes and Lifecycles

Organizations vary by size and complexity, and the processes employed will reflect the nature of their business. The development of software involves many processes such as those for defining requirements; processes for project estimation and planning; processes for design, implementation, and testing; and so on.

It is important that the processes employed are fit for purpose, and a key premise in the software quality field is that the quality of the resulting software is influenced by the quality and maturity of the underlying processes, and compliance with them. Therefore, it is necessary to focus on the quality of the processes as well as the quality of the resulting software.

There is, of course, little point in having high-quality processes unless their use is ingrained in the organization. That is, all employees need to follow the processes consistently. This requires that the employees are trained on the processes, and that process discipline is instilled with an appropriate audit strategy. Data needs to be collected to improve the process. The software process assets in an organization generally consist of

- A software development policy for the organization.
- Process maps that describe the flow of activities.
- Procedures and guidelines that describe the processes in more detail.
- Checklists to assist with the performance of the process.
- Templates for the performance of specific activities (e.g., design, testing).
- Training materials.

The processes employed to develop high-quality software generally include

- Project management process.
- Requirements process.
- Design process.
- Coding process.
- Peer review process.
- Testing process.
- Supplier selection and management processes.
- Configuration management process.
- Audit process.
- Measurement process.
- Improvement process.
- Customer support and maintenance processes.

The software development process has an associated lifecycle that consists of various phases. There are several well-known lifecycles employed such as the waterfall model [9], the spiral model [10], the Rational Unified Process [11], and the popular Agile methodology [12]. The choice of a particular software development lifecycle is determined from the needs of the specific project. The various lifecycles are described in more detail in the following sections.

1.4.1   Waterfall Lifecycle

The waterfall model (Fig. 1.3) starts with requirements such as gathering and definition. It is followed by the system specification (with the functional and non-functional requirements), the design and implementation of the software, and comprehensive testing. The testing generally includes unit, system, and user acceptance testing.

The waterfall model is employed for projects where the requirements can be identified early in the project lifecycle or are known in advance. We are treating the waterfall model as the "V" lifecycle model, with the left-hand side of the "V" detailing requirements, specification, design, and coding and the right-hand side detailing unit tests, integration tests, system tests, and acceptance testing. Each phase has entry and exit criteria that must be satisfied before the next phase commences. There are several variations to the waterfall model.

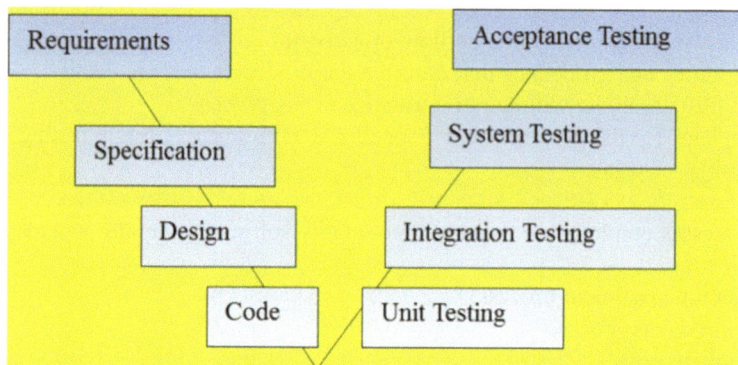

Fig. 1.3 Waterfall V lifecycle model

Many companies employ a set of templates to enable the activities in the various phases to be consistently performed. Templates may be employed for project planning and reporting, requirements definition, design, testing, and so on. These templates may be based on the IEEE standards or industrial best practice.

1.4.2   Spiral Lifecycles

The spiral model (Fig. 1.4) was developed by Barry Boehm in the 1980s [10], and it is useful for projects where the requirements are not fully known at project initiation, or where the requirements evolve as a part of the development lifecycle. The development proceeds in several spirals, where each spiral typically involves objectives and an analysis of the risks, updates to the requirements, design, code, testing, and a user review of the iteration or spiral.

The spiral is, in effect, a re-usable prototype with the business analysts and the customer reviewing the current iteration and providing feedback to the development team. The feedback is analysed and used to plan the next iteration. This approach is often used in joint application development, where the usability and look and feel of the application is a key concern. This is important in web-based development and in the development of a graphical user interface (GUI). The implementation of part of the system helps in gaining a better understanding of the requirements of the system, and this feeds into subsequent development cycles. The process repeats until the requirements and the software product are fully complete.

There are several variations of the spiral model including Rapid Application Development (RAD), Joint Application Development (JAD) models, and the Dynamic Systems Development Method (DSDM) model. The Agile methodology employs sprints (or iterations) of 2–4 weeks duration to implement a number of user stories. A sample spiral model is shown in Fig. 1.4.

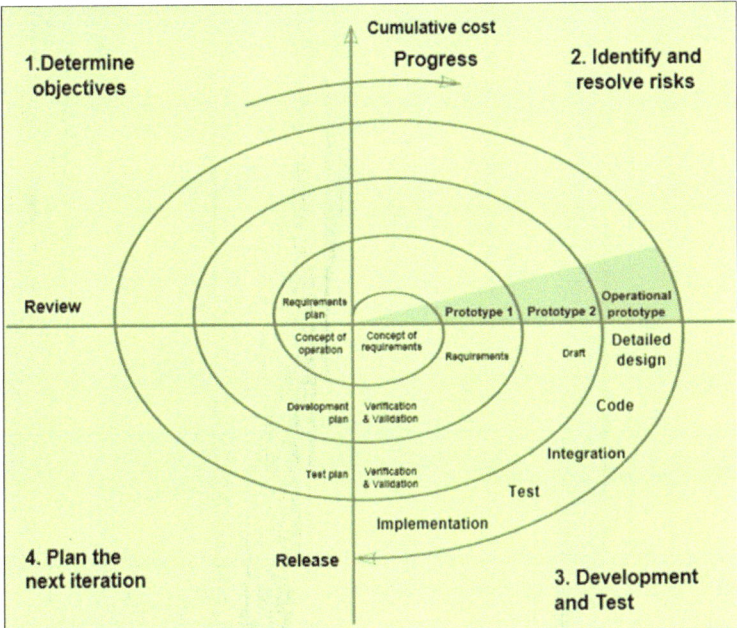

Fig. 1.4 SPIRAL lifecycle model. Public domain

There are other lifecycle models such as the iterative development process that combines the waterfall and spiral lifecycle model. Cleanroom was developed by Harlan Mills (see Chap. 15 of [13]), and includes a phase for formal specification. Its approach to testing is based on the predicted usage of the software product, which allows a software reliability measure to be calculated. The Rational Unified Process (RUP) is discussed in the next section.

1.4.3   Rational Unified Process

The *Rational Unified Process* [11] was developed at the Rational Corporation (now part of IBM) in the late 1990s. It uses the Unified Modelling Language (UML) as a tool for specification and design, where UML is a visual modelling language for software systems that provides a means of specifying, constructing, and documenting the object-oriented system. It was developed by James Rumbaugh, Grady Booch, and Ivar Jacobson, and it facilitates the understanding of the architecture and complexity of the system.

RUP is *use case driven, architecture centric, iterative,* and *incremental,* and includes cycles, phases, workflows, risk mitigation, quality control, project management, and configuration control (Fig. 1.5). Software projects may be very complex, and there are risks that requirements may be incomplete, or that the

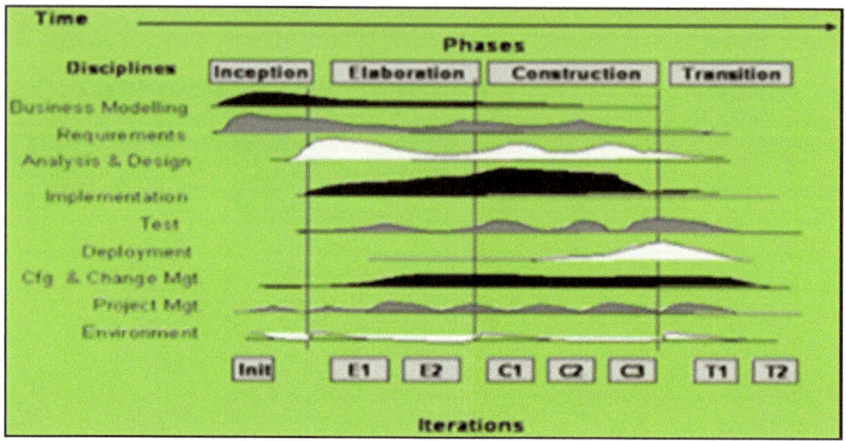

Fig. 1.5 Rational unified process

interpretation of a requirement may differ between the customer and the project team. RUP is a way to reduce risk in software engineering.

Requirements are gathered as use cases, where the *use cases describe the functional requirements from the point of view of the user of the system.* They describe what the system will do at a high level and ensure that there is an appropriate focus on the user when defining the scope of the project. *Use cases also drive the development process,* as the developers create a series of design and implementation models that realize the use cases. The developers review each successive model for conformance to the use-case model, and the test team verifies that the implementation correctly implements the use cases.

The software architecture concept embodies the most significant static and dynamic aspects of the system. The architecture grows out of the use cases and factors such as the platform that the software is to run on, deployment considerations, legacy systems, and the non-functional requirements.

RUP decomposes the work of a large project into smaller slices or mini-projects, and *each mini-project is an iteration that results in an increment to the product.* The iteration consists of one or more steps in the workflow, and generally leads to the growth of the product. If there is a need to repeat an iteration, then all that is lost is the misdirected effort of one iteration, rather than the entire product. Another words, RUP is a way to mitigate risk in software engineering.

1.4.4 Agile Development

Agile is a *software development* methodology that is more responsive to customer needs than traditional methods such as the waterfall model. *The waterfall development model is similar to a wide and slow-moving value stream,* and halfway through the project 100% of the requirements are typically 50% done. *However, for agile development 50% of requirements are typically 100% done halfway through the project.*

This methodology has a strong collaborative style of working and its approach includes

- Aims to achieve a narrow fast flowing value stream.
- User stories and sprints are employed.
- Stories are either done are not done (no such thing as 50% done).
- Iterative and incremental development is employed.
- A project is divided into sprints.
- Entire software development lifecycle is used for implementation of each story.
- Change is accepted as a normal part of life in the Agile world.
- Refactoring and evolutionary design employed.
- Continuous integration is employed.
- Emphasis on quality.
- Stand-up meetings.
- Direct interaction preferred over documentation.
- Rapid conversion of requirements into working functionality.

Ongoing changes to requirements are considered normal in the Agile world, and it is believed to be more realistic to change requirements regularly throughout the project rather than attempting to define all the requirements at the start of the project.

A story may be a new feature or a modification to an existing feature. It is reduced to the minimum scope that can deliver business value, and a feature may give rise to several stories. Stories often build upon other stories and the entire software development lifecycle is employed for the implementation of each story. *Stories are either done or not done, i.e., there is such thing as a story being 80% done.* The story is complete only when it passes its acceptance tests. Stories are prioritized based on a number of factors including

- Business value of story.
- Mitigation of risk.
- Dependencies on other stories.

The Scrum approach is an Agile method for managing iterative development, and it consists of an outline planning phase for the project followed by a set of sprint cycles (where each cycle develops an increment). *Sprint planning* is performed before the start of the iteration, and stories are assigned to the iteration to fill the available time. Each scrum sprint is of a fixed length (usually 2–4 weeks), and it develops an increment of the system. The estimates for each story and their priority are determined, and the prioritized stories are assigned to the iteration. *A short morning stand-up meeting is held daily* during the iteration, and attended by the scrum master, the project manager,[12] and the project team. It discusses the progress made the previous day, problem reporting and tracking, and the work planned for the day ahead. A separate meeting is held for issues that require more detailed discussion.

Once the iteration is complete the latest product increment is demonstrated to an audience including the product owner. This is to receive feedback and to identify new requirements. The team also conducts a retrospective meeting to identify what went well and what went poorly during the iteration. This is for continuous improvement of future iterations. Planning for the next sprint then commences. The scrum master is a facilitator who arranges the daily meetings and ensures that the scrum process is followed. The role involves removing roadblocks so that the team can achieve their goals and communicating with other stakeholders.

Agile employs pair programming and a collaborative style of working with the philosophy that two heads are better than one. This allows multiple perspectives in decision-making and a broader understanding of the issues.

Agile generally employs automated testing for unit, acceptance, performance, and integration testing. Tests are run frequently with the goal of catching programming errors early. They are generally run on a separate build server to ensure that all dependencies are checked. Tests are re-run before making a release. *Agile employs test-driven development with tests written before the code.* The developers write code to make a test pass with ideally developers only coding against failing tests. This approach forces the developer to write testable code.

Refactoring is employed in Agile as a design and coding practice. The objective is to change how the software is written without changing what it does. Refactoring is a tool for evolutionary design where the design is regularly evaluated, and improvements are implemented as they are identified. It helps in improving the maintainability and readability of the code and in reducing complexity. The automated test suite is essential in showing that the integrity of the software is maintained following refactoring.

Continuous integration allows the system to be built with every change. Early and regular integration allows early feedback to be provided. It also allows all of the automated tests to be run thereby identifying problems earlier. Agile is discussed in more detail in Chap. 13.

1.4.5   Continuous Software Development

Continuous software development is in a sense the successor to Agile, and involves activities such as continuous integration, continuous delivery, continuous testing, and continuous deployment of the software. Its objective is to enable technology companies to accelerate the delivery of their products to their customers, thereby

---

[12] Agile teams are self-organizing, and the project manager role is generally not employed for small projects (<20 staff).

delivering faster business benefits as well as reshaping relationships with their customers.

Continuous integration is a coding philosophy with an associated set of practices where each developer submits their work as soon as it is finished, and several builds may take place during the day in response to the addition of significant change. The build has an associated set of unit and integration tests that are automated and are used to verify the integrity of the build, and this ensures that the addition of the new code is of a high quality. Continuous integration ensures that the developers receive immediate feedback on the software that they are working on.

Continuous delivery builds on the activities in continuous integration, where each code that is added to the build has automated unit and system tests conducted. Automated functional tests, regression tests, and possibly acceptance tests will be conducted, and once the automated tests pass the software is sent to a staging environment for deployment.

Continuous testing allows the test group to continuously test the most up-to-date version of the software, and it includes manual testing as well as user acceptance testing. It differs from conventional testing as the software is expected to change over time.

Continuous deployment allows changes to be delivered to end users quickly without human intervention, and it requires the completion of the automated delivery tests prior to deployment to production.

1.5   Activities in Software Development

There are various activities involved in software development including

- Requirements definition.
- Design.
- Implementation.
- Software testing.
- Support and maintenance.

These activities are discussed in the following sections and cover both traditional software engineering and Agile.

1.5.1   Requirements Definition

The user (business) requirements specify what the customer wants and define what the software system is required to do (*as distinct from how this is to be done*). The requirements are the foundation for the system, and if they are incorrect, then the implemented system will be incorrect. *Prototyping may be employed* to assist in the definition and validation of the requirements. The process of determining the requirements, analysing, and validating them and managing them throughout the project lifecycle is termed *requirements engineering*.

The *user requirements* are determined from discussions with the customer to determine their actual needs, and they are then refined into the *system requirements*, which state the *functional* and *non-functional* requirements of the system. The specification of the user requirements needs to be unambiguous to ensure that all parties involved in the development of the system share a common understanding of what is to be developed and tested.

There is no requirements document as such in Agile, and the product backlog (i.e., the prioritized list of functionality of the product to be developed) is the closest to the idea of a requirements document in a traditional project. However, the written part of a user story in Agile is incomplete until the discussion of that story takes place. It is often useful to think of the written part of a story as a pointer to the real requirement, such as a diagram showing a workflow or the formula for a calculation. The Agile *software development* methodology argues that as requirements change so quickly that a requirements document is unnecessary, since such a document would be out of date as soon as it was written.

Requirements gathering in traditional software engineering involves meetings with the stakeholders to gather all relevant information for the proposed product. The stakeholders are interviewed, and requirements workshops conducted to elicit the requirements from them. An early working system (prototype) is often used to identify gaps and misunderstandings between developers and users. The prototype may serve as a basis for writing the specification.

The requirements workshops are used to discuss and prioritize the requirements, as well as identifying and resolving any conflicting requirements. The collected information is consolidated into a coherent set of requirements. Changes to the requirements may occur during the project, and these need to be controlled. It is essential to understand the impacts (e.g., schedule, budget, and technical) of a proposed change to the requirements prior to its approval.

Requirements verification is concerned with ensuring that the requirements are properly implemented (i.e., building it right) in the design and implementation. *Requirements validation* is concerned with ensuring that the right requirements are defined (building the right system), and that they are precise, complete, and reflect the actual needs of the customer.

The requirements are validated by the stakeholders to ensure that they are those desired, and to establish their feasibility. This may involve several reviews of the requirements until all stakeholders are ready to approve the requirements document. Other validation activities include reviews of the prototype and the design, and user acceptance testing.

The requirements for a system are generally documented in a natural language such as "English". Other notations that are employed include the visual modelling language UML (see Chap. 18 of [13]), and formal specification languages such as VDM or Z for the safety-critical field.

The specification of the system requirements of the product is essentially a statement of what the software development organization will provide to meet the business (user) requirements. That is, the detailed user (business) requirements are a statement of what the customer wants, whereas the specification of the system requirements is a statement of what will be delivered by the software development organization.

It is essential that the system requirements are valid with respect to the user requirements, and they are reviewed by the stakeholders to ensure their validity. Traceability may be employed to show that the business requirements are addressed by the system requirements.

There are two categories of system requirements: namely, functional and non-functional requirements. The *functional requirements* define the functionality that is required of the system, and it may include screen shots, report layouts, or desired functionality specified as use cases. The *non-functional requirements* will generally include security, reliability, availability, performance, and portability requirements, as well as usability and maintainability requirements.

1.5.2   Design

The design of the system consists of engineering activities to describe the architecture or structure of the system, as well as activities to describe the algorithms and functions required to implement the system requirements. It is a creative process concerned with how the system will be implemented, and its activities include architecture design, interface design, and data structure design. There are often several possible design solutions for a particular system, and the designer will need to decide on the most appropriate solution.

Refactoring is employed in Agile as a design and coding practice. The objective is to change how the software is written without changing what it does. Refactoring is a tool for evolutionary design where the design is regularly evaluated, and improvements are implemented as they are identified. It helps in improving the maintainability and readability of the code and in reducing complexity. The automated test suite is essential in demonstrating that the integrity of the software is maintained following refactoring.

The design may be specified in various ways such as graphical notations that display the relationships between the components making up the design. The notation may include flow charts, or various UML diagrams such as sequence diagrams, state charts, and so on. Program description languages or pseudo-code may be employed to define the algorithms and data structures that are the basis for implementation.

Function-oriented design is historical, and it involves starting with a high-level view of the system and refining it into a more detailed design. The system state is centralized and shared between the functions operating on that state.

Object-oriented design is based on the concept of *information hiding* developed by Parnas [14]. The system is viewed as a collection of objects rather than functions, with each object managing its own state information. The system state is decentralized, and an object is a member of a class. The definition of a class includes attributes and operations on class members, and these may be inherited from super classes. Objects communicate by exchanging messages.

It is essential to verify and validate the design with respect to the system requirements, and this may be done by traceability of the design to the system requirements and design reviews.

1.5.3   Implementation

This phase is concerned with implementing the design in the target language and environment (e.g., C++ or Java), and it involves writing or generating the actual code. The development team divides up the work to be done, with each programmer responsible for one or more modules. The coding activities often include code reviews or walkthroughs to ensure that quality code is produced, and to verify its correctness. The code reviews will verify that the source code conforms to the coding standards and that maintainability issues are addressed. They will also verify that the code produced is a valid implementation of the software design.

The development of a new feature in Agile begins with writing a suite of test cases based on the requirements for the feature. The tests fail initially, and so the first step is to write some code that enables the new test cases to pass. This new code may be imperfect (it will be improved later). The next step is to ensure that the new feature works with the existing features, and this involves executing all new and existing test cases.

This may involve modification of the source code to enable all of the tests to pass, and to ensure that all features work correctly together. The final step is refactoring the code, and this involves cleaning up and restructuring the code, and improving its structure and readability. The test cases are re-run during the refactoring to ensure that the functionality is not altered in any way. The process repeats with the addition of each new feature.

Software reuse provides a way to speed up the development process. Components or objects that may be reused need to be identified and handled accordingly. The implemented code may use software components that have either being developed internally or purchased off the shelf. Open-source software has become popular in recent years, and it allows software developed by others to be used (*under an open-source license*) in the development of applications.

The benefits of software reuse include increased productivity and a faster time to market. There are inherent risks with customized-off-the-shelf (COTS) software, as the supplier may decide to no longer support the software, or there is no guarantee that software that has worked successfully in one domain will work correctly in a different domain. It is therefore important to consider the risks as well as the benefits of software reuse and open-source software.

1.5.4   Software Testing

Software testing is employed to verify that the requirements have been correctly implemented, and that the software is fit for purpose, as well as identifying defects present in the software. There are various types of testing that may be conducted including *unit testing, integration testing, system testing, performance testing, and user acceptance testing.* These are described below:

Unit and Integration Testing

The unit tests are written and performed by the programmer on the completed unit (or module), prior to its integration with other modules. The objective is to show that the code satisfies the design, and a unit test includes the test objective and the expected results. Code coverage and branch coverage metrics are often generated to give an indication of how comprehensive the unit testing has been. These metrics provide visibility into the number of lines of code executed, as well as the branches covered during unit testing. The developer executes the unit tests, records the results, corrects any identified defects, and re-tests the software.

Test-driven development (TDD) is employed in the Agile world, and this involves writing the unit test cases (and possibly other test cases) before the code, and the code is then written to pass the defined test cases. These tests are automated in the Agile world and are run with every build.

Integration testing is performed by developers on the integrated system once all of the individual units work correctly in isolation. The objective is to verify that all of the modules and their interfaces work correctly together, and to identify and resolve any issues. Modules that work correctly in isolation may fail when integrated with other modules. These tests are automated in the Agile world.

System and Performance Testing

The purpose of system testing is to verify that the system requirements have been correctly implemented. It involves the specification and execution of the system test cases by an independent test group, and the system tests are traceable to the system requirements.

The purpose of performance testing is to ensure that the performance of the system satisfies the non-functional requirements. It may include *load performance testing*, where the system is subjected to heavy loads over a long period of time, and *stress testing*, where the system is subjected to heavy loads during a short time interval. *Performance testing often involves the simulation of many users* using the system and involves measuring the response times for various activities.

The preparation of the test environment may involve ordering special hardware and tools, and needs to be set up early in the project. Any defects identified during system and performance testing will be logged and reported to the developers. System testing may also include security and usability testing.

User Acceptance Testing

UAT testing is usually performed under controlled conditions at the customer site, and its operation will closely resemble the real-life behaviour of the system. The customer will see the product in operation and will judge whether the system is fit for purpose. The objective is to demonstrate that the product satisfies the business requirements and meets the customer expectations. Upon its successful completion the customer is happy to accept the product.

1.5.5 Support and Maintenance

Software systems often have a long lifetime, and the software needs to be continuously enhanced over its lifetime to meet the evolving needs of the customers. This may involve regular new releases with new functionality and corrections to known defects.

Any problems that the customer identifies with the software are reported as per the customer support and maintenance agreement. The support issues will require investigation, and the issue may be *a defect in the software, an enhancement to the software*, or *due to a misunderstanding*. An appropriate solution is implemented to resolve, and testing is conducted to verify that the solution is correct, and that the changes made have not adversely affected other parts of the system. A post-mortem may be conducted to learn lessons from the defect, and to take corrective action to prevent a reoccurrence.[13]

The goal of building a correct and reliable software product the first time is difficult to achieve, and the customer is always likely to find some issues with the released software product. It is accepted today that quality needs to be built into each step in the development process, with the role of software inspections and testing to identify as many defects as possible prior to release and minimize the risk that serious defects will be found post-release.

The effective in-phase inspections of the deliverables will influence the quality of the resulting software, and lead to a corresponding reduction in the number of defects. The testing group plays a key role in verifying that the system is correct, and in providing confidence that the software is fit for purpose and ready to be released. The approach to software correctness involves testing and re-testing, until the testing group believe that all defects have been eliminated. Dijkstra [15] comments on testing are well known:

"Testing a program demonstrates that it contains errors, never that it is correct".

---

[13] This is essential for serious defects that have caused significant inconvenience to customers (e.g., a major telecom outage). It is important to learn lessons to determine what prevented the defect from been identified during peer reviews and testing, and to implement preventive actions.

That is, irrespective of the amount of time spent testing, it can never be said with absolute confidence that all defects have been found in the software. Testing provides increased confidence that the program is correct, and statistical techniques may be employed to give a measure of the software reliability.

Some mature organizations have a quality objective of three defects per million lines of code, which was introduced by Motorola as part of its six-sigma (6σ) program. It was originally applied to its manufacturing businesses and subsequently applied to its software organizations. The goal is to reduce variability in manufacturing processes and to ensure that the processes performed within strict process control limits.

1.6 Software Inspections

Software inspections are used to build quality into software products, and include the Fagan inspections [6], Gilb's approach [7], and Prince 2's approach. Fagan inspections were developed by Michael Fagan at IBM in the mid-1970s. It is a seven-step process that identifies and removes errors in work products. The process mandates that requirement documents, design documents, source code, and test plans are all formally inspected by experts independent of the author of the deliverable.

There are various *roles* defined in the process including the *moderator* who chairs the inspection. The *reader's* responsibility is to read or paraphrase the deliverable, and the *author* is the creator of the deliverable and has a special interest in ensuring that it is correct. The *tester* role is concerned with the test viewpoint.

The inspection process will consider whether the design is correct with respect to the requirements, and whether the source code is correct with respect to the design. Software inspections play a key role in building quality into software, and in reducing the cost of poor quality (see Chap. 8).

1.7 Software Project Management

Software projects have a history of being delivered late- or over-budget, and good project management practices include the following:

- Estimation of cost, effort, and schedule for the project.
- Identifying and managing risks.
- Preparing the project plan/schedule.
- Staffing the project.
- Monitoring progress, budget, schedule, effort, risks, issues, and change requests.
- Taking corrective action/re-planning.
- Communicating progress to affected stakeholders.
- Preparing status reports and presentations.

The project plan will contain or reference several other plans such as the project quality plan, the communication plan, the configuration management plan, and the test plan. Project estimation and scheduling are difficult as previous estimates are often not a good basis for estimation of the current project. Often, unanticipated problems can arise for technically advanced projects, and the estimates may often be optimistic. Gantt charts are employed for project scheduling, and these show the work breakdown for the project, as well as task dependencies and allocation of staff to the various tasks.

The effective management of risk during a project is essential to project success. Risks arise due to uncertainty and the risk management cycle involves identifying and managing risk throughout the project (see Chap. 7). An overview of software project management is presented in Chap. 5.

1.8   CMMI Maturity Model

The CMMI is a framework to assist an organization in the implementation of best practice in software and systems engineering. It is an internationally recognized model for software process improvement and assessment and is used worldwide by thousands of organizations. It provides a solid engineering approach to the development of software, and it supports the definition of high-quality processes for the various software engineering and management activities.

It was developed by the Software Engineering Institute (SEI) who adapted the process improvement principles used in the manufacturing field to the software field. They developed the original CMM model and its successor the CMMI. The CMMI states *what the organization needs to do* to mature its processes rather than *how this should be done.*

It consists of five maturity levels with each maturity level consisting of several process areas. Each process area consists of a set of goals, and these goals are implemented by practices related to that process area. Level two is focused on management practices, level three is focused on engineering and organization practices, level four is concerned with ensuring that key processes are performing within strict quantitative limits, and level five is concerned with continuous process improvement. Maturity levels may not be skipped in the staged representation of the CMMI, as each maturity level is the foundation for the next level. The CMMI and Agile are compatible, and CMMI v1.3 supports Agile software development.

The CMMI allows organizations to benchmark themselves against other organizations. This is done by a formal SCAMPI appraisal conducted by an authorized lead appraiser. The results of the appraisal are generally reported back to the SEI, and there is a strict qualification process to become an *authorized lead appraiser.* An appraisal is useful in verifying that an organization has improved, and it enables the organization to prioritize improvements for the next improvement cycle. The CMMI is discussed in more detail in Chap. 20 of [13].

1.9   Formal Methods

Dijkstra and Hoare have argued that the way to develop correct software is to derive the program from its specifications using mathematics, and to employ *mathematical proof* to demonstrate its correctness with respect to the specification. This offers a rigorous framework to develop programs adhering to the highest quality constraints. However, in practice, mathematical techniques have proved to be cumbersome to use, and their widespread use in industry is unlikely at this time.

Mathematical techniques have been successfully applied to the *safety-critical area* where there is a need for extra rigour in the safety and security critical fields. The mathematical techniques can demonstrate the presence or absence of certain desirable or undesirable properties (e.g., *"when a train is in a level crossing, then the gate is closed"*).

Spivey [16] defines a *"formal specification"* as "the use of mathematical notation to describe in a precise way the properties which an information system must have, without unduly constraining the way in which these properties are achieved". It describes *what* the system must do, as distinct from *how* it is to be done. This abstraction away from implementation enables questions about what the system does to be answered, independently of the detailed code. Further, the unambiguous nature of mathematical notation avoids the problem of ambiguity in an imprecisely worded natural language description of a system.

The formal specification thus becomes the key reference point for the different parties concerned with the construction of the system and is a useful way of promoting a common understanding for all those concerned with the system. The term *"formal methods"* is used to describe a formal specification language, and a method for the design and implementation of computer systems.

The specification is written precisely in a mathematical language. The derivation of an implementation from the specification may be achieved via *stepwise refinement*. Each refinement step makes the specification more concrete and closer to the actual implementation. There is an associated *proof obligation* that the refinement be valid, and that the concrete state preserves the properties of the more abstract state. Thus, assuming the original specification is correct and the proofs of correctness of each refinement step are valid, then there is a very high degree of confidence in the correctness of the implemented software.

Formal methods have been applied to a diverse range of applications, including circuit design, specification of standards, specification and verification of programs, etc. Mathematics to assist software engineers are described in [3, 17]] and software engineering is discussed in [13, 18].

1.10   Review Questions

1. Discuss the Standish Group research results on IT project delivery.
2. What are the main challenges in software engineering?
3. Describe various software lifecycles.
4. What are the advantages and disadvantages of Agile?
5. Describe the purpose of the CMMI. What are the benefits?
6. Describe the main activities in software inspections.
7. Describe the main activities in software testing.
8. Describe the main activities in project management.
9. What are the advantages and disadvantages of formal methods?

1.11   Summary

The birth of software engineering was at the NATO conference held in 1968 in Germany. This conference highlighted the problems that existed in the software sector in the late 1960s, and the term "*software crisis*" was coined to refer to these. The conference led to the realization that programming is quite distinct from science and mathematics, and that software engineers need to be properly trained to enable them to build high-quality products that are safe to use.

The Standish Group conducts research on the extent of problems with the delivery of projects on time and budget. Their research indicates that it remains a challenge to deliver projects on time, on budget, and with the right quality.

Programmers are like engineers in the sense that they build products. Therefore, programmers need to receive an appropriate education in engineering as part of their training. The education of traditional engineers includes training on product design, and an appropriate level of mathematics.

Software engineering involves multi-person construction of multi-version programs. It is a systematic approach to the development and maintenance of the software, and it requires a precise statement of the requirements of the software product, and then the design and development of a solution to meet these requirements. It includes methodologies to design, develop, implement, and test software as well as sound project management, quality management, and configuration management practices. Support and maintenance of the software needs to be properly addressed.

Software process maturity models such as the CMMI have become popular in recent years. They place an emphasis on understanding and improving the software process to enable software engineers to be more effective in their work.

References

1. A. Wesley, *The Mythical Man Month*, (Fred Brooks, 1975)
2. P.Naur, B. Randell, *Software Engineering*. Petrocelli. 1975. IN. Buxton, *Report on two NATO Conferences held in Garmisch, Germany (October1968) and Rome, Italy (October 1969)*
3. G. O' Regan, *Concise Guide to Formal Methods*, (Springer, 2017)
4. F. Brooks, *No Silver Bullet. Essence and accidents of Software Engineering. Information Processing*. (Elsevier, Amsterdam, 1986)
5. G. O'Regan, *Introduction to Software Process Improvement*. (Springer Verlag, London, 2010)
6. M. Fagan, *Design and code inspections to reduce errors in software development*. IBM Syst. J. **15**(3) (1976)
7. T. Gilb, D. Graham, *Software Inspections*, (Addison Wesley, 1994)
8. *Managing Successful Projects with PRINCE2*, (Office of Government Commerce, 2004)
9. W. Royce, Managing the development of large software systems, in *Proceedings of IEEE WESTCON* (26), Pages 1–9, August, 1970
10. B. Boehm, A spiral model for software development and enhancement. *Computer*, (May 1988)
11. J. Rumbaugh et al., *The Unified Software Development Process*, (Addison Wesley, 1999)
12. Kent Beck, *Extreme Programming Explained. Embrace Change*, (Addison Wesley, 2000)
13. G. O' Regan, *Concise Guide to Software Engineering*. 2nd Edition, (Springer, 2022)
14. D. Parnas, On the criteria to be used in decomposing systems into modules. Commun. ACM **15**(12) (1972)
15. E.W. Dijkstra, *Structured Programming*, (Academic Press, 1972)
16. J.M. Spivey, *The Z Notation. A Reference Manual*, (Prentice Hall International Series in Computer Science, 1992)
17. G. O' Regan, *Mathematical Foundations of Software Engineering*, (Springer, 2023)
18. I. Sommerville, *Software Engineering*. 10th Edition, (Pearson, 2017)

Professional Responsibility

2

2.1 Introduction

Parnas has argued that computer scientists need the right education to apply scientific and mathematical principles in their work. He argues, "*software engineers have individual responsibilities as professionals*. They are responsible for designing and implementing high-quality and reliable software that is safe to use. They are also accountable for their own decisions and actions, and have a responsibility to object to decisions that violate professional standards".

Professional engineers have a duty to their clients to ensure that they are solving the real problem of the client. They need to precisely state the problem before working on its solution. Engineers need to be honest about current capabilities when asked to work on problems that have no appropriate technical solution, rather than accepting a contract for something that cannot be done.

The *licensing of a professional engineer* provides confidence that the engineer has the right education, experience to build safe and reliable products. Otherwise, the profession gets a bad name because of poor work carried out by unqualified people. Professional engineers are required to follow rules of good practice and to object when rules are violated. The licensing of an engineer requires that the engineer completes an accepted engineering course and understands the professional responsibilities of an engineer. The professional body is responsible for enforcing

© The Author(s), under exclusive license to Springer Nature Switzerland AG 2025
G. O'Regan, *Guide to Software Project Management*, Undergraduate Topics in
Computer Science, https://doi.org/10.1007/978-3-031-80578-3_2

Table 2.1 Professional responsibilities of software engineers

No	Responsibility
1	Honesty and fairness in dealings with clients
2	Responsibility for actions
3	Continuous learning to ensure appropriate knowledge to serve the client effectively

standards and certification. The term *"engineer"* is a title that is awarded on merit, but *it also places responsibilities on its holder*.

Engineers are required to behave ethically with their clients. The membership of the professional engineering body requires the member to adhere to the code of ethics[1] of the profession, which is given in Table 2.1.

2.2   What is a Code of Ethics?

A professional code of ethics expresses ideals of human behaviour, and it defines the core principles of the organization. Several organizations such as the Association Computing Machinery (ACM), the Institute of Electrical and Electronic Engineers (IEEE), and the British Computer Society (BCS) have developed a code of conduct for their members. Violations of the code by members are taken seriously and are subject to investigations and disciplinary procedures. A professional code of conduct for a professional body or corporation includes

1. Guidelines for responsible behaviour of its members.
2. The guidelines may be detailed and prescriptive or a broad statement of values.
3. Codes of conduct are an addendum to legal requirements.
4. Professional codes are formulated by engineering bodies.
5. Companies formulate corporate codes.
6. Violations of codes are investigated.
7. Members may be disciplined for violating the codes.

There are various types of codes of ethics which are given in Table 2.2.

Business ethics (also called corporate ethics) is concerned with ethical principles and moral problems that may arise in a business environment. They refer to the core principles and values of the organization, and apply throughout the organization. They guide individual employees in carrying out their roles, and ethical issues include the rights and duties between a company and its employees, customers and suppliers (Fig. 2.1).

---

[1] These are core values of many mature software companies, and many organisations have a code of ethics that employees are required to adhere to. However, in some cases, the code of ethics may be window dressing where the core values do not reflect the reality on the ground (e.g., we discuss the Volkswagen emissions scandal in a later chapter).

Table 2.2 Types of professional codes

Code	Responsibility
Aspirational codes	These are the values that the profession or company is committed to and aspires to achieve
Advisory codes	These values help professionals to make moral judgments in different situations, based on the values of the profession or company
Disciplinary codes	These include disciplinary procedures to ensure that the behaviour of professionals adheres to the values specified in the code of ethics

Fig. 2.1 Corrupt legislation. 1896. Public Domain

Many corporation and professional organizations have a written "*code of ethics*" that defines the professional standards expected of all employees in the company. All employees are expected to adhere to these values whenever they represent the company. The human resource function in a company plays an important role in promoting ethics, and in putting internal HR policies in place relating to the ethical conduct of employees, including the prevention of discrimination or sexual harassment in the workplace, and ensuring that employees are treated appropriately (including cultural sensitivities in a multi-cultural business environment).

Companies are expected to behave ethically and not to exploit its workers. There was an infamous case of employee exploitation at the Foxconn plant (an Apple supplier of the *i*Phone) in Shenzhen in China in 2006, where conditions at the plant were so dreadful (long hours, low pay, unreasonable workload, and crammed accommodation) that several employees committed suicide. The scandal raised questions on the extent to which a large corporation such as Apple should protect the health and safety of the factory workers of its suppliers. Further, given the profits that Apple makes from the *i*Phone, is it ethical for Apple to allow such workers to be exploited?

Today, the area of *corporate social responsibility* (CSR) has become applicable to the corporate world, and it requires the corporation to be an ethical and responsible citizen in the communities in which it operates (even at a cost to its profits). It is therefore reasonable to expect a responsible corporation to pay its fair share of tax, and to refrain from using tax loopholes to avoid paying billions in taxes on international sales. Today, environment ethics has become topical, and it is concerned with the responsibility of business in protecting the environment in which it operates. It is reasonable to expect a responsible corporation to make the protection of the environment and sustainability part of its business practices, and so CSR plays a role in ensuring that the corporation behaves ethically within society and has a positive impact on the environment.

Unethical business practices refer to those business actions that don't meet the standard of acceptable business operations, and they give the company a bad reputation. It may be that the entire business culture is corrupt or it may be as a result of the unethical actions of an employee. It is important that such practices be exposed, and this may place an employee in an ethical dilemma (i.e., the loyalty of the employee to the employer versus what is the right thing to do such as exposing an unethical practice).

Some accepted practices in the workplace might cause ethical concerns. For example, it is normal for the employer to monitor email and Internet use to ensure that employees do not abuse it, and so there may be grounds for privacy concerns. On the one hand, the employer is paying the employee's salary and has a reasonable expectation that the employee does not abuse email and the Internet in the workplace. On the other hand, the employee has reasonable rights of privacy provided computer resources are not abused.

The nature of privacy is relevant in the business models of several technology companies. For example, Google specializes in Internet-based services and products, and its many products include *Google Search* (the world's largest search engine), *Gmail* for email, and *Google Maps* (a web mapping application that offers satellite images and street views). Google's products gather a lot of personal data, and create revealing profiles of its users, which can then be exploited for commercial purposes.

A Google search leaves traces on both the computer and in records kept by Google, which has raised privacy concerns as such information may be obtained by a forensic examination of the computer, or in records obtained from Google or the Internet Service Providers (ISP). Gmail automatically scans the contents of emails to add context-sensitive advertisements to them and to filter spam, which raises privacy concerns, as it means that all emails sent or received are scanned and read by some computer. Google has argued that the automated scanning of emails is done to enhance the user experience, as it provides customized search

Table 2.3   Ten commandments on computer ethics

No.	Description
1	Thou shalt not use a computer to harm other people
2	Thou shalt not interfere with other people's computer work
3	Thou shalt not snoop around in other people's computer files
4	Thou shalt not use a computer to steal
5	Thou shalt not use a computer to bear false witness
6	Thou shalt not copy or use proprietary software for which you have not paid
7	Thou shalt not use other people's computer resources without authorization or proper compensation
8	Thou shalt not appropriate other people's intellectual output
9	Thou shalt think about the social consequences of the program you are writing or the system you are designing
10	Thou shalt always use a computer in ways that ensure consideration and respect for your fellow humans

results, tailored advertisements, and the prevention of spam and viruses. Google maps provide location information that may be used for targeted advertisements.

A code of ethics places professional and ethical responsibility on computer professionals including software engineers and project managers, and includes ethical behaviour and responsibilities such as[2]

1. Values of the profession.
2. Behaving with integrity and honesty.
3. Obligations to employer and to clients.
4. Responsibility towards public and society.

2.2.1   What is Computer Ethics?

Computer ethics is a set of principles that guide the behaviour of individuals when using computer resources. Several ethical issues that may arise include intellectual property rights, privacy concerns, as well as the impacts of computer technology on wider society. The Computer Ethics Institute (CEI) is an American organization that examines ethical issues that arise in the information technology field. It published the *ten commandments on computer ethics* (Table 2.3) in the early 1990s [1], which attempted to outline principles and standards of behaviour to guide people in the ethical use of computers.

---

[2] These are core values of many mature software companies, and most companies operating today have a code of ethics that employees are expected to adhere to.

The first commandment says that it is unethical to use a computer to harm another user (e.g., destroy their files or steal their personal data), or to write a program that on execution does so. That is, activities such as spamming, phishing, writing, and spreading malicious software and cyberbullying are unethical. The second commandment is related and may be interpreted that malicious software and viruses that disrupt the functioning of computer systems are unethical. The third commandment says that it is unethical (with some exceptions such as dealing with cybercrime and international terrorism) to read another person's emails, files, and personal data, as this is an invasion of their privacy.

The fourth commandment argues that the theft or leaking of confidential electronic personal information is unethical (computer technology has made it easier to steal personal information). The fifth commandment states that it is unethical to spread false or incorrect information (e.g., fake news or misinformation spread via email or social media). The sixth commandment states that it is unethical to obtain illegal copies of copyrighted software, as software is considered an artistic or literary work that is subject to copyright. All copies should be obtained legally.

The seventh commandment states that it is unethical to break into a computer system with another user's ID and password (without their permission), or to gain unauthorized access to the data on another computer by hacking into the computer system. The eight commandment states that it is unethical to claim ownership of intellectual property created by another. For example, it would be unethical to claim ownership of a program that was written by another.

The ninth commandment states that it is important for companies and individuals to think about the social impacts of the software that is being created, and to create software only if it is beneficial to society (i.e., it is unethical to create malicious software). The tenth commandment states that communication over computers and the Internet should be courteous, as well as showing respect for others (e.g., no abusive language or spreading false statements).

2.2.2 Codes of Conduct

Codes of conduct are values that members of a professional body or employees of a company are expected to adhere to, but may not be legally enforced as such. However, members of a particular profession or employees of a company that violate the codes may be subject to disciplinary procedures by the professional body or their employer. An effective code of ethics helps the corporation to achieve its corporate social responsibilities.

Unfortunately, codes of conduct may sometimes be just *window dressing*, where the aspirations expressed in the code of ethics do not reflect the reality on the ground. The code may give the appearance that work is carried out a certain way (e.g., emissions are below certain thresholds), and that the engineers are ethical in their day-to-day work. However, the reality on the ground may be quite different with unethical work practices taking place but covered up. Further, codes of conduct have been criticized as being vague and contradictory, and this may create uncertainty for the employee or member of the professional as to what is the right action or behaviour is for a given situation.

Moral judgements and ethical decisions occur in various situations in a work environment, and so it would not be feasible for a code of ethics to cover all scenarios. In practice, a code of ethics expresses the moral principles of an organization, and so an employee or software professional needs a *moral compass*, and to recognize situations where ethical decisions need to be made.

There may be conflicts between the loyalty that a person has to their employer and their duty to do the right thing such as protecting the public. No employee desires to be placed in a situation where there is a conflict between what is morally right and their loyalty to their employer, and it is important that organizations establish structures, where serious problems can be reported, discussed openly, and dealt with appropriately. In rare situations, an employee may have no choice but to become a whistle-blower to protect the public, where the organization is intent or proceeding with a very risky approach that potentially endangers life or the environment. However, every effort should be made to avoid this situation as it places the employee in a very difficult position with potential consequences to their career if he or she speaks out (Fig. 2.2).

An employee may have a *conflict of interest* that could affect her professional judgement in a certain situation. For example, suppose that an employee has responsibility for selecting a new software package, and her husband runs one of the firms tendering for the work. Then an ethical employee would inform management of the conflict of interest and remove herself from the selection process to remove any possibility of bias in the selection.

That is, a conflict of interest is an interest which if pursued interferes or conflicts with the obligation of the employee to his/her employer or client. The conflict of interest may corrupt or interfere with the employee's professional judgement and could potentially lead to inappropriate or immoral behaviour. It potentially destroys the trustworthiness of an individual, and so it is important to disclose a potential conflict of interest as soon as it arises.

Fig. 2.2 Whistle-blower

Bribery and corruption are endemic to some countries, and as these are illegal activities in most countries the employee needs to report such activities when they arise. For example, an employee such as a purchasing manager is in a position of influence in an organization and could potentially be offered a *bribe* by another individual or company to influence his/her decision-making. Often, individuals or companies may be subtle in their attempt to gain influence on decision-makers, with gifts or invitations to all-expenses paid events such as golf outings used to build up relationships with decision-makers.

It is important to be cautious with respect to corporate entertainment, and many companies have policies that prohibit or restrict gifts to employees from external organizations or individuals. This helps to prevent employees being inappropriately influenced by others in their decision-making.

2.2.3 Role of a Whistle-Blower

The whistle-blower is a person who speaks out and informs the public on potentially unsafe or criminal acts in an organization. However, speaking out should be the very last step in the process as it could have serious consequences on the employee and their career. The first steps are to establish the facts to determine the extent of the danger and its potential impact on the public, communicating the perceived danger and evidence for the danger within the organization, and exhausting all internal procedures prior to acting by speaking out. The whistle-blower should only speak out when:

1. The organization will do serious harm to the public.
2. The whistle-blower has identified the threat, reported it to management, and concluded that management will not act.
3. The whistle-blower has exhausted all internal procedures.
4. The whistle-blower has convincing evidence that the threat is real.
5. The whistle-blower believes that revealing the threat will prevent harm.

Table 2.4 describes the typical steps in whistle-blowing.

Speaking out may be the ethical thing to do but often it comes at a serious cost to the employee, as he or she may be portrayed as being disloyal to the organization. Further, as the organization will wish to protect itself it may attempt to discredit the employee, and it may even terminate the employment of the employee. The organization may portray the issue as a disgruntled employee whose employment was terminated due to performance issues with the employee's work.

Whistle-blowing can also place a lot of emotional strain on the employee, and even if the employee is not fired it may result in career termination in the organization, with zero prospects of further promotion in the company. It is important that the employee protects himself by gathering all evidence on the existence of danger, as this will be needed at a later stage. It may be prudent for the whistle-blower

Table 2.4 Steps in whistle-blowing

No.	Responsibility
1	Establish the facts and double (or triple check) to ensure that you are factually correct with respect to the danger and gather appropriate solid evidence that will convince any reasonable person of the danger
2	Report the matter and present the factual information to your immediate superior and determine what action (if any) management will take
3	In the case of inaction escalate as appropriate within the organization (organizations vary size/hierarchical structure and so escalation mechanism will differ) until all internal procedures are exhausted
4	In the absence of a reasonable resolution to the situation, or the organization fails to act or find an appropriate solution there may be no alternative but to speak out
5	The whistle-blower reflects on the situation, weighs up the evidence and options, and decides that the only way to prevent harm is to speak out and reveal the danger to the public

to consider the consequences of speaking out and doing the right thing, both on themselves and on others, to ensure that they fully understand the implications of the serious steps that they are taking and can manage the difficult circumstances in the aftermath of speaking out.

It may seem reasonable to suggest that an employee is fulfilling his moral duty if he informs management of the danger, as management are the decision-makers with all the pertinent facts and are thus best to make the final decision. However, such an approach can sometimes lead to loss of life, as with the Space Shuttle Challenger disaster back in 1986, which is discussed in Chap. 3. Robert Boisjoly, an Engineer at Morton Thiokel, was aware of the risks of erosion and failure when the 0-Rings of the Solid Rocket Booster (SRB) are exposed to low temperatures. He argued that the shuttle launch should not take place on the planned date due to the predicted temperatures and advised management at Morton Thiokel of the situation. However, NASA placed pressure on Morton Thiokel to proceed with the launch, and the company gave its go ahead to continue with the launch, which resulted in the death of the crew of the space shuttle.

The IEEE code of ethics is discussed in the next section and it highlights the importance of speaking out in the case of danger. It includes the code: *"disclose promptly factors that might endanger the public or the environment"*.

2.3 IEEE Code of Ethics

The Institute of Electrical and Electronic Engineers (IEEE) is the world's largest technical professional organizations with over 400,000 members in over 160 countries, and it is dedicated to advancing technology for the benefit of mankind. It publishes over 30% of the world's technical literature in electrical engineering, computer science, and electronics as well as technical books and monographs. It is a leading developer of international standards in telecommunications and information technology, and individuals who have made outstanding contributions to engineering and technology may receive the prestigious IEEE Medal.

IEEE has developed a code of ethics for its members designed to ensure that they adhere to the highest ethical standards, and that its members treat others fairly and ensure that they are not discriminated against on the grounds of gender, race, and so on (Table 2.5).

The IEEE Code of Ethics requires its members to promptly disclose any factors that might endanger the public or society, which shows that it recognizes the reality of whistle-blowing and the need for members to speak out when there is danger to the public. The code mentions the importance of avoiding conflicts of interest and disclosing them when they occur, and stresses that unlawful activities such as bribery should be rejected. The code highlights the importance of carrying

Table 2.5 IEEE code of ethics

No.	Description
Highest ethical standards	
1	To hold paramount the safety, health, and welfare of the public; to strive to comply with ethical design and sustainable development practices; to protect the privacy of others; and to disclose promptly factors that might endanger the public or the environment
2	To improve the understanding by individuals and society of the capabilities and societal implications of conventional and emerging technologies, including intelligent system
3	To avoid real or perceived conflicts of interest whenever possible, and to disclose them to affected parties when they do exist
4	To avoid unlawful conduct in professional activities, and to reject bribery in all its forms
5	To seek, accept, and offer honest criticism of technical work, to acknowledge and correct errors, to be honest and realistic in stating claims or estimates based on available data, and to credit properly the contributions of others
6	To maintain and improve technical competence and to undertake technological tasks for others only if qualified by training or experience, or after full disclosure of pertinent limitations
Treating people fairly	
7	To treat all persons fairly and with respect, and to not engage in discrimination based on characteristics such as race, religion, gender, disability, age, national origin, sexual orientation, gender identity, or gender expression
8	To not engage in harassment of any kind, including sexual harassment or bullying behaviour
9	To avoid injuring others, their property, reputation, or employment by false or malicious actions, rumours or any other verbal or physical abuses
Following the code	
10	To support colleagues and co-workers in following this code of ethics, to strive to ensure the code is upheld, and to not retaliate against individuals reporting a violation

out roles only when one is qualified to do so, and to continue to improve one's technical competence. It emphasizes that people should be treated fairly and with respect, without discrimination on gender, ethnicity, etc., and that harassment and injury to others should be avoided.

2.4 British Computer Society Code of Conduct

The British Computer Society (BCS) is a professional organization for information technology and computer science that was founded by in 1957, and its first president was Sir Maurice Wilkes.[3] It has over 68,000 members in 150 countries, and it has played an important role in educating IT professionals. The BCS provides awards such as the Lovelace Medal[4] to individuals, who have made outstanding contributions to the computing field.

The BCS has developed a code of conduct that defines the standards expected of BCS members, and it applies to all grades of members during their professional work. Any known breaches of the BCS codes by a member are investigated by the BCS, and appropriate disciplinary procedures followed. The main parts of the BCS code of conduct are listed in Table 2.6.

The BCS Code of Ethics requires its members to be conscious of the public health and environment. It states that one should only carry out those roles that one is qualified to do so, and one should continue to improve one's technical competence. It states the importance of avoiding conflicts of interest and that unlawful activities such as bribery should be rejected. It emphasizes that members should seek to improve professional standards and support other members in their professional development.

2.5 ACM Code of Professional Conduct and Ethics

The Association of Computing Machinery (ACM) is the world's largest educational and scientific computing society, and it delivers resources that advance computing as a science. It has over 100,000 members around the world, and it includes several special interest groups (e.g., SIG AI is a special interest group on AI, and SIG SOFT is a special interest group on software engineering). The ACM has defined a code of ethics and professional conduct for its members, and the Code is summarized in Table 2.7.

The ACM Code of Ethics is comprehensive and requires its members to report any dangers that might cause damage or injury. The code mentions the importance

---

[3] Sir Maurice Wilkes developed the EDSAC computer at Cambridge University, which was one of the earliest stored-program computers. It was operational from May 1949.

[4] Ada Lovelace was an English mathematician who collaborated with Babbage on applications for the Analytic Engine.

Table 2.6 BCS code of conduct

Area	Description
Public interest	Due regard to public health, privacy, security, and environment Due regards to legitimate rights of third parties Conduct professional activities without discrimination Promote equal access to IT
Professional competence and integrity	Only do work within professional competence Do not claim competence that you do not possess Continuous development of knowledge/skills Understand/knowledge/comply with legislation Respect other viewpoints Avoid injuring others Reject bribery and unethical behaviour
Duty to relevant authority	Carry out professional responsibilities with due care and diligence Avoid conflicts of interest Accept professional responsibility for your work Do not disclose confidential information Accurate information on performance of products
Duty to the profession	Uphold reputation of profession and BCS Seek to improve professional standards Act with integrity Notify BCS if convicted of criminal offence Support other members in their professional development

of respecting intellectual property as well as privacy and confidentiality and carrying out roles only when one is qualified to do so. Conflicts of interest should be avoided, and their work should be to the highest professional standards. Members should seek to improve their technical competence, and people should be treated fairly and with respect. Finally, members should notify the ACM of any violations of the code.

We shall discuss the professional responsibilities of some specific roles (e.g., software testing) in our discussion of ethical software engineering in Chap. 3.

2.6   Precautionary Principle

The precautionary principle argues that if there is an identifiable risk of serious or irreversible harm, then it may be appropriate to place the burden of proof on the organization proposing the potentially risky activity to show that it is safe, and for inaction until a proof of safety has been provided.

The main problem with the precautionary principle is that it potentially forbids too much, and opponents have argued that several innovations used today would not have been implemented if the precautionary principle had been adhered to.

Table 2.7 ACM code of conduct

No.	Area	Description
1. *General principles*		
1.1	Contribute to society and human well-being	Computer professionals must strive to develop computer systems that will be used in socially responsible ways with minimal negative consequences
1.2	Avoid harm to others	Computer professionals must follow best practice to ensure that they develop high-quality systems that are safe for the public. The professional has a responsibility to report any signs of danger in the workplace that could result in serious damage or injury
1.3	Be honest and trustworthy	The computer professional will give an honest account of their qualifications and any conflicts of interest. The professional will make accurate statement on the system and the system design and will exercise care in representing ACM
1.4	Be fair and act not to discriminate	Computer professionals are required to ensure that there is no discrimination in the use of computer resources, and that equality, tolerance, and respect for others are respected
1.5	Respect property rights/intellectual property	The professional must not violate copyright or patent law, and only authorized copies of software should be made. The integrity of intellectual property must be protected, and credit for another person's ideas or work must not be taken
1.6	Respect the privacy of others	The professional must ensure that any personal information gathered for a specific purpose is not used for another purpose without the consent of the individuals. User data observed during normal system operation must be treated with the strictest confidentiality
1.7	Respect confidentiality	The professional will respect all confidentiality obligations to employers, clients, and users
2. *Professional responsibility*		
2.1	Quality of processes/product	Computing professionals should strive to achieve the highest quality work throughout the process
2.2	Maintain high standards	It is essential to maintain high standards of technical knowledge and competence, and to upgrade skills on an ongoing basis

(continued)

Table 2.7 (continued)

No.	Area	Description
2.3	Respect rules	Computing professionals must adhere to rules including national and international laws and regulations
2.4	Professional review	Peer reviews play an important role in building quality into a work product, and computing professions should seek reviews of their work as well as participating in reviews
2.5	Comprehensive evaluations	Computing professionals are required to be thorough and comprehensive in their evaluation of computer systems including analysis and management of risk
2.6	Areas of competence	Computing professionals should only undertake work for which they have the required competence
2.7	Foster public awareness	Computing professionals should share technical knowledge with the public and foster public awareness and understanding of computing
2.8	Authorised use of resources	Computing professionals should only access computer systems and software unless they are authorized to do so
2.9	Secure systems	Computing professionals should develop robust and secure systems, as well as mitigation techniques and policies
3. Professional leadership		
3.1	Public good	The leader should ensure that the public good is the central concern during all professional computing works
3.2	Social responsibilities	Leaders should encourage computing professionals in meeting relevant social responsibilities
3.3	Quality of working life	Leaders should enhance the quality of working life of workers

(continued)

Table 2.7 (continued)

No.	Area	Description
3.4	Support principles of Code	Leaders should pursue policies that are consistent with the Code and communicate them to the relevant stakeholders
3.5	Support growth of professionals	Leaders should ensure that opportunities are available to computing professionals to improve their knowledge and skill
3.6	Modifying/Retiring Systems	Leaders should exercise care when modifying or retiring systems
3.7	Special care	Leaders have a responsibility to be good stewards of systems that become part of the infrastructure of society
4. Compliance		
4.1	Uphold code	Computing professionals should adhere to the principles in the Code and strive to improve them, and to express their concern to any individuals thought to be violating the code
4.2	Violations of code	ACM members who recognize a breach in the Code should consider reporting the violation to the ACM

Further, its opponents argue that its demands for incontrovertible proof of no damage or harm is impractical, and that it is more sensible to demand that there are reasonable grounds for believing that there is no harm.

The precautionary principle may also be applied to unknown threats, where the principle permits preventive measures to be taken prior to fully knowing the seriousness of the threat. That is,

1. There is a threat
2. The threat is uncertain
3. Action is required
4. Action is taken

2.7 Review Questions

1. Explain professional responsibility and accountability.
2. What is a code of ethics?
3. Describe the main features of the IEEE code of conduct.
4. Describe the main features of the BCS code of conduct.
5. Describe the main features of the ACM code of conduct.

6. What is the role of a whistle-blower?
7. Give examples of conflicts of interest that could arise in the work place.
8. What is the precautionary principle?

2.8   Summary

Software engineers have responsibilities as computer professionals in that they are responsible for designing and implementing high-quality and reliable software that is safe for the public to use. They are also accountable for their own decisions and actions and have a responsibility to object to decisions that violate professional standards.

Professional engineers have a duty to their clients to ensure that they are solving the real problem of the client. They need to precisely state the problem before working on its solution. Engineers need to be honest about current capabilities when asked to work on problems that have no appropriate technical solution, rather than accepting a contract for something that cannot be done.

Professional engineers are required to follow rules of good practice and to object when rules are violated. The licensing of an engineer requires that the engineer completes an accepted engineering course and understands the professional responsibility of an engineer. The professional body is responsible for enforcing standards and certification. That is, the term *"engineer"* is awarded only to those that have achieved a certain minimum level of competence, and the term places responsibilities on its holder.

Several professional organizations such as the British Computer Society, IEEE, and ACM have developed a code of ethics for their members to adhere to. These codes provide guidelines for the responsible behaviour of their members, and members may be disciplined for violating the code of ethics. A code of ethics places professional and ethical responsibilities on software engineers.

A whistle-blower is a person who speaks out and informs the public on potentially unsafe or criminal acts in an organization. Speaking out may be the ethical thing to do but it often comes at a serious cost to the employee.

Reference

1. R. C. Barquin, *In Pursuit of a 'Ten Commandments' for Computer Ethics*, (Computer Ethics Institute, 1992)

Ethical Software Engineering

3

Key Topics

Safety and ethics
Therac-25
Space shuttle disaster
Volkswagen scandal
Ethical project management
Ethical software testing
Ethical design and development

3.1 Introduction

Software engineering is a discipline that is concerned with the development of software, and it includes activities such as requirements gathering and definition, software design and development, and software testing to verify the correctness of the software. It is a team-based activity with several roles involved such as project managers, system analysts, developers, and testers. Software engineering is much more than programming, and it involves rigorous engineering practices to define the right requirements, and to design and implement an appropriate solution that is fit for purpose and satisfies the requirements.

Technical decisions need to be made in software engineering, and often these decisions affect people's lives, with potential harmful impacts on others and society. This means that the ethical impacts of technical decisions need to be considered as part of the software engineering process, and so the ethical software engineer needs to examine both the technical and the ethical dimensions of decisions that affect wider society. At a minimum ethical, software engineers should

G. O'Regan, *Guide to Software Project Management*, Undergraduate Topics in Computer Science, https://doi.org/10.1007/978-3-031-80578-3_3

- Do no harm
- Do not take bribes
- Be fair to others

A fundamental principle of ethics is based on the Hippocratic Oath "Do *no harm*", which may be seen to be breached where there are violations of ethics. For example, the Volkswagen emissions scandal (discussed later in the chapter) led to the deception of the public and harm to society, the company, and its employees. The actions of Volkswagen were unethical and illegal.

We discussed the professional responsibilities of software engineers in Chap. 2, as well as the code of ethics/conduct of several professional bodies such as IEEE, ACM, and BCS. The codes of ethics provide guidance on the interaction of technology and values, and software engineers and project managers need to be aware of their ethical responsibilities throughout the software development process, and to act when ethical standards are in danger of being violated.

3.2 Safety and Ethics

The release of an unreliable software product may result in damage to property or injury (including loss of life) to a third party. Consequently, companies need to be confident that their software products are fit for purpose prior to their release. It is essential that software that is widely used is dependable, which means that the software is available whenever required, and that it operates safely and reliably without any adverse side effects.

Today, billions of devices and computers are connected to the Internet, and this has led to a growth in attacks on computers. It is essential that computer security is carefully considered, and that software developers and managers are aware of the threats facing a system, and develop techniques to eliminate them. That is, software developers need to be able to develop secure dependable systems that can deal with and recover from external attacks.

A safety-critical system is a system whose failure could result in significant economic damage or loss of life. There are many examples of safety-critical systems such as aircraft flight control systems, nuclear power stations, and missile systems. It is essential to employ rigorous processes in the design and development of safety-critical systems, and software testing alone is usually insufficient in verifying the correctness of these systems.

The safety-critical industry takes the view that any change to safety-critical software creates a new program. The new program is therefore required to demonstrate that it is reliable and safe to the public, and so extensive testing needs to be performed. Additional techniques such as formal verification and model checking may be employed to provide an extra level of assurance in the correctness of these systems.

Safety-critical systems need to be reliable, dependable, and available for use whenever required. The software must operate correctly and reliably without any adverse side effects. The consequence of failure (e.g., the failure of a weapons system) could be massive damage, leading to loss of life or endangering the lives of the public. We discuss two important case studies on disasters that occurred in the mid-1980s, and these are the Therac-25 disaster and the Space Shuttle Challenger disaster.

3.2.1 Therac-25 Disaster

The Therac-25 was a computer-controlled radiation therapy machine that was developed by the Atomic Energy of Canada (AECL) in the early 1980s. This linear accelerator treated cancer patients by exposing them to a beam of particles that would destroy malignant tissue (Fig. 3.1).

The machine consisted of hardware and software, and whereas the role of software on the earlier Therac-20 machine was limited, software played a more important role in the Therac-25 machine. Its role was to perform many of the safety-critical checks for the Therac-25, whereas this was performed by hardware on the earlier Therac-20 machine. The software on the Therac-25 radiation machine was responsible for

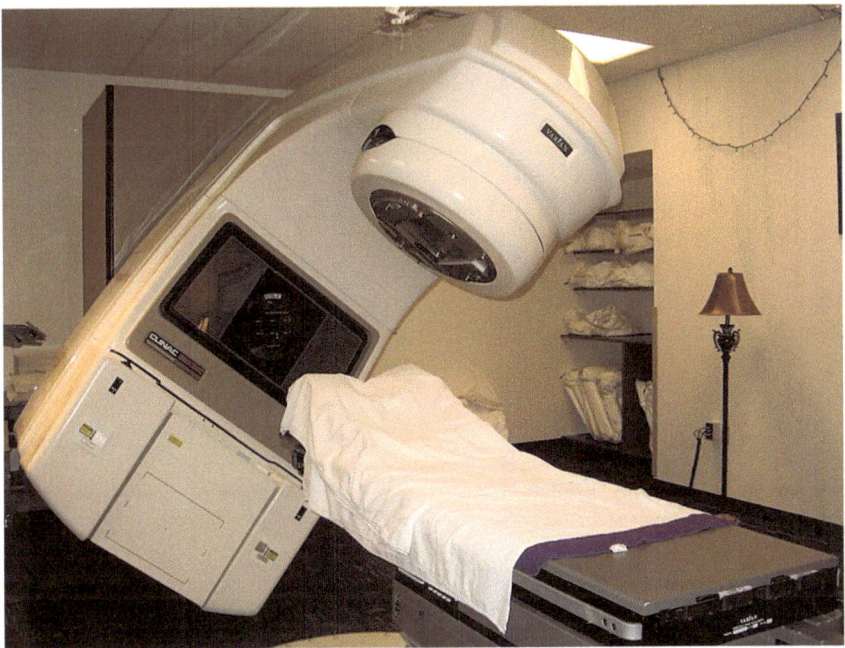

Fig. 3.1 A radiotherapy machine

- Monitoring the status of the machine.
- Accepting treatment input.
- Setting up the machine for the treatment.
- Turning on treatment beam.
- Turning off treatment beam.
- Detecting hardware malfunction.

There were six major accidents with the machine in the mid-1980s (1985–1987), where patients were given massive overdoses of radiation. The machine malfunctioned, and several patients received doses that were hundreds of times more than the appropriate dose, resulting in the death of three people and serious injuries to three others.

The machine continued in use for over 18 months after the first accident, with AECL believing that an accident was impossible with the machine, and it took no action with respect to the first accident. The second accident occurred a month later, and AECL sent an engineer on site to investigate the incident. He was unable to reproduce the problem, but AECL made some hardware and software changes and claimed that this solved the problem, as well as increasing the reliability of the machine a multiple of times.

AECL's response to the third action was denial of the problem, where they stated that the malfunction could not have been caused by the Therac-25 machine. They claimed that the fourth accident was as the result of a wiring problem. Finally, because of the fifth accident, and FDA investigations into the operation of the Therac-25 machine, AECL finally launched a thorough investigation. The FDA ruled that the Therac-25 machines were defective, and advised AECL to prepare a corrective action plan, and to advise their customers of the problems with the machine.

The corrective action plan was prepared by AECL and presented to the FDA. It led to serious concerns in the FDA with respect to the software engineering practices employed in AECL, and the risks that these posed to the delivery of a high-quality product that was safe for the public. There was a lack of software engineering and testing documentation for the software development, and the testing of the software was judged to be inadequate. The FDA directed AECL to do extensive testing on the system each time a small software change was made to ensure the safety of the software. The main reasons for the Therac-25 disaster include

- Initial failure to believe end users.
- Poor investigation of malfunction of the machine.
- Overconfidence of engineers in its correctness.
- Poor software design and development.
- Poor resolution of software defects.
- Inadequate testing.

The Therac-25 disaster led to the deaths of three people and serious injury to three others (see Ref. [1]) Software engineering practices were immature in the 1980s, but this is no excuse for what happened. It is basic common sense that a proper investigation should have been done after the first accident, and that all existing machines should have been judged unsafe until proved otherwise. That is, all Therac-25 machines should have removed from operational use until the cause of the problem had been correctly identified, and appropriate solutions implemented to prevent a reoccurrence.

3.2.2 Space Shuttle Challenger Disaster

The Space Shuttle Challenger disaster is an important case study on engineering safety and workplace ethics. The disaster occurred in January 1986, when the space shuttle broke apart 73 s into its flight, and all the seven members of the crew were killed. The Rogers Commission was formed to investigate the accident, and it found that the Challenger disaster was caused by a failure in the O-Rings sealing a joint on the right solid rocket booster. The report also criticized the decision-making process that led to the launch stating that it was deeply flawed, with conflicts between engineering data and management judgements (Fig. 3.2).

Robert Boisjoly, an Engineer at Morton Thiokel, launched strong objections to the launch, as he was aware of the risks of erosion and failure when the 0-Rings of the Solid Rocket Booster (SRB) are exposed to low temperatures. He argued that the shuttle launch should not take place on the planned date due to the predicted temperatures.

Both the NASA project team and the management team at Morton Thiokel had the opportunity to prevent the challenger disaster by postponing the launch. During the conference call on the evening prior to the launch the entire Morton Thiokel team recommended a postponement of the launch, as they recommended a minimum launch temperature of 52° F. Temperatures were forecast to drop to 30° F overnight which was likely to compromise the safety of the launch. They had expected NASA to rubber stamp the decision, but they were wrong, and NASA stated that the Morton Thiokel briefing was based on emotion rather than factual data. NASA requested Morton Thiokel to review their data again to determine if the data showed that it was unsafe to proceed, and the conference call was rescheduled to later in the evening.

For a launch to take place all subcontractors must sign-off on going ahead, and NASA seems to have encouraged (perhaps pressurized) Morton Thiokel to recommend the launch unless they could prove that it was unsafe to do so. The conference call had been delayed allowing Morton Thiokel management to consider all of the data, and the result of the Morton Thiokel management meeting (which excluded participation from Boisjoly) was to proceed with the launch. Morton Thiokel stated that its data was inconclusive at the conference call with NASA, and all subcontractors agreed to proceed with the launch. Boisjoly later called the Morton Thiokel decision to go ahead to be unethical.

Fig. 3.2 Space challenger disaster

Separatism is the idea that scientists and engineers provide the technical input and advice to management concerning a particular engineering situation, and management decide how best to proceed. That is, managers act as the decision-maker taking all inputs into account to make a value judgement on the best way to proceed. This approach generally works fine in engineering, but problems arise when managers are trying to balance conflicting values such as achieving a strict delivery constraint and the safety of an operation, and where management believes (or encourages their subordinates to support their belief) that there is a small but manageable risk. It is essential to have openness and transparency in decision-making, where decisions are made on the objective facts and data, and risks are kept to an absolute minimum and are manageable.

The *precautionary principle* was discussed in Chap. 2 and requires that a particular course of action be demonstrated to be safe prior to being conducted. This was the normal *modus operandi* of NASA, but NASA changed the burden of proof the night before the launch to demand that Morton Thiokel prove to NASA management that it was unsafe to proceed with launch. However, once Morton Thiokel gave their approval and ignored the input of Robert Boisjoly, it could be argued that Boisjoly had a moral responsibility to be a whistle-blower given the likelihood that safety would be compromised due to the forecasted low temperatures for the launch. Boisjoly may have taken the position that he had advised management of the dangers with launch (following the principle of separatism), and that it was the responsibility of management to act by postponing the launch.

3.3   Ethical Software Design and Development

Ethical software design and development is concerned with ethical issues that may arise during technology development, such as questions as to how the technology will be used, and whether it could lead to harm to individuals and society. The design of a technology determines how it will be used, and this means that there needs to be an ethical dimension to the design process, where ethical values are considered as well as the desired functionality.

David Lean[1] directed the movie *"The Bridge on the River Kwai"* in 1957, and the film was based on the historical construction of the Thailand-Burma railway that took place during the Japanese occupation of Burma in the Second World War. British prisoners of war were ordered to construct the bridge, and initially the British and their leader, Colonel Nicholson, resisted participation in its construction. However, Colonel Nicholson later became obsessed with designing and building a proper bridge that would last well beyond the war, and that would be a tribute to the skill and ingenuity of British engineers (Fig. 3.3).

---

[1] David Lean was an influential film director who directed well-known movies such as Lawrence of Arabia, Doctor Zhivago, A Passage to India and Ryan's Daughter.

Fig. 3.3 Bridge over the River Kwai in Kanchanburi, Thailand

They build a solid bridge over the river and on the day that it was due to open with the first train due to pass over Nicholson finally realized the gravity of what he has done (i.e., collaborating with the enemy and contributing to their plans for further aggression). He blows up the bridge sending the train into the river. That is, the purpose of the technology (i.e., the completed bridge) needed to be considered, as a completed bridge would cause harm to others in that it would have facilitated an expansion of Japanese aggression to other countries. Further, it was unethical for Nicholson to collaborate with his enemy who wished to harm him and his country, and his collaboration conflicted with his duties to the British army.

Software design is the process where certain functions are translated into a blueprint for a system that can fulfil these functions. It is a systematic process that uses technical and scientific knowledge, and there may need for trade-offs with conflicting ethical values. There are often several design choices for a particular technology, and different designs may vary in the extent to which they deal with individual ethical values. The goal is to choose the design that best meets the most important ethical values and technology considerations, and this means that responsible choices must be made in the selection of the most appropriate design. It involves activities such as

- Problem analysis.
- Requirements analysis and definition (may include prototyping).
- Architectural design (may include design options and decision).
- Low level design.

- Implementation.
- Testing.
- Maintenance.

Value-centred design is an approach to design that involves taking human values into account during the design process, and solving value conflicts through engineering design and technological innovation. It involves investigating and determining the values that are relevant to the project, and understanding conflicts to make trade-offs. There is a need to analyse designs to determine the extent to which they meet individual values, and to develop innovative designs to meet particularly relevant moral values. Value-centred design involves

- Reasoning/clarifying values underlying conflicting design requirements.
- Social cost-benefit analysis (including monetary costs for safety).
- Evaluation criteria (including value criteria, weightings may be employed).
- Thresholds for what is acceptable for each criterion.
- Evaluation of options.
- Selected option.

There may be conflicts between ethical values when choosing between two or more design options, and where the different designs score well on different criteria. This is where designers are unable to do justice to all ethical values simultaneously, and often the resolution of these moral dilemmas requires a trade-off and fining a balance between competing values. A trade-off decision is where a choice needs to be made between at least two options, in which at least two moral values are relevant as choice criteria, and so finding the right balance in the trade-off decisions may be a challenge (Fig. 3.4).

Software designers have a responsibility to create ethical designs that satisfy the requirements, and to ensure that their designs are robust and protect the safety of the public. Ethics is an important design concern that should be considered, and this will determine how well the product fits within the ethical boundaries. There may be several ethical values that may be relevant, including safety, accessibility, usability, sustainability, privacy, security, honesty, fairness, and loyalty. The evaluation of each design option should rate the extent to which the relevant moral values are addressed by that option as well as the technical criteria.

Data management is an important part of ethical software engineering, where personal data ownership as well as data rights, access rights, privacy and security rights need to be considered and protected. Software designers need to follow best practice in privacy and security in collecting, processing, and protecting data. An ethical system needs to be accessible, and its design should consider its accessibility for different categories of users, such as those with visual or hearing impairments, or those with different levels of language ability or education.

The ethical design of a software system should give an open and accurate account of the system and should satisfy all relevant legal and regulatory requirements. We discuss the Volkswagen diesel gate emissions scandal in the next

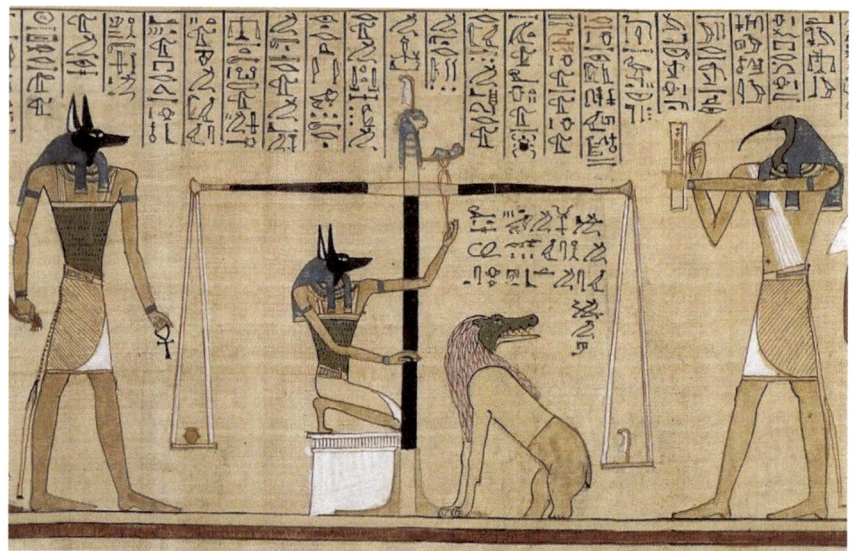

Fig. 3.4 Balancing an ethical life against a feather in Egyptian religion

section, where the unethical conduct of the company and its management involved tasking software designers to develop a "*defeat device*" to cheat the vehicle emissions tests.

Ethical software designers need to be conscious of the algorithms that they create to ensure that they are unbiased, and do not discriminate against minority groups in society. This is especially important in machine learning algorithms based on pattern matching that are employed in the AI field, where *biased algorithms* may lead to discrimination such as in controversies including the Amazon hiring algorithm which discriminated against females, and predictive policing algorithm which led to racial profiling and discrimination against minorities.

Software designers should consider the ultimate purpose of the project including its benefits to society as well as harm of the technology. We discussed the purpose of the "Bridge over the river Kwai", and argued that its design and construction would lead to harm to the Allies in their war against Japan. Social media and various other apps are deliberately designed to be *addictive* to their users, where the software captures the attention of the human at a primal level, and the company reaps financial gain from the addiction of the users. Humans have become addicted to their smartphones, and check their phone hundreds of times a day, and their addiction has been caused by addictive software design. This poses questions on the ethics of this addictive design, and whether the consequences of design as well as the end product should be considered in ethical decision-making.[2]

The system needs to be designed for security, as it is difficult to add security after the system has been implemented. Security engineering is concerned with the development of systems that can prevent malicious attacks and recover from them. Software developers need to be aware of the threats facing a system and develop solutions to manage them. Security loopholes may be introduced in the development of the system, and so care needs to be taken to prevent these as well as preventing hackers from exploiting security vulnerabilities.

There is a need to conduct a risk assessment of the security threats facing a system early in the software development process, and this will lead to several security requirements for the system. That is, the requirements of the system should specify security and privacy requirements, and the software design and development must implement them to ensure that security and privacy are not breached. Security testing (including penetration testing) is carried out to identify any flaws in the security mechanisms of the computer system, and to verify that the security requirements, such as confidentiality, availability, and integrity, are satisfied. However, the successful completion of security testing does not guarantee that there are no security vulnerabilities in the system. Hackers will still attempt to steal confidential data and to disrupt the services being offered by a system.

3.3.1 Volkswagen Emissions Scandal

The Volkswagen *Diesel gate* scandal arose as a result of the German company deliberately programming its turbocharged direct injection (TDI) diesel engines to activate their emission controls only during laboratory emission tests. This meant that the vehicles' NO_x emissions passed the US regulatory requirements during laboratory tests, whereas the actual emissions were over 40 times higher in real-world driving (Fig. 3.5).

Volkswagen deployed this software in over 11 million vehicles worldwide including roughly half a million vehicles in the United States from 2009 to 2015. It became evident in 2014 that there were discrepancies in emissions between European and US models, and regulators in several countries launched an investigation into Volkswagen. Several senior executives resigned or were suspended, and Volkswagen spent billions in recalling the affected vehicles and rectifying the issues with the emissions.

---

[2] The rise of the Internet has led to giant technology companies such as Facebook, Apple, Amazon, and Google, and the business model (for some of these companies) is based upon gathering data about the users, and selling this data to advertisers (surveillance capitalism). Often, software developers are so focused on providing technical solutions that they do not consider the wider picture of the technology that they are creating, and the potential negative impacts of technology on society.

Fig. 3.5 Volkswagen Beetle Type 82E

Volkswagen pleaded guilty to criminal charges in 2017, and they admitted to developing a "defeat device" to enable diesel models to pass US emission tests and deliberately concealing its use. Volkswagen was fined $2.8 billion for rigging the vehicles to cheat on the emission tests. The scandal had cost Volkswagen $33 billion in fines, penalties, financial settlements, and buyback costs by mid-2020. Martin Winterkorn resigned his position of the CEO of Volkswagen in 2015, and he was charged with fraud and conspiracy in the United States in 2018.

The scandal highlighted how software-controlled machinery is prone to cheating, and it has opened a debate on whether there is a need for a mechanism to independently verify software that is employed to satisfy safety, legal, or regulatory requirements. That is, should all such software code be published for scrutiny by independent regulators and/or independently certified?

The Volkswagen scandal is deeply concerning as it demonstrates the failure of corporate business ethics to act as a barrier to the pursuit of business self-interest. Volkswagen is a prestigious German company, and it is extraordinary that the professionalism that Germany is renowned for could be tarnished in this way. Unfortunately, sometimes the code of ethics of an organization are just window dressing for the public, rather than being embraced and engrained in the day-to-day work practices of corporate life. Why did engineers fail to consider their ethical responsibilities? Why did they fail to question the implementation of this device? Why were there no whistle-blowers to speak out against these unethical practices?

Was there a lack of moral courage among the engineers? Were there appropriate structures in place for whistle-blowers to discuss ethical concerns? Volkswagen's actions were illegal and deeply unethical, and its good name has been tarnished.

A corporate environment is generally focused on the business and product implementation rather than on critical reflection on the wider implications of the technology. Engineers are often busy with their lives outside the office while trying to build a career within the office and speaking out may not be viewed as career advancing. Further, a hierarchical work environment does not actively encourage speaking out on issues outside of product development, with corporate enterprises often *command-driven operations*, with power assigned within the hierarchy, and subordinates may fear the consequences of speaking out.

Engineers are often focused on getting the software to perform correctly to meet its specification, and so often may not consider the wider societal impacts of the technology. However, it is in the interest of both corporations and their employees to consider the bigger picture, and to actively consider ethical issues in the design process. Otherwise, they could well pay the price for their inaction later with significant damage to the reputation of the corporation and financial loss.

3.4   Ethical Software Testing

Software testers are professionals and need to always behave ethically during testing. The ISTQB Code of Ethics for test professionals is based on the IEEE and ACM code of ethics and it states that

Certified software testers shall act consistently in the public interest.
They act in the best interests of their client and employer.
They ensure that their deliverables meet the highest professional standards.
They maintain independence and integrity in professional judgements.
They shall promote an ethical approach to the management of software testing.
They shall advance the integrity and reputation of the profession.
They shall be supportive of colleagues and cooperate with software developers.
They shall participate in lifelong learning and promote ethics in their profession.

Comprehensive testing reduces the risk of serious quality problems with the software, but it is impossible to test everything due to time constraints. This means that the testers need to focus their testing on the areas of greatest risk with the software, and on the parts of the system that the users are most likely to be using. It is essential that the testers have the appropriate expertise, that the right test environment is set up, that they have prepared test plans and test specification to test the software, and that they have all the required tools in place.

Ethical issues may arise during testing if the project is behind schedule, and when there is pressure applied to the test team to stay with the original project delivery schedule. It may be that the available time for testing is insufficient to verify the correctness of the software, or the limited time could lead to testers missing serious defects. This could lead to the quality of the released software being compromised, and the test manager needs to resist any pressure that poses risks to quality and needs to raise concerns at senior level where appropriate.

It is essential that the customer be informed of all quality problems with the software to ensure that they can manage any associated risks. The final test report should summarize the testing that has been done, the results of the testing, the open problems, the problem arrival rate, and known risks with the software. The final test report generally includes a recommendation from the test manager to release the software, and such a recommendation should be based on the key facts with a clear statement that all risks can be managed.

There may be conflicts when the project manager wishes to release the software on schedule, and where the test manager has concerns or believes that it is unsafe to do so based on the key testing status and risks. It is essential in such situations that the decision made is based on the facts and risks, and objective data should support the decision that is made.

3.5   Review Questions

1. What is ethical software engineering?
2. Explain how the Therac-25 disaster occurred.
3. Explain how the challenger disaster occurred.
4. What is ethical software design?
5. What is value-centred design?
6. What is ethical software testing?
7. What is ethical project management?
8. Explain the concept of separatism.
9. What are the ethical considerations in the development of safety-critical systems?

3.6   Summary

Ethical software engineering is concerned with ethical issues that may arise during software development, such as questions as to how the technology will be used, and whether it could lead to harm to individuals and society.

Ethics and professional responsibility apply to many areas in software engineering. There is a need for ethical project management where project managers have a *responsibility* for the decisions that they make (or fail to make), and the actions that they take (or fail to take). Further, they should be aware of regulations and laws that govern their work.

There is an ethical dimension to the design process, where ethical values need to be considered as well as the desired functionality. Ethical issues may arise during testing if the project is behind schedule, and when there is pressure applied to the test team to stay with the original project delivery schedule.

The space shuttle challenger disaster in the mid-1980s is an important case study on engineering safety and workplace ethics. The disaster was caused by a failure in the O-Rings sealing, and the decision-making that led to the launch was deeply flawed.

The Volkswagen dieselgate emissions scandal involved the German company deliberately programming a "defeat device" to enable diesel models to pass US emission tests and concealing its use.

Reference

1. N. Leveson, C. Turner, An investigation of the Therac-25 accidents. Computer (26), 18–41 (1993)

Legal and Ethical Responsibilities of Project Managers

4

Key Topics

Ethics
Law of tort
Lawsuits
Professional responsibility
Professional negligence
Test outsourcing
Software licenses
Computer crime
Hacking

4.1 Introduction

Ethics is a practical branch of philosophy that deals with moral questions such as what is right or wrong, and how a person should behave in a given situation in a complex world. Ethics explore what actions are right or wrong within a specific context or within a certain society, and seek to find satisfactory answers to moral questions. The origin of the word "ethics" is from the Greek word ἠθικός, which means habit or custom.

There are various schools of ethics such as the *relativist* position (as defined by Protagoras), which argues that each person decides on what is right or wrong for them; *cultural relativism* argues that the particular society determines what is right or wrong based upon its cultural values; *deontological ethics* (as defined by Kant) argues that there are moral laws to guide people in deciding what is right or wrong; and *utilitarianism* which argues that an action is right if its overall effect is to produce more happiness than unhappiness in society.

Professional ethics define a code of conduct that governs how members of a profession deal with each other and with third parties. A professional code of ethics expresses ideals of human behaviour, and it defines the fundamental principles of the organization, and is an indication of its professionalism. We discussed the code of ethics of the ACM, BCS, and IEEE in Chap.2, and violations of the code by members are taken seriously and are subject to investigations and disciplinary procedures (see Chap. 2).

Business ethics define the core values of the business, and are used to guide employee behaviour. Should an employee accept gifts from a supplier to a company as this could lead to a conflict of interest? A company may face ethical questions on the use of technology. For example, should the use of a new technology be restricted because people can use it for illegal or harmful actions as well as beneficial ones?

Consider mobile phone technology, which has transformed communication between people, and thus is highly beneficial to society. What about mobile phones with cameras? On the one hand, they provide useful functionality in combining a phone and a camera. On the other hand, they may be employed to take indiscreet photos without permission of others, which may then be placed on inappropriate sites. In other words, how can citizens be protected from inappropriate use of such technology, and how should such technology be regulated?

4.2   Professional Responsibilities of Project Managers

Software projects have a history of being delivered late- or over-budget, and software project management is concerned with the effective management of software projects to ensure the delivery of a high-quality product, on time and on budget, to the customer.

Project managers are professionals, and they must behave professionally and ethically during the project. Project management professionals have a responsibility for the decisions and actions that they make (or fail to make). They should accept only those assignments for which they have the required competence, and commitments made should be fulfilled.

Project managers have a duty to show respect to others and to be fair in decision-making, and they should refrain from participating in decision-making where there is a potential conflict of interest. Finally, it is the duty of project managers to act in a truthful and honest manner in their communication and conduct, and not to deceive others.

The project manager is accountable for the success of the project, and endeavours to balance budget, schedule, effort, and quality. This could potentially lead to ethical dilemmas when the project manager is tempted to cut corners to enable the project to be delivered on time and on budget. This could potentially result in quality being compromised, health and safety being compromised, privacy being compromised, and so on. The code of ethics of the Project Management Institute is discussed in the next section.

4.2.1   PMI Code of Ethics for Project Managers

Project managers are professionals, and they must behave professionally and ethically at all times during the project. The *Project Management Institute* (PMI) has defined a code of ethics and professional behaviour for project management, which defines the expectations of the behaviour of project management professionals. These core values include

Professional responsibility
Respect
Fairness
Honesty

Project management professionals have a *responsibility* for the decisions that they make (or fail to make), and the actions that they take (or fail to take). They should accept only those assignments for which they have the required competence, and commitments made should be fulfilled. Errors or omissions should be corrected promptly, and any proprietary information provided should be protected. Further, any unethical or illegal conduct should be reported to management, and project management professions should be aware of regulations and laws that govern their work.

Project managers have a duty to show *respect* to others including sensitivity of behaviour in working with others from different cultural backgrounds. This involves always behaving professionally, listening to others' point of view, and seeking to understand them, and working through conflicts and disagreements with others.

Project managers have a duty to be *fair* in decision-making with decisions made objectively and impartially, and they should refrain from participating in decision-making where there is a potential conflict of interest. Further, favouritism and discrimination are not allowed.

Finally, it is the duty of project managers to act in a truthful and *honest* manner in their communication and conduct, and not to engage in or condone behaviour that attempts to deceive others (e.g., making misleading or false statements).

The project manager is accountable for the success of the project, and larger projects have more opportunities for ethics being compromised than smaller projects. Project managers endeavour to balance budget, schedule, effort, and quality, which may potentially lead to ethical dilemmas when the project manager is tempted to cut corners to enable the project to be delivered on time and on budget. This could potentially result in quality being compromised, health and safety being compromised, privacy being compromised, and so on.

The selection of a subcontractor could pose a conflict of interest to the project manager, where the project manager knows one of the candidate subcontractors from a previous working relationship or family relationships. It is therefore important that in such a situation that the project manager excludes herself from the supplier selection to ensure that there is no conflict of interest.

Project management involves ethical decision-making, and good project governance is a good enabler of ethical project management. It enables the key project stakeholders to be kept informed of the key project status and the key decisions being made regularly during the project.

4.3   Legal Aspects of Project Management

Legal aspects of software project management are concerned with the application of the legal system to project management and software projects. It includes intellectual property law covering patents, copyright, trademarks, and trade secrets. Patents provide legal protection for intellectual ideas, copyright law protects the expression of an idea, trademarks provide legal protection of names or symbols, and trade secrets protect commercially sensitive secret information. There are potential legal impacts on a software development organization should the software be inadequately tested, and where the quality of the testing is deemed to be negligent leading to loss or damage to another party.

Software test tools are generally subject to a license, where a software license is a legal agreement between the copyright owner and the licensee that governs the use or distribution of software to the user. The two most common categories of software licenses that may be granted under copyright law are those for proprietary software and those for free open-source software.

Electronic commerce includes transactions to place an order, the acknowledgement of the order, the acceptance of the order where a legal contract now exists between both parties, and order fulfilment. We discuss the legal aspects of bespoke software development and test outsourcing, where a legal contract is prepared between the supplier and the customer. This will generally include a statement of work that stipulates the deliverables to be produced, and it may also include a service level agreement and an Escrow agreement.

4.3.1   Legal Impacts of Failure

Software license agreements generally provide limited warranties on the quality of the licensed software, with limited remedies to the customer when the software is defective. The software vendor typically promises that the software will conform to the software documentation for a specified period (the *warranty period*), and the software warranty generally excludes problems that are not caused by the software or are beyond the software vendor's control.

The customers are generally provided with limited remedies in the case of defective software (e.g., the replacement of the software with a corrected version, or termination of the user's right to use the defective software and a partial refund of the license fee). The payment of compensation for loss or damage is generally excluded in the software licensing agreement.

Software licensing agreements are generally accompanied by a comprehensive disclaimer that protects the software vendor from any liability (however remote) that might result from the use of the software. It may include statements such as *"the software is provided 'as is', and that the customers use the software at their own risk"*.

A limited warranty and disclaimer limits the customer's rights and remedies if the licensed software is defective, and so the customer may need to consider how best to manage the associated risks. However, there are various lawsuits that could potentially be launched against a software provider and these are discussed in the next section.

4.3.2   Lawsuits and Professional Negligence

A lawsuit is a proceeding by one party (or several parties) against another party (or several parties) in a civil court. The basic principles of litigation are where the plaintiff sues another person(s) (i.e., the defendant) for being negligent, and where the negligence of the defendant caused injury or damage to the property of the plaintiff. It involves proving in a court of law that:

The defendant had a duty of care.
The defendant breached this duty of care.
The breach caused harm to the plaintiff or the property of the plaintiff.

The plaintiff is entitled to compensation of the full value of the injury or the damage to the property if the case is successfully proved. Further, if there is clear evidence that the defendant acted maliciously or fraudulently then punitive damages may be awarded to the plaintiff to punish the defendant. Punitive damages are generally awarded in a small percentage of lawsuits, and they may be appealed to a higher court.

There are several types of lawsuit that may be brought against a software company (the defendant) which are given in Table 4.1.

4.3.3   Legal Breach of Contact in Outsourcing

The legal agreement between the company and the subcontractor specifies the terms to be satisfied and the obligations on both parties for the duration of the contract. These include the deliverables to be produced, the timelines, the responsibilities of both parties, and the financial payments to be made at agreed milestones. A contract is legally binding on both parties with both having defined obligations and should one party fail to deliver according to the terms of the agreement then they may be in breach of the contract.

A *material breach* is where one party does not fulfil their obligations under the contract or delivers a significantly different result from that defined in the

Table 4.1 Types of lawsuits

Type	Description
Criminal	This type of lawsuit is brought by the state against the software company (or developers or testers) for committing a criminal act (e.g., tampering with a computer or loading a virus onto a computer)
Tort	This type of lawsuit is brought by an individual(s) against a company/developers for committing some wrong to you or your computer (e.g., releasing a virus onto your computer)
Negligence	The company has a duty of care to take reasonable measures to make the product safe to ensure that there are no personal injuries or damage to property
Malpractice	This is where the quality of service is judged against a professional standard and deemed to be negligent, with mistakes made in the delivery of the service that would not be made by an ordinary professional in the field
Strict liability	A product defect caused a personal injury or damage to property, and the burden of proof required is to demonstrate that the program was defective and that the defect caused the accident (e.g., the failure of the program controlling the breaks in an automobile led to an accident)
Fraud	The company made a statement of fact to you when it knew that the statement was false (and where you relied on the statement to make an economic decision such as buying a defective product)
Regulatory	The regulatory sector (e.g., FDA) places requirements on how software should be developed and tested to ensure that it is safe for the public to use
Breach of contract	A software contract specifies the obligations that both parties have to each other (as well as implied terms such as implied warranty)

contract. An *anticipatory breach* is where one party has indicated that they will not be fulfilling their obligations under the contract, and while an actual breach has not yet occurred there is an intention to be in breach of the contract. Both parties will generally discuss and attempt to resolve any such breaches, and it is generally easy to resolve *minor breaches*. However, if both parties are unable to resolve their dispute over a material breach in the contract, then one party may decide to sue the other party for being in breach of contract. However, legal disputes tend to be expensive and time-consuming, and it is in the best interest of both parties to come to a resolution of their dispute without the involvement of their lawyers.

The plaintiff will bring the lawsuit to court claiming a material breach in the contract, and the plaintiff will need to show that there was a legally binding contract between both parties, that the plaintiff fulfilled all of his obligations under the contract (unless there was a legitimate reason not to), that the defendant failed to honour the terms of the legal agreement, and that the defendant's actions led to loss being suffered by the plaintiff. This is described in more detail in Chap. 10.

4.3.4 The Law of Tort

The *law of tort* refers to a civil wrong where one party (the *defendant*) is held accountable for their actions (by the *plaintiff*). There are several actions that the defendant could be held accountable, e.g., negligence, trespass, misstatement, product liability, defamation, and so on. For example, the defendant may be accused of negligence and a breach of his duty of care, where damage that was reasonably foreseeable was caused by negligence.

The impact of a flaw in the software may be catastrophic (e.g., the failures of the defective Therac-25 machine led to several fatalities and were discussed in Chap. 3), and so a software development organization must take all reasonable precautions to prevent the occurrence of defects (as otherwise it may be sued for negligence). This is especially true in the safety-critical domain, where defects could cause major damage or even loss of life. Reasonable precautions consist of having appropriate software engineering practices in place to allow the organization to consistently produce high-quality software.

A quality management system indicates that the organization takes software quality seriously, and has a sound software development process in place that serves the needs of the organization and its customers. Software quality assurance includes processes for software inspections and testing, checklists for verifying quality, milestone and customer reviews, quality audits, and so on.

The organization will require evidence or records to prove that the quality management system is in place, that it is appropriate for the organization, and that it is fully operational within the organization. This generally requires records and an audit trail of the various quality activities to be maintained. The records enable the organization to prepare a legal defence to show that it took all reasonable steps in software development, especially if a customer decides to take legal action for negligence against the software provider following a serious problem with the software at the customer site.

The presence of records may be used to indicate that all reasonable steps were taken, and the records typically include lists of all the deliverables in the project; minutes of project meetings; records of reviews of requirements, design, and software code; records of test plans, testing, and test results; and so on.

4.3.5 Legal Aspects of Outsourcing

The outsourcing of software development is common in the software engineering field, and this is where the development or testing (or both) is outsourced to an independent external organization. Bespoke (or custom) software is software that is developed for a specific customer or organization, and it needs to satisfy the defined customer requirements. The organization will need to be rigorous in its selection of the appropriate supplier, as it is essential that the supplier selected has the capability of delivering high-quality and reliable software on time and on budget.

Fig. 4.1 Legal contract. Creative commons

This means that the capability of the supplier is clearly understood and the associated risks are known prior to selection. The selection is based on objective criteria such as cost, the approach, the ability of the supplier to deliver the required solution, the supplier capability, and while cost is an important criterion, it is just one among several other important factors (Fig. 4.1).

Once the selection of the supplier is finalized a legal agreement is drawn up between the contractor and supplier, which states the terms and condition of the contract as well as the statement of work. The *statement of work* (SOW) details the work to be carried out, the deliverables to be produced, when they will be produced, the personnel involved their roles and responsibilities, any training to be provided, and the standards to be followed. The agreement will need to be signed by both parties, and may (depending on the type of agreement) include (Fig. 4.2):

Legal Contract
Statement of Work
Implementation Plan
Training Plan
User Guides and Manuals
Customer Support to be provided
Service Level Agreement

Escrow Agreement
Warranty Period

A *service level agreement* (SLA) is an agreement between the customer and service provider which specifies the service that the customer will receive as well as the response time to customer issues and problems. It will also detail the penalties should the service performance fall below the defined levels.

An *Escrow agreement* is an agreement made between two parties where an independent trusted third party acts as an intermediary between both parties. The intermediary receives money from one party and sends it to the other party when contractual obligations are satisfied. Under an Escrow agreement the trusted third party may also hold documents and source code.

Occasionally, it will be just the testing part of a project that is outsourced, and test outsourcing is concerned with the selection and management of an appropriate supplier to perform the testing. It is essential that the selected test organization is capable of carrying out the required testing to the defined quality standard, as well as being capable of completing the testing within the budget and schedule constraints.

The legal contract specifies the obligations of the supplier, and should the supplier fail to honour its commitments it may well be in breach of contract. This means that the binding agreement has not been honoured, and there may be a need to seek legal remedy if a *material* breach of the contract has occurred. The first step is dialogue between both parties with the objective of finding a reasonable resolution, but if both parties are unable to agree a way forward the first party may seek a legal remedy in a civil court. Software outsourcing is discussed in more detail in Chap. 10.

4.3.6 Licenses for Tools and Software

The project team (including developers and testers) often employ specialized tools for various parts of the process, and the project manager needs to ensure that the tools have appropriate licenses. The tools may be developed in-house, but it is more common to employ proprietary tools or open-source tools. A software license is a legal agreement between the copyright owner and the licensee, which governs the use or distribution of software to the user (licensee). Computer software code is protected under copyright law in most countries, and a typical software license grants the user permission to make one or more copies of the software, where the copyright owner retains exclusive rights to the software under copyright law.

The two most common categories of software licenses that may be granted under copyright law are those for *proprietary software*, and those for *free open-source software* (FOSS). The rights granted to the licensee are quite different for each of these categories, where the user has the right to copy, modify, and distribute (under the same license) software that has been supplied under an open-source license, whereas proprietary software typically does not grant these rights to the user.

The *licensing of proprietary software* typically gives the owner of a copy of the software the right to use it (including the rights to make copies for archival purposes). The software may be accompanied with an end-user license agreement (EULA) that may place further restrictions on the rights of the user. There may be restrictions on the ownership of the copies made, and on the number of installations allowed under the term of the distribution. The ownership of the copy of the software often remains with the copyright owner, and the end user must accept the license agreement to use the software.

The most common licensing model is per single user, and the customer may purchase a certain number of licenses over a fixed period. Another model employed is the license per server model (for a site license), or a license per dongle model, which allows the owner of the dongle use the software on any computer. A license may be perpetual (it lasts forever), or it may be for a fixed period of time (typically 1 year).

The software license may include support and maintenance for a period of time (typically 1 year), and this often includes the provision of updated versions of the software during the period, as well as technical support. The two parties may sign a service level agreement (SLA), which stipulates the service that will be provided by the service provider. The SLA will often include timelines for the resolution of serious problems, as well as financial penalties that will be applicable where the customer service performance does not meet the levels defined in the SLA.

Free and open-source licenses are often divided into two categories depending on the rights to be granted in distribution of the modified software. The first category aims to give users unlimited freedom to use, study, and modify the software, and if the user adheres to the terms of an open-source license such as the Free Software Foundation (FSF) GNU or General Public License (GPL), the freedom to distribute the software and any changes made to it. The second category of open-source licenses gives the user permission to use, study, and modify the software, but not the right to distribute it freely under an open-source license (it could be distributed as part of a proprietary software license).

4.3.7   Privacy and the Law

Individuals may take a lawsuit against another when their privacy is violated such as when another person pries or stalks them, or publishes a defamatory article about them. The area of privacy has become very important in the software field with the rise of data gathering on the Internet. Data collection laws focus on how data is collected, used, and shared, and data protection includes the right to information self-determination. The web is full of privacy policies that specify what type of personal data will be collected, how it will be processed and used, how it is shared, and what can be done about it. There are three main areas that impact upon an individual's privacy:

- The Media.
- Surveillance.
- Personal data.

Media laws protect an individual against intrusion, where another party may be held liable for the invasion of the individual's privacy (e.g., phone tapping, snooping, examining a person's bank account, and so on). The tort of the public disclosure of private facts prevents others from widely spreading private facts such as the individual's face or identity for their own benefit, and there are slander and libel laws to protect an individual's good name and reputation, and to prevent defamation of character.

There are laws and rights to regulate surveillance with search warrants required in most countries to search the home of a private individual, as well as the right to seize personal property. Warrants are generally required to obtain personal electronic records held by telecommunication companies (e.g., the calls made and received as well as meta-data such as geo-location data), and warrants may be required to obtain records held by Internet technology companies (e.g., emails, websites visited, searches, and other electronic messages).[1]

Countries vary in their laws for the protection of security and privacy, but many countries recognize that the security and privacy commitments made by a company in their policies should be fully implemented. Further, companies should be held accountable for any security breaches that occur that lead to data security or privacy being compromised, and the company may be liable for any losses suffered by individuals as a result of the breach.

Further, people must not be misled about the functionality of a website or mobile app that places their security or privacy at risk, and users must give their consent to any changes to the privacy policy that would allow for the collection of additional personal data, and users must be informed about the extensiveness of tracking and data collection.

4.3.8 EU GDPR Privacy Law

Europe has been active in the development of data protection regulation, and the European General Data Protection Regulation (EU GDPR 2016/679) is a comprehensive data protection framework that became operational in 2018. Privacy and data protection are regarded as fundamental human rights in the EU, and GDPR aims to give individuals control over their personal data. It has had a huge impact on privacy laws of other countries around the world, and it also protects the transfer of personal data outside of the EU, as it prohibits its transfer to countries that do not provide an equivalent or adequate data protection framework as GDPR.

---

[1] The term "surveillance capitalism" denotes the widespread collection and moneterization of data captured through monitoring the user's online behaviour.

GDPR consists of a data governance framework that attempts to place privacy on a par with other laws. It creates protections that follow the data, and it places responsibilities on companies in managing privacy and information. GDPR applies whenever personal data is processed, and it starts from the presumption that the processing of the personal data is illegitimate. This means that companies carry the burden of legitimizing their actions, and they must be able to show that they have a legitimate basis for processing data. That is, they must be able to show that they have the consent of the data subject, or that the processing is necessary as a result of the contract that exists between them and the data subject, or where they have a legitimate interest, and where the interest of the data controller prevails over that of the data subject. The company must be able to demonstrate adherence to the fair information practice.

This means that data must be obtained legitimately and is used in the manner of the purpose for which it was acquired, and there must be openness and transparency so that individuals will know how their data will be used. There should be special protections for sensitive data with the ability to opt in for consent (e.g., race, sexual orientation, political beliefs), and there must be standards for enforcement to ensure compliance with the standards. The *Data Privacy Impact Assessment* (DPIA) is mentioned in GDPR, and it is needed if the processing of personal information is likely to result in a high risk to the rights and freedoms of individuals. This assessment helps to ensure that companies are complying with privacy requirements.

The standard for informed consent is very high which means that it is freely given and informed. GDPR also gives very strong data subject rights, including the right to access data, data portability, the right to rectify data, the right to erase data, the right to object to processing, and the right to restrict processing. These provide solid rights for the data subjects to exercise control over their personal data.

Other laws that have become important include the EU Digital Services Act (DSA), which protects digital space against illegal content as well as protecting fundamental rights of users. For more detailed information on legal and ethical aspects of computing see Ref. [1].

4.4   Review Questions

1. What is intellectual property law?
2. Describe the behaviours of the ethical project manager.
3. How can a software company demonstrate that it took all reasonable steps to deliver a high-quality software product, and that the testing was fit for purpose?
4. Explain the different types of software licensing.

5. Explain the legal aspects of bespoke software development.
6. What happens when one party in an outsourcing project believes that a material breach of the contract has occurred?
7. What types of lawsuits could be brought against a software company?
8. Explain the difference between ethical and malicious hackers.
9. What is computer crime?
10. Explain the importance of ethics in project management.
11. Describe the PMI code of ethics and professional behaviour.

4.5   Summary

Business ethics is concerned with ethical principles and moral problems that arise in a business environment. They refer to the core principles and values of the organization, and apply throughout the organization. They guide individual employees in carrying out their roles, and ethical issues include the rights and duties between a company and its employees, customers and suppliers.

Project managers are professionals and need to behave professionally and ethically at all times during the project. The Project Management Institute has defined a code of ethics and professional behaviour for project management, which defines the expectations of the behaviour of project management professionals. The core values for the ethical conduct for project management professionals include responsibility, respect, fairness, and honesty.

Legal aspects of software project management are concerned with the application of the legal system to the project management and computing fields. It includes intellectual property law including patents, copyright, trademarks, and trade secrets; bespoke software development; test outsourcing; licensing of software; professional negligence in the development and testing of software; and computer crime.

A lawsuit is a proceeding by a party against another party in a civil court where the plaintiff sues another person for being negligent, and the negligence of the defendant caused injury or damage to the property of the plaintiff.

Bespoke software (or custom software) is software that is developed for a specific customer or organization, and needs to satisfy specific customer requirements. The legal contract specifies the obligations of the supplier, and should the supplier fail to honour its commitments it may well be in breach of contract. This may result in the first party seeking a legal remedy in a civil court.

A software license is a legal agreement between the copyright owner and the licensee, which governs the use or distribution of software to the user (licensee). Computer software code is protected under copyright law, and the license grants the user permission to make one or more copies of the software. Software license agreements generally provide limited remedies to the customer when the software is defective. However, there may be legal implications if the software has been inadequately developed and tested.

Reference

1. G. O' Regan, *Ethical and Legal Aspects of Computing*, (Springer, 2024)

Overview of Software Project Management

5

Key Topics

Business case
Estimation
Scheduling
Risk management
Project board and project governance
People management
Project reports
Project metrics
Remote project management
Outsourcing
Quality management
Prince 2
PMP and PMBOK

5.1 Introduction

Software projects have a history of being delivered late- or over-budget, and software project management is concerned with the effective management of software projects to ensure the successful delivery of a high-quality product, on time and on budget, to the customer. *A project is a temporary group activity designed to accomplish a specific goal such as the delivery of a product to a customer. It has a clearly defined beginning and end in time.*

Project management involves good project planning and estimation, the management of resources, the management of issues and change requests that arise during the project, managing quality, managing risks, managing the budget,

© The Author(s), under exclusive license to Springer Nature Switzerland AG 2025
G. O'Regan, *Guide to Software Project Management*, Undergraduate Topics in
Computer Science, https://doi.org/10.1007/978-3-031-80578-3_5

monitoring progress, taking appropriate action when progress deviates from expectations, communicating progress to the various stakeholders, and delivering a high-quality product to the customer. It involves

- Defining the business case for the project.
- Defining the scope of the project and what it is to achieve.
- Estimation of the cost, effort, and schedule.
- Determining the start and end dates for the project.
- Determining the resources required.
- Assigning resources to the various tasks and activities.
- Determining the project lifecycle and phases of the project.
- Staffing the project.
- Preparing the project plan.
- Scheduling the various tasks and activities.
- Preparing the initial project schedule and key milestones.
- Obtaining approval for the project plan and schedule.
- Identifying and managing risks.
- Monitoring progress, budget, schedule, effort, risks, issues, change requests, and quality.
- Taking corrective action.
- Re-planning and rescheduling.
- Preparing project status reports and presentations.
- Communicating progress to affected stakeholders.

The scope of the project needs to be determined, and the estimated effort for the various tasks and activities established. The project plan and schedule will then be developed and approved by the stakeholders, and these are maintained during the project. The project plan will contain or reference several other plans such as the project quality plan, the communication plan, the configuration management plan, and the test plan.

Project estimation and scheduling are difficult as software projects are often breaking new ground and differ from previous projects. That is, historical estimates may often not be a good basis for estimation for the current project. Often, unanticipated problems may arise for technically advanced projects, and the estimates may be overly optimistic.

Gantt charts are generally employed for project scheduling, and these show the work breakdown for the project as well as task dependencies and allocation of staff to the various tasks.[1]

---

[1] The American mechanical engineer and management consultant, Henry Gantt, developed Gantt charts in the early twentieth century.

The effective management of risk during a project is essential to project success. Risks arise due to uncertainty and the risk management cycle involves[2] risk identification, risk analysis and evaluation, identifying responses to risks, selecting and planning a response to the risk, and risk monitoring.

Once the risks have been identified they are logged (e.g., in the Risk Log or a risk repository tool). The likelihood of each risk arising and its impact is then determined. The risk is assigned an owner and an appropriate response to the risk determined.

Once the planning is complete the project execution commences, and the focus moves to monitoring progress, managing risks and issues, re-planning as appropriate, providing regular progress reports to the project board, and so on.

Two popular project management methodologies are the *Prince* 2 methodology, which was developed in the U.K., and *Project Management Professional* (PMP) developed by the *Project Management Institute* (PMI) in the United States. PMP has an associated project management body of knowledge (PMBOK).

5.2 Project Start-Up and Initiation

There are many ways in which a project may arise, but it is always essential that there is a clear rationale for the project. A telecom company may wish to develop a new version of its software with attractive features to gain market share. An internal IT department may receive a request from its business users to alter its business software to satisfy new legal or regulatory requirements. A software development company may be contacted by a business to develop a bespoke solution to meet its needs, and so on.

All parties must be clear on what the project is to achieve, and how it will be achieved. It is fundamental that there is a *business case* for the project (this is the reason for the project), as it clearly does not make sense for the organization to spend a large amount of money without a sound rationale for the project. In other words, the project must make business sense (e.g., it may have a financial return on the investment or it may be to satisfy some business or regulatory requirement).

At the project start-up the initial scope and costing for the project are estimated, and the feasibility of the project is determined.[3] The project is authorized,[4] and a project board is set up for project governance. The project board verifies that there is a sound business case for the project, and a *project manager* is appointed to manage the project.

---

[2] These are the risk management activities in the Prince2 methodology.

[3] This refers to whether the project is technically and financially feasible.

[4] Organizations have limited resources, and as many projects may be proposed it will not be possible to authorize every project, and so several projects with weak business cases may be rejected.

The *project board* (or steering group) includes the key stakeholders and is accountable for the success of the project. The project manager provides regular status reports to the project board during the project, and the project board is consulted when key project decisions need to be made.

The project manager is responsible for the day-to-day management of the project, and good planning is essential to its success. The approach to the project is decided,[5] and the project manager *kicks off the project* and mobilizes the project team. The detailed requirements and estimates for the project are determined, the schedule of activities and tasks established, and resources are assigned for the various tasks and activities.[6] The project manager prepares the project plan, which is subject to the approval of the key stakeholders. The initial risks are identified and managed, and a risk log (or repository) is set up for the project. Once the planning is complete project execution commences.

5.3   Estimation

Estimation is an important part of project management, and the accurate estimates of effort, cost, and schedule are essential to delivering a project on time, on budget, and with the right quality.[7] Estimation is employed in the planning process to determine the effort and resources required, and it feeds into the scheduling of the project. The problems with over- or under-estimation of projects are well known, and good estimates allow

- Accurate calculation of the project cost and its feasibility.
- Accurate scheduling of the project.
- Determining the resources required for the project.
- Measurement of progress and costs against the estimates.

Poor estimation leads to

- Projects being over- or under-estimated.
- Projects being over- or under-resourced (impacting staff morale).
- Negative impression of the project manager.

Consequently, estimation needs to be rigorous, and there are several well-known estimation techniques available (e.g., work breakdown structures, function points, and so on). Estimation applies to both the early and later parts of the project, with

---

[5] For example, it may be decided to outsource the development to a third-party provider, purchase an off-the-shelf solution, or develop the solution internally.

[6] The project scheduling is usually done with the Microsoft Project tool.

[7] The consequences of underestimating a project include the project being delivered late, with the project team working late nights and weekends to recover the schedule, quality being compromised with steps in the process omitted, and so on.

the later phases of the project refining the initial estimates, as a more detailed understanding of the project activities is then available. The new estimates are used to reschedule and to predict the eventual effort, delivery date, and cost of the project. The following are guidelines for estimation:

– Sufficient time needs to be allowed to do estimation.
– Estimates are produced for each phase of software development.
– The initial estimates are high level.
– The estimates for the next phase should be solid whereas estimates for the later phases may be high level.
– The estimates should be conservative rather than optimistic.
– Estimates will usually include contingency.
– Estimates should be reviewed to ensure their adequacy.
– Estimates from independent experts may be useful.
– It may be useful to prepare estimates using various methods and to compare.

Project metrics are often employed to measure the accuracy of the estimates, and these are reported regularly during the project. They include

– Effort estimation accuracy.
– Budget estimation accuracy.
– Schedule estimation accuracy.

Next, we discuss several estimation techniques including the work breakdown structure, the analogy method, and the Delphi method.

5.3.1   Estimation Techniques

Estimates need to be produced consistently, and it would be inappropriate to have an estimation procedure such as *"Go ask Fred"*,[8] as this clearly relies on an individual and is not a repeatable process. There are several approaches to project estimation which are given in Table 5.1.

5.3.2   Work Breakdown Structure

This is a popular approach to project estimation (*it is also known as decomposition*) and involves the following:

– Identify the project deliverables to be produced during the project.
– Estimate the size of each deliverable (in pages or LOC).

---

[8] Unless "Go Ask Fred" is the name of the estimation methodology, or the estimation tool employed.

Table 5.1 Estimation techniques

Technique	Description
Work breakdown structure	Identify the project deliverables to be produced during the project. Estimate the size of each deliverable (in pages or LOC). Estimate the effort (number of days) required to complete the deliverable based on its size and complexity. Estimate the cost of the completed deliverable
Analogy method	This involves comparing the project to a previously completed project (that is like the proposed project). The historical data and metrics for schedule, effort, and budget estimation accuracy are considered, as well as similarities and differences between the projects to provide effort, schedule, and budget estimates
Expert judgement	This involves consultation with experienced personnel to derive the estimate. The expert(s) can factor in differences between past project experiences, knowledge of existing systems as well as the specific requirements of the project
Delphi method	The *Delphi Method* is a consensus method used to produce accurate schedules and estimates. It was developed by the Rand Corporation and improved by Barry Boehm. It uses experts independent of the project manager or third-party supplier
Planning poker	This is a popular consensus-based estimation technique that is used in Agile, and it is used to estimate the effort required to implement a user story
Function points	*Function Points* were developed by Allan Albrecht at IBM in the late 1970s. Each functional requirement is analysed and assigned a number of function points (based on its size and complexity). This total number of function points is a measure of the estimate for the project
Cost predictor models	These include various cost prediction models such as *Cocomo* and Slim. The Costar tool supports Cocomo, and the Qsm tool supports Slim

– Estimate the effort (number of days) required to complete the deliverable based on its complexity and size, and experience of team.
– Estimate the cost of the completed deliverable.
– The estimate for the project is the sum of the individual estimates.

The approach often uses productivity data that is available from previously completed projects. The effort required for a complex deliverable is higher than that of a simple deliverable (where both are of the same size). The project planning section in the project plan (or a separate estimation plan) will include the lifecycle phases, and the deliverables/tasks to be carried out in each phase. It may include a table similar to Table 6.5 for traditional projects.

5.4   Project Planning and Scheduling

A well-managed project has an increased chance of success, and good planning is an essential part of project management. The project manager and the relevant stakeholders will consider the appropriate approach for the project and determine whether a solution should be purchased off the shelf, whether to outsource the software development to a third party supplier, or whether to develop the solution internally. A simple process map for project planning is presented in Fig. 6.1.

Estimation is a key part of project planning, and the effort estimates are used for scheduling of the tasks and activities in a project-scheduling tool such as *Microsoft Project* (Fig. 5.1).

The schedule will detail the phases (or sprints in Agile) of the project, the key project milestones, the activities and tasks to be performed in each phase as well as their associated timescales, and the resources required to carry out each task. The project manager will update the project schedule regularly during the project.

Projects vary in size and complexity and the formality of the software development process employed needs to reflect this. The project plan defines how the project will be carried out, and it generally includes sections such as

– Business case.
– Project scope.

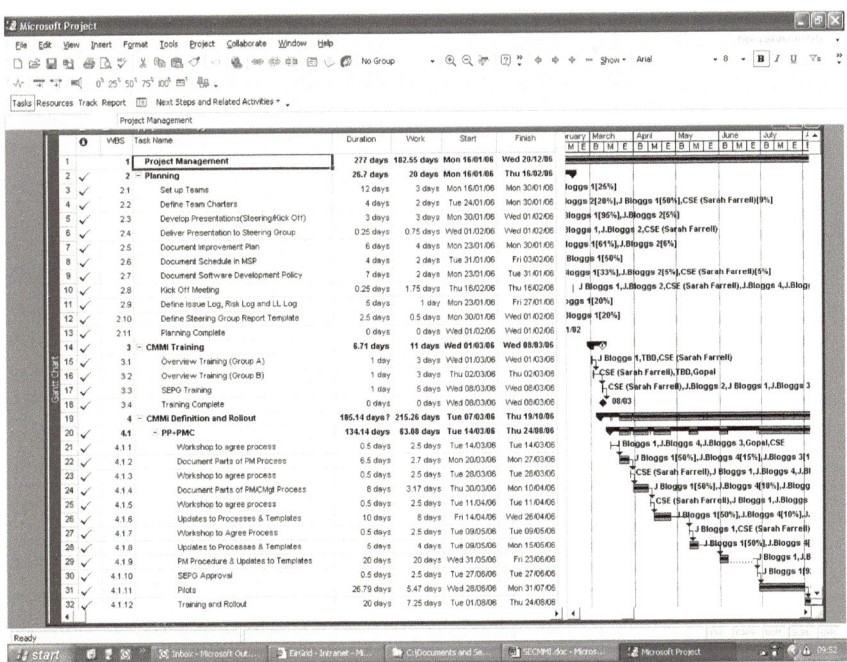

Fig. 5.1   Sample Microsoft project schedule

- Project goals and objectives.
- Key milestones.
- Project planning and estimates.
- Key stakeholders.
- Project team and responsibilities.
- Knowledge and skills required.
- Communication planning.
- Financial planning.
- Quality and test planning.
- Configuration management.

Communication planning describes how communication will be carried out during the project, and it includes the various project meetings and reports that will be produced; financial planning is concerned with budget planning for the project; quality and test planning is concerned with the planning required to ensure that a high-quality product is delivered; and configuration management is concerned with identifying the configuration items to be controlled, and systematically controlling changes to them throughout the lifecycle. It ensures that all deliverables are kept consistent following approved changes (see Chap. 12).

The project plan is a key project document, and it needs to be approved by all stakeholders. The project manager needs to ensure that the project plan, schedule, and technical work products are kept consistent with the requirements. Another words, if there are changes to the requirements then the project plan and schedule as well as all other affected deliverables need to be updated accordingly.

Checklists are useful in verifying that the tasks have been completed. The sample project management checklist given in Table 5.2 is a way to verify that project planning is being appropriately performed and that project controls are in place.

5.5   Risk Management

Risks arise due to uncertainty, and *risk management is concerned with managing uncertainty*, and especially the management of any undesired events. Risks need to be identified, analysed, and controlled in order for the project to be successful, and risk management activities take place throughout the project lifecycle.

Once the initial set of risks to the project have been identified, they are analysed to determine their *likelihood of occurrence* and their *impact* (e.g., on cost, schedule, or quality). These two parameters determine the *risk category*, and the most serious risk category refers to a risk with a high probability of occurrence and a high impact on occurrence.

Countermeasures are defined to reduce the likelihood of occurrence and impact of the risks, and contingency plans are prepared to deal with the situation of the risk actually occurring. Additional risks may arise during the project, and the project manager needs to be proactive in their identification and management.

Table 5.2 Sample project management checklist

No.	Item to check
1	Is the project plan complete and approved by the stakeholders?
2	Does the project have a sound business case?
3	Are the Risk Log, Issue Log, and Lessons Learned Log set up?
4	Are estimates available for the project? Are they realistic?
5	Is the project appropriately resourced?
6	Is the Microsoft Schedule available for the project?
7	Is the project schedule up to date?
8	Has quality planning been completed for the project?
9	Has project communication been appropriately planned?
10	Has the change control mechanism been set up for the project?
11	Are all project deliverables under configuration management control?
12	Are the responses to the risks and issues appropriate?
13	Is the project directory set up for the project?
14	Are the key milestones defined in the project plan?

Risks need to be reviewed regularly especially following changes to the project. These could be changes to the business case or the business requirements, loss of key personnel, and so on. Events that occur may affect existing risks (including the probability of their occurrence and their impact) and may lead to new risks. Countermeasures need to be kept up to date during the project. Risks are reported regularly throughout the project.

The project manager will maintain a risk repository (this may be a tool or a risk log) to record details of each risk, including its type and description, its likelihood and its impact (yielding the risk category), as well as the response to the risk.

The risk management cycle is concerned with identifying and managing risks throughout the project lifecycle. It involves identifying risks, determining their probability of occurrence and impact should they occur, identifying responses to the risks, and monitoring and reporting. The risk management activities are discussed in more detail in Chap. 7.

5.6 People Management in Projects

People management is an integral part of project management, and the success of a project is dependent on a functioning high-performance team. Good people management results in the best performance from the team, where team members deliver high-quality work throughout the project. This means that the project manager needs to be a strong people manager, as well as being a competent project management professional.

The project manager is responsible for inspiring and motivating the project team, and the team may be in the same physical location or operate remotely. Often project teams today (in the post-COVID world) consist of hybrid and remote teams, rather than being in the same physical location. It is essential that team building activities take place and that team members are given orientation on the overall purpose of the project, and their role and responsibilities. Team orientation is straightforward where team members are in the same physical location, as social team building activities may take place to bring the team into a cohesive unit. However, it is more difficult to build the same supportive team culture for remote or hybrid teams.

It takes time for the project team to perform as a team and the project manager needs to devote time to getting to know each team member, understanding them and their skill set, planning improvements to their skill set, explaining their role and responsibilities in the project, as well as getting commitment from the team member. Good people management skills help in building a good rapport with all team members and in having a positive work environment with committed team members working in harmony together to complete the project activities. A good work environment helps in improving productivity, as team members are working in harmony together to achieve the project goals. The project team development phases often include

- Forming
- Storming
- Norming
- Performing

The project manager needs to be active in motivating team members and addressing natural drops in project commitment levels that may arise during the project. It is essential that team members feel a part of the project and that they feel that their contribution is important and recognized, as this will help in maintaining their commitment to the project. Conflicts may arise between team members during a project, and the project manager needs to play a role in resolving such situations. The project manager needs to manage people issues such as

- Communication issues
- Clash of personalities
- Unrealistic expectations
- Workplace culture

The project manager must be proactive in monitoring completion of the deliverables of team members, ensuring that the project is kept on schedule, and giving feedback on performance to team members.

5.7   Quality Management in Projects

There are various definitions of "quality" such as Juran's definition that quality is *"fitness for purpose"*, and Crosby definition of quality as *"conformance to the requirements"*. The Crosby definition is useful when asking whether we are building it right as in requirements verification, whereas the Juran definition is useful when asking whether we are building the right system as in requirements validation.

It is a fundamental premise in the quality field that it is more cost-effective to build quality into the product, rather than adding it later during the testing phase. Therefore, quality needs to be considered at every step during the project, and each deliverable needs to be reviewed to ensure its fitness for purpose. The review may be like a *software inspection*, a *structured walkthrough,* or another appropriate methodology.

The project plan will include a section on quality planning for the project (this may be a reference to a separate plan). The quality plan will define how the project plans to deliver a high-quality project, as well as the quality controls and quality assurance activities that will take place during project execution. The quality planning for the project needs to ensure that the customer's quality expectations will be achieved.

The project manager has overall responsibility for project quality, and the quality department (if one exists) will assign a quality engineer to the project, and the quality engineer will promote quality and its importance to the project team, as well as facilitating quality improvement. The project manager needs to ensure that sound software engineering processes are employed, as well as ensuring that the defined standards and templates are followed.

It is an accepted principle in the quality field that good processes and conformance to them is essential for the delivery of a high-quality product. The quality engineer (where one exists) will conduct process audits to ensure that the processes and standards are followed consistently during the project. An audit report is published, and any audit actions are tracked to closure.

Software testing is conducted to verify that the software correctly implements the requirements, and a separate project test plan will define the various types of testing to be performed during the project. These will typically include unit, integration, system, performance, and acceptance testing, and the results from the various test activities enable the fitness for purpose of the software to be determined, as well as judging whether it is ready to be released or not.

The project manager will report the various project metrics (including the quality metrics) in the regular project status reports, and the quality metrics provide an objective indication of the quality of the product at that moment in time.

The cost of poor quality may be determined at the end of the project, and this may require a time recording system for the various project activities. The effort involved in detecting and correcting defects may be recorded, and a COPQ chart as shown in Fig. 14.31 may be presented.

Poor quality may arise with the software due to several factors. For example, it may be due to inadequate reviews or testing of the software. It could be due to inadequate skills or experience of the project team, or poorly defined or understood requirements.

The project manager will conduct a lessons-learned meeting at the end of the project to identify and record all the lessons learned from the project. These may be published as a lessons-learned report and shared with relevant stakeholders as part of continuous improvement. Quality management for projects is discussed in more detail in Chap. 8.

5.8   Project Monitoring and Control

Project monitoring and control is concerned with monitoring project execution and taking corrective action when project performance deviates from expectations. The progress of the project is monitored against the plan, and corrective actions taken as appropriate. The key project parameters such as budget, effort, and schedule as well as risks and issues are monitored, and the status of the project communicated regularly to the affected stakeholders.

The project manager will conduct progress and milestone reviews to determine the actual progress, with new issues identified and monitored. The appropriate corrective actions are identified and are tracked to closure. Project monitoring and control involves

– Monitor the project plan/schedule.
– Monitor the key project parameters.
– Conduct progress/milestone reviews.
– Re-plan as appropriate.
– Monitor risks/take appropriate action.
– Analyse issues and change requests/take appropriate action.
– Track corrective action to closure.
– Monitor resources and manage.
– Report the project status to management and project board.

The project manager will monitor progress, risks, and issues during the project, and take appropriate corrective action. The status of the project will be reported in the regular status reports sent to management and the project board, with the status reviewed regularly with management during the project. A sample process map for project monitoring and control is presented in Fig. 9.2, and project management and control is discussed in more detail in Chap. 9.

Table 5.3   Activities in managing issues and change requests

Activity	Description of issue/change request
Log issue or change request	The project manager logs the issue or change request. It is assigned a unique reference number and priority (severity) and categorized into an issue (problem) or change request
Assess impact	This involves analysis to determine the impacts such as technical, cost, schedule, and quality. The risks need to be identified
Decision on implementation	A decision is made on how to deal with the issue or change request. The CCB is often involved in the decision to authorize a change request
Implement solution	The affected project documents and software modules are identified and modified accordingly
Verify solution	Testing (unit, system, and UAT) is employed to verify the correctness of the solution
Close issue/CR	The issue or change request is closed

5.9   Managing Issues and Change Requests

The management of issues and change requests is an important part of project management. An *issue* can arise at any time during the project (e.g., a supplier to the project may go out of business, an employee may resign, specialized hardware for testing may not arrive in time, and so on), and an issue refers to a problem that has occurred which may have a negative impact on the project. The severity of the issue is an indication of its impact on the project, and the project manager needs to manage it appropriately.

A *change request* is a stakeholder request for a change to the scope of the project, and it may arise at any time during the project. The impacts of the change request (e.g., technical, cost, and schedule) need to be carefully considered, as a change introduces new risks to the project that may adversely affect cost, schedule, and quality. It is therefore essential to fully understand the impacts to make an informed decision on whether to authorize or reject the change request. The project manager may directly approve small change requests, with the impacts of a larger change request considered by the project *change control board* (CCB).

The activities involved in managing issues and change requests are summarized in Table 5.3.

5.10   Remote Project Management

Remote project management is concerned with managing remote and hybrid teams to ensure that the project objectives are achieved. Traditional project management involves teams based in the same physical location, whereas often today teams may operate in hybrid mode with some employees working in the office and other employees and teams working remotely in different physical locations (possibly in other parts of the world). This means that today remote employees play important roles in the success of projects, and remote project management has become more important in managing hybrid and remote teams. A *hybrid team* is a flexible work structure with some employees working remotely and others working from the office.

The management of remote teams requires modern communication including video conferencing, shared files, and documents, as well as effective team communication and messaging apps. It is more challenging to build a team culture with remote teams, and so while creating the hybrid team is the easy part, the building of a cohesive and effective team is more difficult. This is since it is much harder to build up a team bond and trust among team members who are not in the same physical location. The project manager will stay engaged with the team throughout the project with virtual meetings, and remote project management is like traditional project management except that the project is executed remotely. It is a flexible methodology that can support various approaches such as traditional software engineering and Agile.

The first step in assembling a remote team is to determine the remote structure that is required, and then to find the people with the appropriate technical and soft skills that are required to carry out the project. The project manager needs to communicate clear expectations to the team members at project initiation, including the process to be followed, work hours, project goals, their responsibilities, the tools that will be employed for collaboration, and so on. The project manager will keep the team engaged through regular virtual team meetings, and the team members will check in daily with the project manager to advise on progress made, and this could take the form of a virtual stand-up meeting.

5.11   Outsourcing

Outsourcing is a common business practice where a company contracts out business functions such as manufacturing, software development, and call centres to third-party providers. The outsourcing of a business function to a distant country is termed *offshoring*, whereas outsourcing may also be done domestically, and *nearshoring* is where the outsourcing is to a nearby country. The main benefits of outsourcing include

- Cost savings due to reduction in business expenses.
- Availability of expertise not available in-house.
- Additional skilled personnel to supplement in-house staff.
- Allows company to focus on core business activities.
- Makes business more flexible.
- Increased efficiencies.

Outsourcing involves handing control of various business functions over to a third party, and this leads to business risks such as the quality of the service may be below expectations, or the third party may go out of business, or that there may be risks to confidentiality and security. There are several disadvantages associated with outsourcing such as

- Managing the day-to-day relationship with offshore team.
- Differences in times zones.
- Risks to quality, confidentiality, and security.
- Differences in culture and language.

Many large projects involve total or partial outsourcing of the software development, and it is therefore essential to select a supplier that can deliver high-quality and reliable software on time and on budget. We discuss the selection and management of a supplier in more detail in Chap. 10.

5.12   Project Board and Governance

The *project board*[9] (or steering group) is responsible for directing the project, and it is directly accountable for the success of the project. It consists of senior managers and staff in the organization who have the authority to make resources available, to remove roadblocks, and to get things done (Fig. 5.2).

It is consulted whenever key project decisions need to be made, and it plays a key role in project governance.[10] The project board ensures that there is a clear business case for the project, and that the capital funding for the project is adequate and well spent. The project board may cancel the project at any stage during project execution should there cease to be a business case, or should project spending exceed tolerance and go out of control.[11]

The project manager reports to the project board and sends regular status reports to highlight progress made as well as key project risks and issues. The project board meets at an appropriate frequency during the project (with extra sessions held should serious project issues arise).

There are several roles on the project board (an individual may perform more than one role). The responsibilities of the project board members are given in Table 5.4.

---

[9] The project board in the Prince 2 methodology includes roles such as the project executive, senior supplier, senior user, project assurance, and the project manager. These roles have distinct responsibilities.

[10] Another words, the right decisions are made by the right people with the right information.

[11] The project plan will usually specify a *tolerance level* for schedule and spending, where the project may spend (perhaps less than 10%) more than the allocated capital for the project before seeking authorization for further capital funding for the project.

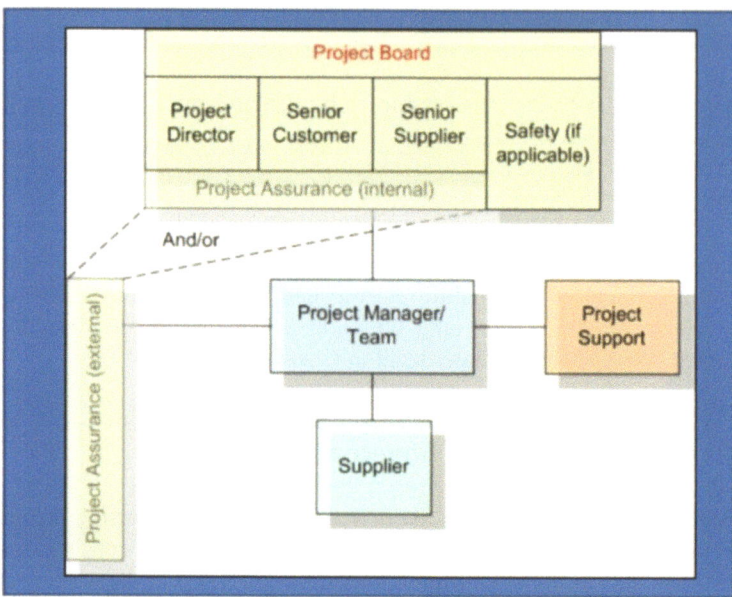

Fig. 5.2 Prince 2 project board

Table 5.4 Project board roles and responsibilities

Role	Responsibility
Project director	Ultimately responsible for the project. Provides overall guidance to the project
Senior customer	Represents the interests of users
Senior supplier	Represents the resources responsible for implementation of project (e.g., IS manager)
Project manager	Link between project board and project team
Project assurance	Internal role (optional) that provides an independent (of project manager) objective view of the project
Safety (optional)	Ensure adherence to health and safety standards

5.13   Project Reporting

The frequency of project reporting is defined in the project plan (or the communications plan). The project report advises management and the key stakeholders of the current status of the project, and includes key project information such as

– Completed deliverables (during period)
– New risks and issues

- Schedule, effort, and budget status (e.g., RAG metrics[12])
- Quality and test status
- Key risks and issues
- Milestone status
- Deliverables planned (next period)

The project manager discusses the project report with management and the project board and presents the status of the project as well as the key risks and issues. The project manager will present a recovery plan (exception report) to deal with the situation where the project has fallen significantly outside the defined project tolerance (i.e., it is significantly behind schedule or over-budget).

The key risks and issues will be discussed, and the project manager will explain how the key issues are being dealt with, and how the key risks will be managed. The new risks and issues will also be discussed, and the project board will carefully consider how the project manager plans to deal with these and will provide appropriate support.

The project board will carefully consider the status of the project as well as the input from the project manager before deciding on the appropriate course of action (which could include the immediate termination of the project if there is no longer a business case for it).

5.14   Project Closure

A project is a temporary activity, and once the project goals have been achieved and the product handed over to the customer and support group, it is ready to be closed. The project manager will prepare an end of project report detailing the extent to which the project achieved its targeted objectives. The report will include a summary of key project metrics including key quality metrics and the budget and timeliness metrics.

The success of the project is judged on the extent to which the defined objectives have been achieved, and on the extent to which the project has delivered the agreed functionality on schedule, on budget and with the right quality. This is often referred to as the project management triangle (Fig. 5.3).

The project manager presents the end project report to the project board, including any factors (e.g., change requests) that may have affected the timely delivery of the project or the allocated budget. The project is then officially closed.

The project manager then schedules a meeting with the team which reviews the lessons learned from the project. The key lessons learned are summarized in the lessons-learned report. Any actions identified are assigned to individuals and followed through to closure, and the lessons-learned report is made available

---

[12] Often, a colour coding mechanism is employed with a red flag indicating a serious issue, amber highlighting a potentially serious issue, and green indicating that everything is ok.

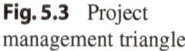

Fig. 5.3 Project management triangle

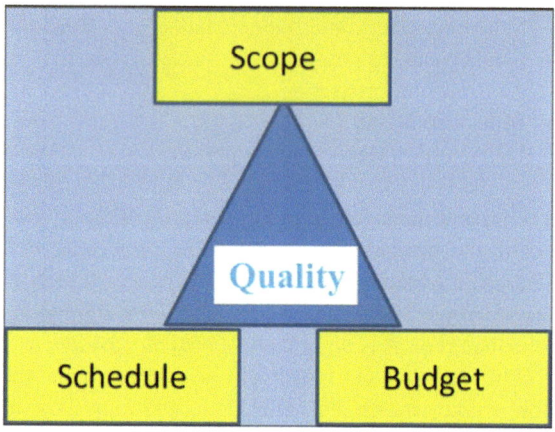

to other projects (with the goal of learning from experience). The project team is disbanded, and the project team members are assigned to other duties. The activities involved in closing the project are discussed in more detail in Chap. 11.

5.15 Prince 2 Methodology

Prince 2 (*projects in controlled environments*) is a popular project management methodology that is widely used in the U.K., Australia, and Europe. It is a structured, process-driven approach to project management, with processes for project start-up, initiating a project, controlling a stage, managing stage boundaries, closing a project, managing product delivery, planning, and directing a project. It has procedures to coordinate people and activities in a project, as well as procedures to monitor and control project activities (Fig. 5.4).

These key processes are summarized in Table 5.5. Prince 2 has supported Agile since 2015, and more detailed information on Prince 2 is in Ref. [1].

5.16 Project Manager Professional

Project manager professional (PMP) is an internationally recognized project management qualification offered by the Project Management Institute (PMI), and it is popular in the United States, Canada, and the Middle East. It involves an exam based on PMI's project management body of knowledge (PMBOK).

The project management body of knowledge is a body of knowledge for project management, and the PMBOK guide is a subset of the project management body of knowledge. It was first published by the PMI in the US in 1996, and its sixth edition provides support for Agile [2].

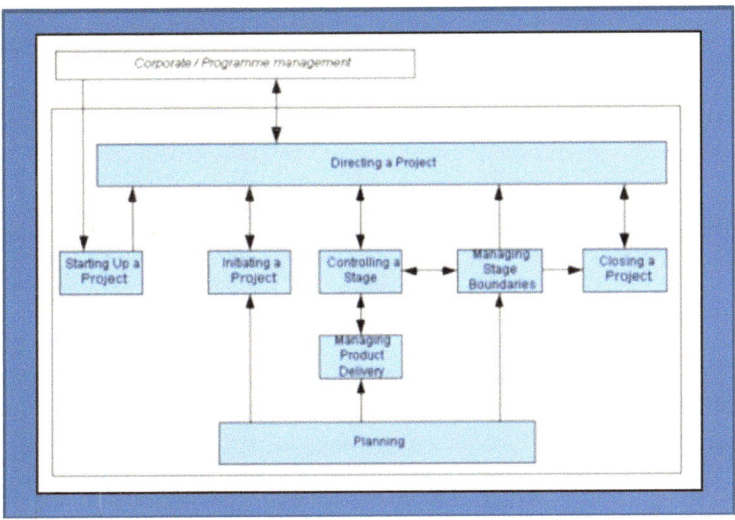

Fig. 5.4 Prince 2 processes

Table 5.5 Key processes in Prince 2

Process	Description
Start-up	Project manager and project board appointed, project approach, and project brief defined
Initiating	Project and quality plan complete, business case and risks refined, project files set-up, and project authorized
Controlling a stage	Stage plan prepared, quality and risks/issues managed, progress reviewed and reported
Managing stage boundary	Stage status reviewed and next stage planned, actual products produced versus original stage plan compared, stage or exception report produced
Closing a project	Orderly closure of project with project board, end project report, and lessons learned report
Managing product delivery	Covers product (deliverable) creation by the team or a third-party supplier. Ensure that the planned deliverables meet quality criteria
Planning	Prince 2 employs product-based planning that involves identifying the products (deliverables) required, and the activities and resources to provide them
Directing a project	The project board consists of senior management, and it controls the project. It has the authority to authorize and define what is required from the project, commitment of resources and funds, and management direction

Table 5.6 PMBOK process groups

Process	Description
Initiating	Define a new project and obtain authorization to start the project
Planning	This involves establishing the scope of the project and defining the plan to achieve the project's objectives
Executing	This involves executing the activities defined in the project plan
Monitoring and Control	This involves tracking progress and performance of the project and taking corrective action where appropriate
Closing a project	These processes perform an orderly closure of the project

It is process based with the work performed as processes, and it provides guidelines for managing projects, as well as describing the project management lifecycle and its related processes. PMP has five groups of processes, and these are given in Table 5.6.

PMBOK has ten knowledge areas on project management, and these are described in Table 5.7.

Table 5.7 PMBOK knowledge areas

Knowledge area	Description
Project integration Management	The processes to identify and coordinate the various processes and project management activities
Project scope Management	The processes to ensure that the project includes all the work required to complete the project (and only that)
Project schedule Management	The processes to manage the timely completion of the project
Project cost management	The processes involved in planning, estimating, budgeting, and controlling costs so that the project can be completed within the approved budget
Project quality management	The processes and activities of the organization that determine the quality policies, objectives, and responsibilities so that the project satisfies the quality expectations
Project resource management	The processes to organize, manage, and lead the project team
Project communications management	The processes involved in determining the information needs of those involved in the project and fulfilling them
Project risk management	The processes involved in analysing, response planning, and controlling risk in a project
Project procurement management	The processes concerned with the purchase of products or services external to the project team
Project stakeholder management	This involves identifying all stakeholders affected by the project and analysing/managing their expectations

Table 5.8 Functions of project management office

Function	Description
Project Governance	This is a project oversight function to ensure that the *right decisions* are made by the *right people*, based on the *right information*
Transparency	This ensures that all relevant information that is required for decision-making is available and accurate
Reusability	The PMO will maintain a repository of best practice from previous successful projects such as lessons learned and a collection of templates to allow project management tasks to be consistently performed
Delivery support	The PMO provides support to the projects during project delivery by streamlining projects, and offering training, mentoring, and quality assurance
Traceability	This involves managing documentation, project history, and organization knowledge

5.17   Project Management Office

A project management office (PMO) is a group or department in an organization that defines and maintains the standards for project management for the organization. The PMO will aim to standardize and enhance project management within the organization so that the projects being carried out have a defined and repeatable process. The PMO will act a centre of expertise on project management within the organization, and it will be consulted by projects for guidance and documentation on project management. It defines the project management metrics to be used and reported by the projects.

The PMO standardizes the project management methodology in the organization, and the project management practices may be based on industrial best practice such as Prince 2 or PMP, or developed internally within the organization. The PMO identifies the tools required to support the process, and it provides training on project management throughout the organization. It may also monitor and report on active projects and portfolios taking place in the organization, and it may have responsibility for reporting progress to senior management for strategic decisions on whether specific projects should continue or be terminated.

The project management office provides several functions such as project governance, transparency, and reusability (Table 5.8).

5.18   Programme Management

Programme management is the process of managing a group of related projects in a coordinated manner to obtain benefits not available from managing them individually. It is often used in managing very large projects such as business transformation, which often involves fundamental changes in the way that business is conducted. A *programme* is a set of related projects, and programme management coordinates their planning and execution. A project manager is responsible for the planning and execution of a single project, and for ensuring that their project is successfully delivered on time and budget, whereas the programme manager is responsible for the success of the entire programme.

Programme management provides an environment where the projects may be run successfully, and it provides a layer above the management of projects. The programme manager has oversight of the importance and status of all the projects in the programme, and supports project-level activity to ensure that the programme goals are achieved.

The programme manager is responsible for the programme and does not micromanage projects, as this is a project manager's responsibility. The programme manager needs to coordinate and prioritize the resources across the projects, and needs to deal with issues, roadblocks, links, and interdependencies between the projects, as well as managing the overall risks and cost of the programme.

5.19   Project Portfolio Management

A portfolio is a collection of projects and programmes that will deliver business benefit or operational efficiencies in an organization. *Project portfolio management* (PPM) *is focused on doing the right projects at the right time*, and so it is the process of selecting the right projects and programmes to do, the right time to do them, and managing them effectively.

PPM differs from programme and project management that are focused on execution and delivery (i.e., doing the projects and programmes right), whereas PPM focuses on ensuring that it does the right projects that deliver business value. Organizations have limited resources and it is not possible to do all projects, and so only the best projects that deliver real business benefit should be done. This means that rigorous project selection should be employed to ensure that only those projects that are aligned to the organization's strategic direction and deliver the greatest business benefit should be selected.

PPM ensures that project execution is aligned with the organization strategy with each selected project playing a role in carrying out its strategy. This ensures that the benefits provided from the execution of the projects provide the greatest financial return on the investment made. It ensures that the portfolio is balanced with pet projects that have a limited business return avoided, and it avoids a focus on short-term results.

PPM must ensure that there is a balance between the implementation of change initiatives and maintaining business as usual.

5.20   Review Questions

1. What is a project? What is project management?
2. Describe various approaches to estimation.

3. What activities take place at project start-up and initiation?
4. What skills are required to be a good project manager?
5. What is the purpose of the project board? Explain project governance.
6. What is the purpose of risk management? How are risks managed?
7. Describe the main activities in project management.
8. What is the difference between a risk and an issue?
9. What is the purpose of project reporting?
10. How is quality managed in a project?

5.21   Summary

Project management is concerned with the effective management of projects, and the goal is to deliver a high-quality product, on time and on budget, to the customer. It involves good project planning and estimation, managing resources, managing changes and issues that arise, managing quality, managing risks, managing the budget, monitoring progress and taking corrective action, communicating progress, and delivering a high-quality product to the customer.

The scope of the project needs to be determined, and estimates established. The project plan is developed and approved by the stakeholders, and it will contain or reference several other plans. It needs to be maintained during the project. Project estimation and scheduling are difficult as often software projects are quite different from previous projects. Gantt charts are often employed for project scheduling, and these show the work breakdown for the project, as well as task dependencies and the assignment of staff to the various tasks.

The effective management of risk during a project is essential to project success. Risks arise due to uncertainty and the risk management cycle involves risk identification, risk analysis and evaluation, identifying responses to risks, selecting and planning a response to the risk, and risk monitoring.

Once the planning is complete the project execution commences, and the focus moves to monitoring progress, re-planning as appropriate, managing risks and issues, providing regular progress reports to the project board, and so on. Finally, there is an orderly close of the project.

References

1. Office of Government Commerce, *Managing Successful Projects with PRINCE2*, (2004)
2. PMBOK Guide. *A Guide to the Project Management Body of Knowledge*, 6th Edition, (Project Management Institute, 2017)

Software Project Planning

6

6.1   Introduction

A new project often arises due to the identification of a problem or business opportunity. The organization decides to undertake a project to take advantage of the
problem/opportunity, and a project team is formed to implement and deliver an
appropriate solution. Often, there may be many potential projects that could take
place in an organization, but as every organization has limited resources available
it needs a rigorous way to select only those projects that are worth doing. These
are the projects that will deliver the greatest business benefit, and so only those
projects that are viable and worth doing should be authorized, and those with a
limited or zero business benefit should be rejected.

This means that the organization needs a process to evaluate each potential
project in a rigorous way to ensure that it is worth undertaking. One way of doing
this is through the business case process, which evaluates the benefits of a project
in relation to its costs. A business case is prepared for each proposed project,

© The Author(s), under exclusive license to Springer Nature Switzerland AG 2025   97
G. O'Regan, *Guide to Software Project Management*, Undergraduate Topics in
Computer Science, https://doi.org/10.1007/978-3-031-80578-3_6

and the analysis of the costs and benefits of the proposed projects (as described in their business cases) is done, with the projects that will deliver the greatest business benefit selected and all others rejected.

The business case provides the rationale for the project, and the project should only proceed if it has a valid business case aligned to its business strategy. The project should be terminated if its business case ceases to exist as otherwise resources are wasted. The business case describes the problem or opportunity in more detail, and it may also identify a preferred solution for its implementation. It is essential to identify clear, unambiguous, and achievable objectives that the project is to solve, and this will make it easier to determine if the project has been successful in meeting its expectations as well as gaining approval for the project.

The project is kicked off and the project management team appointed. The team includes the project board to oversee the project, and a project manager to manage the project. The project board needs to have the right people with sufficient influence and authority in the organization to remove roadblocks that may arise and to make timely decisions. The members need to reflect the interests of all parties involved in the project (e.g., users and suppliers). All involved in the project need to be clear on what the project is to achieve and how it will be achieved, and everyone must be clear on their responsibilities in achieving the project objectives. The approach to the project is decided, e.g., whether to build or buy depending on whether the project team has the right competence to develop a particular software system internally (or component of it), or whether there is a need to outsource (or purchase off the shelf) the required software (see Chap. 10 for details on supplier selection and management). The supplied software may be the complete solution to the project's requirements, or it may need to be integrated with other software produced for the project. The initial project risks, customer's quality expectations, and project's acceptance criteria are defined.

Project planning is an essential part of project management, and it defines what the project intends to achieve and how it will do so. The project plan will enable the schedule, cost, quality, changes in scope, and risks to be managed. The scope of the project needs to be determined, and estimates of the effort for the various tasks and activities established. The project plan and schedule need to be approved by the stakeholders, and the project plan will contain or reference several other plans such as the project quality plan, the communication plan, the training plan, the project test plan, and the configuration management plan.

Project planning involves defining the scope of the project and the business requirements, developing the work breakdown structure (WBS) and estimates of the effort required for the various tasks and activities, and preparing the initial project schedule and defining the key project milestones (this involves determining the deliverables to be produced and the delivery timelines). The initial project risks are determined, and planning for how quality will be built into the project deliverables is defined. Project planning involves

- Defining the business case for the project
- Defining the scope of the project and what it is to achieve

- Defining the key success factors for the project
- Determining the approach to be taken for the project
- Determining the key stakeholders
- Determining the project lifecycle and phases of the project
- Estimation of the cost, effort, and schedule
- Determining the start and end dates for the project
- Determining the key project milestones
- Preparation of financial budget
- Determining the resources required
- Determining the knowledge, skills, and training required
- Staffing the project and assigning resources to the tasks and activities
- Preparing the project plan
- Preparing the initial project schedule
- Identifying initial project risks
- Preparing quality plan
- Preparing test plan
- Preparing configuration management plan
- Preparing deployment plan
- Obtaining approval for the project plan and schedule

The project planning activities take place during the project start-up and initiation phase, and re-planning activities take place during project execution.

6.2 Project Start-up and Initiation

There are many ways in which a project may be triggered but often it is as the result of a problem or business opportunity that the project will address. For example, an e-commerce company may wish to develop a new version of its software with attractive features to dazzle users and increase sales. An internal IT department may receive a request from its business users to enhance its business software in order to satisfy new legal or regulatory requirements. A software development company may be contacted by a business to develop a bespoke software solution to meet its needs, and so on.

All parties must be clear on why the project is needed, what the project is to achieve, and how it will be achieved. It is essential that there is a coherent *business case* for the project, where the business case is the fundamental rationale for the project. The business case defines the problem or opportunity in detail, and a preferred solution is identified for implementation. Clearly, an organization needs to be able to justify spending a large amount of money, and so the project must make business sense. In other words, the project must yield a financial return on the investment made, or the project must satisfy some essential business or regulatory requirements.

At the project start-up, the initial scope and costing for the project are determined, and the technical and financial feasibility of the project is determined. A project brief (also called project charter) may be produced to provide a shared understanding of the project, and this describes the objectives of the project and may be used to authorize the project. The project board is set up for project governance and it is responsible for authorizing and directing the project. It verifies that there is a sound business case for the project, and a *project manager* is appointed by the board to manage the project.

The *project board* (or steering group) oversees the project and includes roles such as the *project executive* (this role may also be called the project sponsor), the *senior user*, and *senior supplier*. The actual members of the project board need to be chosen carefully, as it is essential that they have the appropriate authority and influence in the organization to get things done, to make resources available, to make timely decisions, and to remove roadblocks that arise during project execution. That is, the project board includes the key stakeholders, and it is accountable for the success of the project. The project manager provides regular status reports to the project board during the project, and the project board is consulted when key project decisions need to be made.

The project manager is responsible for the day-to-day management of the project, and for determining the approach to be taken for the project. It may be appropriate to outsource the development to a third-party provider due to a lack of in-house expertise, it may be possible to purchase an off-the-shelf solution, or it may be decided to develop the solution internally.

A project is a temporary activity with a definite start and an end date. The project manager *kicks off the project* and mobilizes the project team. The detailed requirements and estimates for the project are determined, the schedule of activities and tasks established, and resources are assigned to the various tasks and activities. The project scheduling is generally done with the Microsoft Project tool, and the schedule defines the deliverables that will be produced, when they will be produced, and who produces them. The project manager prepares the project plan, which is subject to the approval of the key stakeholders, and it describes how the project will achieve its objectives and how the desired customer quality expectations will be achieved. The initial risks are identified and managed, and a risk log (or repository) is set up for the project. Once the planning and requirements are complete project execution commences.

Often, the initial requirements for a project arise due to a problem that the business or customer needs to solve. This leads to a project to implement an appropriate solution, and the first step is to determine the scope of work and the actual requirements for the project, and whether the project is feasible from the cost, time, and technical considerations. The process of determining the requirements for a proposed system involves discussions with the relevant stakeholders to determine their needs, and to explicitly define what functionality the system should provide, as well as any hardware and performance constraints.

Next, we describe various activities in the project start-up and initiation phase such as preparing the project brief and business case, developing the requirements, estimation, preparing the project plan, and so on in more detail, and we start with a discussion on the role of the project board.

6.3   Project Board

The project board is responsible for directing the project, and it is directly account-able for the success of the project. It consists of senior managers and staff in the organization who have the authority to make resources available, to remove roadblocks, and to get things done. The project sponsor (also called the project executive or project director) has overall responsibility for the project and is a member of the project board. S/he ensures that the project is aligned to the organi-zation's strategy, and has responsibility for monitoring the budget and controlling the spending. The membership of the project board is summarized in Fig. 5.2 and the roles of the members are described in Table 5.4.

The project board includes key stakeholders such as the senior user who repre-sents the interests of the customer and users, and the senior supplier who represents the interest of the developers of the system. The project executive has overall responsibility for the project, and is supported by the senior user and senior sup-plier. The project executive and board will ensure that the business case is valid and aligned to the business, and will support the project manager during project execution.

The project board is accountable for the success of the project, and the project executive may delegate some of his/her responsibilities to the project manager. The project manager provides regular status reports to the project board during project execution to highlight progress made as well as key project risks and issues. The project board meets at an appropriate frequency during the project (with extra sessions held should serious project issues arise), and the project manager will escalate events that are beyond his/her control to the project board for resolution.

The project board is consulted whenever key project decisions need to be made, and it plays a key role in project governance. The project board ensures that there is a valid business case for the project, and that the capital funding for the project is adequate and well spent. The project board may cancel the project at any stage during project execution should there cease to be a business case, or should project spending exceed project tolerance and go out of control.

The members of the project board are chosen carefully, as the members of the project board need to have the appropriate authority and influence in the organiza-tion to be effective in getting things done (e.g., making resources available, making timely decisions, and removing roadblocks). That is, they must be the right people with the right influence to make the right decisions based on the right information.

6.4   Preparing the Project Brief and Business Case

A project often starts with a short document termed the project brief (or project charter) that provides a brief definition of the project and its goals. The project brief communicates what needs to be done during the project, and what the project intends to achieve. This includes its scope and objectives, its key timelines, and the stakeholders involved. The project brief is often revisited during project execution,

Table 6.1 Some sections in the project brief

Section	Description
Project goals and objectives	This section states the key goals and objectives of the project
Project scope	The scope of the project consists of the functionality that will be provided (i.e., it is a statement about the functional requirements)
Proposed timelines	This defines the proposed timelines (e.g., the key project milestones such as the start and end dates of the project)
Risks	The key risks identified at this stage are listed, and these need to be managed
Benefits	The key benefits that will result once the project is successfully implemented by the project team
Outline business case	A short description of the business case

with other deliverables extending and refining it. Table 6.1 describes sections that may be in the project brief.

The business case describes the reason and justification for the project, and it needs to be aligned to the business strategy. It is based on the expected costs of the project, the associated risks, and the expected business benefits and savings. A project should proceed only if it has a valid business case, and the project should be terminated if its business case ceases to exist. The business case describes the problem or opportunity, the options that are available as a solution to the problem or opportunity, and the preferred solution. The preferred solution is subjected to an investment appraisal to determine the return on investment (ROI). Table 6.2 presents sections that may be present in a business case.

Next, we discuss investment analysis and appraisal of the project in more detail.

6.4.1   Investment Appraisal

It is important that the project makes business sense and provides a financial benefit to the organization. A project will generally result in extra income being earned by the company in future years, but it requires the commitment of financial resources now for its implementation. The project should cover its cost in the sense that the net present value of the future payments (NPV) should exceed the cost of the project. Table 6.3 presents various terms often used in investment analysis.

Present Value
The time value of money is the concept that the earlier that a cash payment is received the greater its value to the recipient. Similarly, the later that the cash payment is made, the lower its value to the payee, and the lower its cost to the payer.

This is clear if we consider the example of a person who receives $1000 now and a person who receives $1000 five years from now. The person who receives

Table 6.2 Some sections in business case

Section	Description
Description of problem/business opportunity	This explains why the project is needed, and it gives a description of the problem that the project will solve, or the business opportunity that the project will take advantage of
List of potential solutions	This provides an overview of the various options that are available and a description of each option
Preferred solution	This identifies the preferred solution and summarizes why it is more appropriate than the others
Analysis (costs, timescales, risks, and benefits)	The benefits of the proposed project are described and may be summarized in a requirements/benefit matrix. The negative benefits (where the project is not done) may be listed and these could include loss of market share or legal penalties The estimated costs and timescales of the preferred solution are outlined, and the key risks and issues for the project are described
Investment analysis	This involves performing a cost-benefit analysis of the project, and calculating the net present value of future benefits versus its costs. The method of EVA and NPV may be employed in the analysis (see Sect. 3.4.1)
Implementation plan	This summarizes the implementation plan for the project

$1000 now is able to invest it and to receive compound interest on the principal, whereas the other person who receives $1000 in 5 years earns no interest during the period. Further, the inflation during the period means that the purchasing power of $1000 is less in 5-year time than it is today.

The general formula for the future value of a principal P invested for n compounding periods at a compound rate r of interest per compounding period is

$$A = P(1 + r)^n$$

The present value of a given amount A that will be received in the future is the principal ($P = PV$) that will grow to that amount where there are n compounding periods and the rate of interest is r for each compounding period. The present value of an amount A received in n compounding periods at an interest rate r for the compounding period is given by

$$P = \frac{A}{(1 + r)^n}$$

Table 6.3 Terminology in investment appraisal

Section	Description
Net benefit/Net benefit after tax	Net benefit reflects the total benefits less the total cost in any 1 year. Net cash benefits reflect the net cash benefit after tax has been deducted
Discount rate %	The discount rate reflects two measures (risk and interest). It reflects the cost of borrowing money and the company's attitude to risk It is used to convert money expected in the future back to the present (i.e., today's money), and is based on the time value of money (i.e., the fact that a sum of money received now is worth more than that sum of money received in the future)
Net present value (NPV) of net benefit	The Net Present Value (NPV) of a project is the financial value of the project in today's money. It takes the time value of money into account and is calculated using the discount rate The sum of the discounted benefits less than the project costs is computed to give the extra profit that the company will make. A negative NPV means that the project does not cover its costs, a NPV of zero means that the project breaks even
Cost of capital	The cost of capital refers to the rate that investors expect to receive in return for investing in the company. It may be determined by calculating the cost of debt, which is the after-tax interest rate on loans and bonds An alternative more complex approach involves estimating the cost of equity from analysing shareholder's expected return implicit in the price they have paid to buy or hold their shares
Economic value added (EVA)	The EVA reflects the value of the project and is the net benefit after tax minus the total cost of capital. It determines if a business is earning more than its true cost of capital. A negative EVA means that the project doesn't generate any real profit whereas a positive EVA generates a profit. The higher the EVA, the more attractive the project will be
Payback period (years)	The payback time is the period of time (expressed in years) that it takes to recover all project costs. This may be done on a discounted/non-discounted basis
Internal rate of return (IRR)	The internal rate of return (IRR) is the discount rate (interest rate) at which the present value of the future cash flows of an investment equals the cost of the investment. Alternatively, it can be seen as the % to which the discount rate needs to rise for the project to only break even. The higher the IRR the more attractive the project

We can also write the present value formula as $PV = P = A(1 + r)^{-n}$.

Example (Present Value)
Find the principal that will amount to $10,000 in 5 years at 8% per annum compounded quarterly.

Solution (Present Value)
The term is 5 years $= 5 * 4 = 20$ compounding period. The nominal rate of interest is $8\% = 0.08$ and so the interest rate i per compounding period is $^{0.08}/_4 = 0.02$. The present value is then given by

$$PV = A(1 + i)^{-n} = FV(1 + i)^{-n}$$
$$= 10000\,(1.02)^{-20}$$
$$= \$6729.71$$

6.4.2 Investment Appraisal Example

A business is considering embarking on a process improvement project that will deliver financial savings over 3 years. The costs and savings are summarized in Table 6.4, and the business wishes to determine whether it should authorize or reject the project based on these. The discount rate used by the company is 8% (compounded annually). Should the project be authorized or rejected? Would the project cover its costs if the discount rate is 10%?

Solution (Investment Analysis)

The total cost of the project is £74,000 and so we need to determine if the total savings cover the costs. That is, we determine the present value of savings E_1, E_2, and E_3 where $E = E_1 + E_2 + E_3$ and compare this to the costs to make the decision.

$$E_1 = 35000(1.08)^{-1} = 35000 * 0.9259 = 32,407$$

Table 6.4 Projected costs and savings

Cost area	Amount	Savings	Amount
Consultancy	£15,000	Year 1	£35,000
Training	£12,000	Year 2	£30,000
Materials	£6,000	Year 3	£25,000
Effort	£37,000	–	–
Expenses	£4,000	–	–
Total costs	£74,000	–	–

$$E_2 = 30000(1.08)^{-2} = 30000 * 0.8573 = 25,720$$

$$E_3 = 25000(1.08)^{-3} = 25000 * 0.7938 = 19,845$$

$$E = E_1 + E_2 + E_3 = £32,407 + £25,720 + £19,845 = £77,972$$

The NPV is the total savings less than the total costs $= S - V = £3,972$, and so the project should be authorized.

For the second part, we proceed in a similar manner and calculate that

$$E_1 = 31,818$$

$$E_2 = 24,793$$

$$E_3 = 18,783$$

$$E = E_1 + E_2 + E_3 = £75,394$$

The total savings are still in excess of the projected costs (£1,394), and so the project should be authorized.

For a more detailed information on mathematics used in business see Ref. [1].

6.5   Project Requirements

The user requirements specify what the customer wants and define what the software system is required to do, as distinct from how this is to be done. The requirements are the foundation for the system, and if they are incorrect then the implemented system will be incorrect. The process of determining the requirements, analysing and validating them, and managing them throughout the project lifecycle is termed requirements engineering.

The process of determining the requirements involves discussions with the relevant stakeholders to determine their needs for the proposed system, and to explicitly define what functionality the system should provide, as well as any hardware and performance constraints. The user requirements are determined from discussions with the customer to determine their actual needs, and they are then refined into the system requirements, which state the functional and non-functional requirements of the system. The specification of the user requirements needs to be unambiguous to ensure that all parties involved in the development of the system share a common understanding of what is to be developed and tested.

Requirements management is concerned with managing changes to the requirements of the project, and in maintaining consistency between the requirements and the project plans and the associated work products. It is important that changes to the requirements are controlled, and that the impacts of the changes are fully understood prior to authorization. Once the system requirements have been approved, any proposed changes to the requirements are subject to formal change control.

The direction of a project is regularly evaluated in the Agile world, where ongoing changes to the requirements are a normal part of the process. For traditional projects changes to requirements are subject to a formal change control process, so that the impact of the proposed change is clearly understood. There is more detailed information on requirements engineering in Chap. 5 of [2].

6.6   Project Estimation

Estimation is an important part of project management, and the accurate estimates of effort, cost, and schedule are essential to delivering a project on time and on budget, and with the right quality.[1] Estimation is employed in the planning process to determine the effort and resources required, and it feeds into the scheduling of the project. The problems with over- or under-estimation of projects are well known, and good estimates allow

- Accurate calculation of the project cost and its feasibility
- Accurate scheduling of the project
- Accurate scheduling of resources for the project
- Measurement of progress and costs against the estimates

Poor estimation leads to

- Projects being over- or under-estimated
- Projects being over- or under-resourced (impacting staff morale)
- Quality being compromised
- Project being delivered late
- Negative impression of the project manager and team

Consequently, estimation needs to be rigorous, and there are several well-known techniques available (e.g., work breakdown structures, function points, and so on). Estimation applies to both the early and later parts of the project, with the later phases of the project refining the initial estimates, as a more detailed understanding of the project activities is then available. The new estimates are used to reschedule and to predict the eventual effort, delivery date, and cost of the project. The following are guidelines for estimation:

---

[1] The consequences of under-estimating a project include the project being delivered late, with the project team working late nights and weekends to recover the schedule, quality being compromised with steps in the process omitted, and so on.

- Sufficient time needs to be allowed to do estimation
- Estimates are produced for each phase of software development
- The initial estimates are high level
- The estimates for the next phase should be solid whereas estimates for the later phases may be high level
- The estimates should be conservative rather than optimistic
- Estimates will usually include contingency
- Estimates should be reviewed to ensure their adequacy
- Estimates from independent experts may be useful
- It may be useful to prepare estimates using various methods and to compare

Project metrics may be employed to measure the accuracy of the estimates (see Chap. 14). These metrics are reported during the project and include

- Effort estimation accuracy
- Budget estimation accuracy
- Schedule estimation accuracy

6.6.1   Estimation Techniques

Estimates need to be produced consistently, and it would be inappropriate to have an estimation procedure that relies on an individual and is not a repeatable process. We mentioned several estimation techniques in Chap. 5 (see Table 5.1):

- Work breakdown structure
- Analogy method
- Expert judgement
- Delphi method
- Cost predictor models
- Function points
- Planning poker

Work breakdown structures and function points are described in more detail below.

6.6.2   Work Breakdown Structure

This is a popular approach to project estimation (*it is also known as decomposition*) and involves the following:

- Determine the project deliverables to be produced during the project
- Estimate the size of each deliverable (in pages or LOC)
- Estimate the effort (number of days) required to complete the deliverable based on its complexity and size, and experience of team

Table 6.5 Example work breakdown structure

Lifecycle phase	Project deliverable or task description	Est. size	Est. effort	Est. cost
Planning and requirements	Project plan	40	10 d ays	$5000
	Project schedule	20	5 days	$2500
	Business requirements	20	10 days	$5000
	Test plan	15	5 days	$2500
	Issue/Risk log	3	2 days	$1000
	Lessons learned log	1	1 day	$500
Design	System requirements	15	5 days	$2500
	Technical/DB design	30	10 days	$5000
Coding	Source code	5000 (LOC)	10 days	$5000
	Unit tests/results	200	2 days	$1000
Testing	ST specs	30	10 days	$5000
	System testing		10 days	$5000
	UAT specs	30	10 days	$5000
	UAT testing		10 days	$5000
Deployment	Release notes/procedures	20	5 days	$2500
	User manuals	50	10 days	$2500
	Support procedures	15	10 days	$2500
	Training plan	25	5 days	$2500
Project closure	End project report	10	2 days	$1000
	Lessons learned report	5	2 days	$1000
Contingency	10%	–	13.4	$6700
Total			147.4	$73,700

- Estimate the cost of the completed deliverable (from effort)
- The estimate for the project is the sum of the individual estimates

Productivity data from previous projects may be used. The effort required for a complex deliverable is higher than that of a simple deliverable (where both are of the same size). The project planning section in the project plan (or a separate estimation plan) will include the lifecycle phases, and the deliverables/tasks to be carried out in each phase. It may include a table similar to Table 6.5.

6.6.3 Function Points

Function points were developed by Allan Albrecht at IBM in the late 1970s, and provide a quantitative measure of the amount of functionality in a system [3]. It involves determining the functional requirements and categorizing each functional requirement into one of several types such as input, output, inquiries, and internal and external files. Each functional requirement is assessed to determine its complexity, and a number of function points are assigned to the requirement. The sum of the function points of the functional requirements is a measure of the amount of functionality of the system. That is, function points provide a *functional size measurement* of the software (FSM), and the FSM is a measurement of the effort required for the project.

Function points provide a count of all the functionalities provided to the customer, and function points are calculated by counting screens, reports, queries, and files/database tables. There are two types of functions, namely, data functions and transaction functions, with data functions made up of internal and external resources that affect the system. Transaction functions are made up of the processes that are exchanged between the user, the external applications, and the application being measured, and there are three types, namely, external input, external output, and external inquiry.

Function point analysis may be applied to all phases of development from requirements to implementation, to the application only, or to an enhancement to the software after its release to the customer. An International Function Point User Group (IFPUG) was founded in the mid-1980s, and it has been responsible for the evolving definition and application of functional size measurement method that led to an ISO standard for function points (ISO/IEC 20,926:2009) in 2009. The reader is referred to the IFUPG for more detailed information (https://www. ifpug.org/).

6.7   Project Plan

There is the well-known adage that states, *"Fail to plan, plan to fail"*.[2] A well-managed project has an increased chance of success, and good planning is an essential part of project management. A simple process map for project planning is presented in Fig. 6.1.

The project plan defines how the project will be carried out, and it generally includes sections which are given in Table 6.6.

The project plan is a key project document, and it needs to be approved by all stakeholders. The project manager needs to ensure that the project plan and schedule are kept up to date, and that they are kept consistent with the requirements. Another words, if there are changes to the requirement then the project plan and schedule will need to be updated accordingly.

---

[2] This quotation is adapted from Benjamin Franklin (an inventor and signatory to the American declaration of independence. His precise quote was "By failing to prepare, you are preparing to fail").

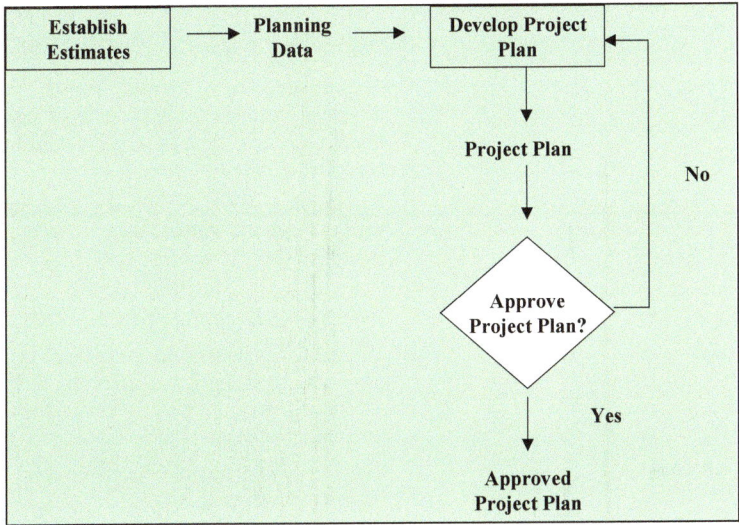

Fig. 6.1 Simple process map for project planning

6.7.1 The Communication Plan

Communication planning describes how communication will be carried out during the project, and it defines all the parties with an interest in the project and the method and frequency of communication between them and the project. The communication may be verbal, email, written reports, presentations, and meetings. A matrix is often employed to summarize the communication plan for the project, and Table 6.7 presents a sample communication plan.

6.7.2 The Project Quality Plan

The project quality plan defines how the project intends to achieve the customer's quality expectations, and the responsibilities for quality of those within and external to the project are defined. The standards from the customer's quality management system and the supplier's quality management system may be combined, with some aspects relating to the customer's quality system and the remainder to the supplier's quality system.

The project quality plan will describe how quality will be built into the project deliverables and final product. The quality control procedures are defined and these include well-defined quality controls such as peer reviews and testing to ensure quality is consistently produced. Metrics may be employed to measure performance (see Chap. 14).

Table 6.6 Some sections in the project plan

Section	Description
Business case	The business case is the reason why the project is taking place, and it may be for legal/regulatory reasons, financial savings, quality improvement, productivity improvements, and so on
Project goals and objectives	The specific goals and objectives of the project need to be clearly stated. They need to be consistent with the business case
Scope of project	The scope of the project defines what is in scope and what is outside scope for the project
Project approach	The approach taken by the project may be to purchase a solution off the shelf from a software vendor, outsource the development, or develop the solution internally
Key stakeholders	The key stakeholders including their roles and responsibilities are listed
Project team/Organization structure	The teams and personnel required for the project as well as their responsibilities are defined, and this may be presented as a table or in a visual diagram
Key success factors	The key success factors for the project define what the project must achieve to be successful
Project lifecycle phases	For traditional waterfall-type projects the phases may be similar to Planning and Requirements, Design, Coding, Testing, Deployment and Project Closure. For an Agile project there may be several fixed interval sprints
Assumptions, constraints, and dependencies	The known assumptions, constraints, and dependencies for the project are listed
Estimation and WBS	The estimation approach for the project may involve listing the project deliverables (per lifecycle phase) and the estimated effort required for each deliverable (WBS approach). Other approaches (e.g., function points) may be employed
Key milestones	The key project milestones may include end of lifecycle milestones such as planning and requirements complete, design and code complete, testing complete, deployment complete, and project closure complete. For an Agile project the key milestones may be at the end of each sprint
Initial project schedule	The initial project schedule is created in Microsoft project or a similar scheduling tool

(continued)

Table 6.6 (continued)

Section	Description
Financial budget	The financial budget details the authorized expenditure for the project such as capital expenditure, staff costs, contractor costs, consultancy costs, and contingency
Project tolerances	The project tolerances stipulate the % deviation from the approved budget and schedule that is allowed, and the project manager is required to advise the project board should the project tolerances be exceeded, and to seek authorization for additional expenditure
Tools required	The specific tools that are required for the project are listed
Initial project risks	Risk management takes place throughout the project and existing risks will be monitored regularly and new risks identified, assessed, and managed. The initial project risks are identified and a Risk log (or RAID log) created
Knowledge, skills required	The knowledge and skills required by the project team are specified
Training Planning	The training required to address gaps in the knowledge/skills of the project team is identified and provided
Quality planning	This section (it may be a reference to a separate document) will specify the customer quality expectations, and will detail how quality will be built into the project deliverables. Each deliverable is subject to a review or walkthrough prior to its approval
Test planning	This section (it may be a reference to a separate test plan) will detail the various types of testing to be performed, who will perform them, when they will be performed, and the test environment required
Communication planning	This section defines the responsibilities for communication and reporting during the project (it may be a reference to a separate plan). It will include meetings, presentations, reports, and verbal communication
Deployment planning	This section (it may be a reference to a separate deployment plan) specifies the activities associated rolling out new applications including release notes, installation procedures, training, and customer support procedures

(continued)

Table 6.6 (continued)

Section	Description
Configuration management planning	This section (it may be a reference to a separate configuration management plan) defines the configuration management planning for the project. This involves defining the configuration items to be placed under configuration management control, setting up a directory structure for the project deliverables, and controlling changes to the configuration items
Project meetings	Project meetings take place regularly (usually weekly) with the project team to check progress against the plan and to identify any new risks or issues
Project issues	The project issues may be logged in an Issue Log (a spreadsheet for tracking issues), a RAID log, or a tool. Issues are then managed
Project change control	A change control board (consisting of project manager and relevant stakeholders) is set up to consider change requests to the project, and all requests are assessed to determine their impacts (technical/schedule/budget) prior to their approval/rejection
Lessons learned	The lessons learned during the project (i.e., what went well and what went poorly) will be recorded in a spreadsheet or a tool

There may be a software quality assurance role assigned to the project, and if so this person will audit the project activities and deliverables (including any suppliers) to ensure that the defined processes are followed and that the deliverables produced follow the required standards. The quality assurance role will raise quality issues to the affected parties, and where necessary issues may be escalated to management for resolution.

Table 6.8 presents an excerpt of a quality plan matrix for the project deliverables, and it lists each deliverable to be produced during the project as well as the quality criteria to be satisfied to accept the project deliverable. It defines the quality controls to ensure that quality is built into the deliverable as well as the party responsible for accepting the deliverable.

6.7.3   Project Test Plan

Testing is a sub-project of the project, and the test manager will generally create the project test plan and schedule (this may be done by the project manager for small projects). The test manager will track the test schedule to completion and

Table 6.7   Some sections in the communication plan

Interested party	Information required	Purpose	Responsibility	Frequency	Method
Project Board	Progress	Keep informed	Project manager	Monthly	Reports
					Meetings
	Exceptions			Ad Hoc	Verbal/email
Project manager	Business decisions	Assess impact on project	Project board	Ad Hoc	Verbal/email
	Progress updates	Keep up to date	Project team	Weekly	Meetings/email/verbal
	Supplier updates	Keep up to date	Supplier	Weekly	Meetings/email/verbal
	Testing progress	Keep up to date	Test manager	Weekly	Meetings/email/verbal
Project team	Progress updates	Awareness of progress	Project Manager	Weekly	Meetings/email/verbal
Third-party supplier	Project changes	Assess impacts	Project Manager	Weekly/Ad hoc	Meetings/email/verbal
Test manager	Project changes	Assess impacts	Project manager	Weekly/Ad hoc	Meetings/email/verbal

Table 6.8   Quality plan matrix for project deliverables

Deliverable	Description	Produced by	Quality criteria	Quality control/audit process	Accepted by
Project plan	Plan	Project manager	Fit for purpose	Review	Project board
Project schedule	Schedule	Project manager	Fit for purpose	Review	Project board
Requirements document	Requirements	Systems analyst	Fit for purpose	Review	Requirements manager
Design	Design	Developer	Fit for purpose	Review	Development manager
Code	Code	Developer	Fit for purpose	Review	Development manager
Testing specification	Test specs	Tester	Fit for purpose	Review	Test manager
Deployment plan	Deployment	Customer support analyst	Fit for purpose	Review	Customer support manager

will regularly update the project manager during the project. The test plan defines
how the testing will be carried out, and it generally includes sections such as

- Scope of testing
- Types of testing to be performed
- Roles and responsibilities
- Key stakeholders
- Resources required (hardware and human)
- Training, knowledge and skills required
- Key milestones (for testing)
- Schedule (for test activities, deliverables, and estimates)
- Key assumptions/risks
- Communication planning and test reporting
- Budget planning
- Defect logging and re-testing
- Test acceptance criteria
- Configuration management

There will usually be dedicated test plans for unit, system, and UAT testing, which
are prepared as part of test case analysis and design. The project manager will track
the testing milestones to ensure that the project remains on track.

6.7.4   Financial Plan

The project budget is a detailed estimate of the projected financial costs to
complete the project, and includes human resource costs; the cost of hardware,
software, tools, and training; and subcontractor costs (Table 6.9). It is common to
include some contingency in the estimates (e.g., 10%).

Table 6.9 Project budget

Item	Amount
Internal staff	€150,000
Subcontractors	€50,000
Consultancy	€60,000
Hardware	€5,000
Software	€2,000
Tools	€1,000
Training	€2,000
Subtotal	*€270,000*
Contingency: 10%	€27,000
Total	**€297,000**

Table 6.10 Training plan

Course	Cost	Date	Plan attendees	Actual attendees	Absent
Prince 2	£2000	22.06.20	Elodie, Mary and Lilly	Elodie and Mary	Lilly
Agile	£2000	29.06.20	Mary and Connie	Mary and Connie	–
Java	£1500	22.06.20	Pilar	Pilar	–
RUP	£2000	22.06.20	Jo and Sheila	Jo and Sheila	–
ISEB software testing	£1500	29.06.20	Jo and Liz	Jo and Liz	–

The project manager will track the spending in the project to ensure that the project remains on budget. The PM will advise the project board should the actual project spending exceed project tolerance.

6.7.5 Configuration Management Plan

The configuration management plan is concerned with identifying the configuration items to be controlled, and systematically controlling changes to them throughout the project lifecycle. It ensures that all project deliverables are kept consistent following approved changes to the requirements. That is, if there is a change to the requirements then all affected deliverables (e.g., design, code, test plans, etc.) need to be modified accordingly and kept consistent with the requirements. Configuration management is described in more detail in Chap. 12.

6.7.6 Training Plan

The knowledge and skills required for the project are identified, and the training needs to be determined. Training is planned accordingly and Table 6.10 sketches a training plan for the project.

6.7.7 Deployment Plan

The deployment plan describes the activities involved in the deployment of the software at the customer site. It outlines the responsibilities of the project personnel, and the steps involved in the installation or upgrade of the software at the customer site, as well as training and support that will be provided. The plan includes sections such as

– Roles and responsibilities

- Release notes/procedures
- Preparation of environment
- Installation instructions
- Rollback instructions
- Training for customers
- Customer support procedures

6.8   Schedule and Resource Management

The effort estimates are used for scheduling of the tasks and activities in a project-scheduling tool such as *Microsoft Project* (Fig. 5.1). The schedule will detail the phases in the project, the key project milestones, the activities, and tasks to be performed in each phase as well as their associated duration, and the resources required to carry out each task. The project manager will update the project schedule regularly during the project to reflect the actual progress made, as well as adjusting the schedule whenever changes occur during the project such as the addition of new resources to the project, which could result in the allocation of tasks to the new individual.

There are several types of project schedule that may be employed in the project, including the master schedule, the milestone schedule, and the detailed schedule. The *Master project schedule* provides a high-level summary of the project schedule, and it summarizes and tracks the key project activities and deliverables together with their associated timeline. The *Milestone project schedule* summarizes and tracks the major project milestones. A *Detailed project schedule* identifies and tracks every project activity, and the most common type of project schedule is the Gantt chart (Fig. 5.1).

The allocation of resources to carry out the various tasks and activities requires care to ensure that the tasks are allocated to the individuals with the appropriate skill set, and that individuals are not over-allocated (i.e., scheduled to do more work during a given time than is available to them). The project manager will need to reschedule whenever there are over-allocated resources, and this involves adjusting (decreasing) the amount of time that a resource is working on a specific task, and possibly assigning extra resources to the task.

One important resource management technique is resource levelling which aims to smooth the allocation of resources to ensure that resources are neither over- nor under-allocated. The Microsoft Project tool has resource levelling functionality to deal with conflicts and over-allocation of resources.

6.9   Risk Management Planning

Risks arise due to uncertainty, and risk management is concerned with managing uncertainty and any undesired events that may arise during the project. Risks need to be identified, analysed, and controlled in order for the project to be successful, and risk management activities take place throughout the project lifecycle. The project manager will maintain a risk repository (this may be a tool or a risk log) to record details of each risk including its type and description, its likelihood and its impact, as well as the response to the risk.

Countermeasures are defined to reduce the likelihood of occurrence and impact of the risks, and contingency plans are prepared to deal with the situation of the risk actually occurring. Additional risks may arise during the project, and the project manager needs to be proactive in their identification and management.

Risks need to be reviewed regularly especially following changes in the project, as events that occur may affect existing risks (including the probability of their occurrence and impact), and may lead to new risks. Countermeasures need to be defined and kept up to date during the project. Risks are reported regularly throughout the project. Chapter 7 discusses risk management in more detail.

6.10 Review Questions

1. What is a project?
2. What is a business case?
3. What is the role of the project board?
4. Explain the responsibilities of the project executive, the senior user, and senior supplier.
5. Explain how to determine whether a proposed project makes business sense (i.e., whether it will pay for itself).
6. How are the requirements gathered and defined?
7. How are changes to the requirements managed? Why is it important to keep project deliverables consistent with the requirements?
8. What is the difference between requirements verification and validation?
9. What is the purpose of estimation?
10. What are the popular approaches to estimation?
11. Explain how estimates are produced using the work breakdown structure.
12. What is the purpose of project planning? Describe the main parts of a project plan.
13. What is the purpose of project scheduling?

6.11 Summary

A project is generally undertaken to take advantage of a problem/opportunity, and a project team is formed to implement and deliver an appropriate solution. Only those projects that will deliver the greatest business benefit should be authorized, with those with a limited or zero business benefit rejected. The business case provides the rationale for the project, and the project should only proceed if it has a valid business case.

The project is kicked off and the project board oversees the project, and the project manager is responsible for managing the project. The project board needs to have the right people with sufficient influence and authority to remove roadblocks that arise and to make timely decisions. It needs to be clear on what the project is to achieve and how it will be achieved. The approach to the project is decided (e.g., whether to build or buy), and the initial project risks, customer's quality expectations, and project's acceptance criteria are defined.

The project plan defines what the project intends to achieve and how it will do so. The scope of the project is determined, and estimates of the effort for the various tasks and activities established. The project plan and schedule are developed and approved by the stakeholders, and the project plan may contain or reference several other plans.

The effective management of risk during a project is essential to project success. Risks arise due to uncertainty and the risk management is concerned with managing uncertainty and undesired events.

References

1. G. O'Regan, *A Guide to Business Mathematics*, (Taylor and Francis, 2022)
2. G. O' Regan, *Concise Guide to Software Engineering*, 2nd Edition, (Springer, 2022)
3. A. Albrecht, Measuring application development productivity. in *Proceedings of the Joint SHARE, GUIDE, and IBM Application Development Symposium, Monterey, California, October 14–17*, (IBM Corporation, 1979), pp. 83–92

Risk Management

7

Key Topics

Risk category
Risk likelihood
Risk impact
Risk response
Risk log

7.1 Introduction

The effective management of risk is an important part of project management, and it is essential that the project can manage its exposure to risk, and that it is well prepared for any unanticipated events that may arise during project execution. Otherwise, there is a danger of major impacts on the project schedule or significant additional costs to the project. A risk that materializes is a project issue that needs to be dealt with, and the project should have effective risk mitigation and contingency plans prepared for the most serious project risks. The project manager needs to be proactive in identifying risks that may occur during the project to ensure that they can be controlled and dealt with effectively, and that the project will not be adversely affected.

Risks arise due to uncertainty, and *risk management is concerned with managing uncertainty*, and especially the management of any undesired events that may occur during project execution. The future is uncertain and events may occur that cause disruption. A risk is an undesirable event that may occur during the project, and should the risk materialize it has a measurable impact on the project. Some risks have a very low probability of occurrence (e.g., an earthquake, a volcanic eruption, or tsunami), but may have a very high impact should they materialize. For example,

© The Author(s), under exclusive license to Springer Nature Switzerland AG 2025   121
G. O'Regan, *Guide to Software Project Management*, Undergraduate Topics in
Computer Science, https://doi.org/10.1007/978-3-031-80578-3_7

a natural disaster such as an earthquake could have a devastating impact on the geographical region and as well as on the project.

Risks need to be identified, analysed, and controlled in order for the project to be successful, and risk management activities take place throughout the project lifecycle. Once the initial set of risks to the project has been identified, they are analysed to determine their *likelihood of occurrence* and their *impact* (e.g., on cost, schedule or quality). These two parameters determine the *risk category*, and the most serious risk category refers to a risk with a high probability of occurrence and a high impact on occurrence (i.e., box I in Fig. 7.1).

Countermeasures are defined to reduce the likelihood of occurrence and impact of the risks, and contingency plans are prepared to deal with the situation of the risk actually occurring. Additional risks may arise during the project, and the project manager needs to be proactive in their identification and management.

Risks need to be reviewed regularly especially following changes to the project such as changes to the business case or the business requirements, loss of key personnel, and so on. Events that occur may affect existing risks (including the probability of their occurrence and their impact), and may lead to new risks. Countermeasures need to be kept up to date during the project. Risks are reported regularly throughout the project.

There is an ISO standard (ISO 31000:2018) on the implementation of risk management, and it provides a framework and a process for managing risk. It includes best practice and guidance on risk management. The ISO 31010:2019 is a standard for risk assessment techniques, and it provides guidance on the selection and application of techniques for assessing risk in a wide range of situations.

The Capability Maturity Model Integrated (CMMI) is a framework for the implementation of best practice in software and system engineering, and it has a process area that is dedicated to risk management. The Prince 2 project management methodology has a rigorous approach to risk management, and this chapter has been influenced by Prince 2's approach to risk management [1].

Fig. 7.1 Risk categories

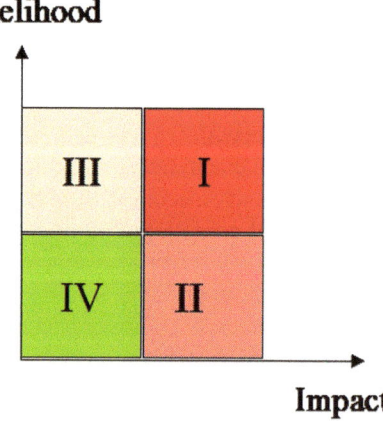

7.2   Risk Management Cycle

The risk management cycle is concerned with identifying and managing risks throughout the project lifecycle. It involves identifying risks, determining their probability of occurrence and impact should they occur, identifying responses to the risks, and monitoring and reporting. The Prince 2 risk management cycle is summarized in Fig. 7.2.

Historical data and discussions with stakeholders often help in identifying the initial risks, and the risks are then classified into types such as business and technical risks. The probability and impact of each risk is determined, and responses to the risk are identified and implemented. The risks are regularly monitored and reported during the project and the cycle repeats. The process of risk management throughout the project lifecycle is illustrated in Fig. 7.3.

The risk management activities are described in more detail in Table 7.1.

The project manager will maintain a risk repository (this may be a tool or a spreadsheet such as a risk log or a RAID log) to record details of each risk, its

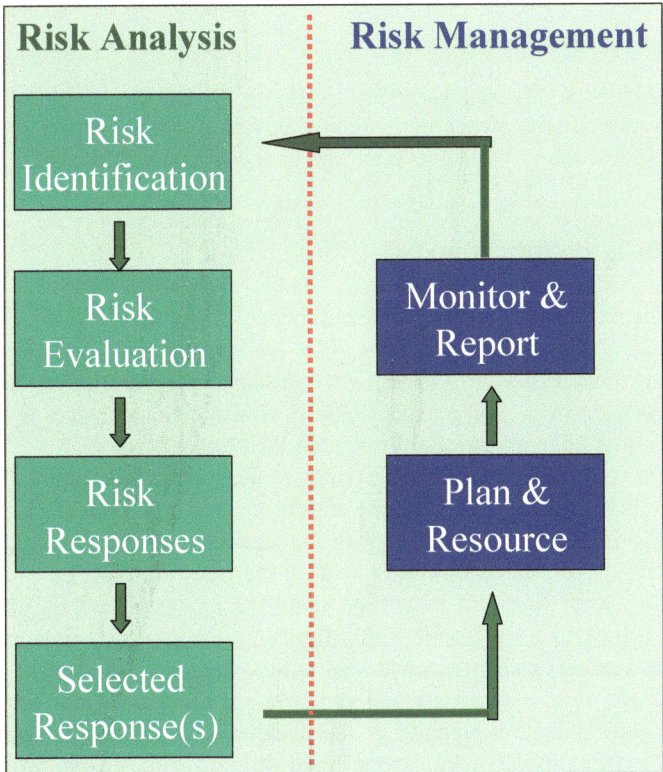

Fig. 7.2 Risk management

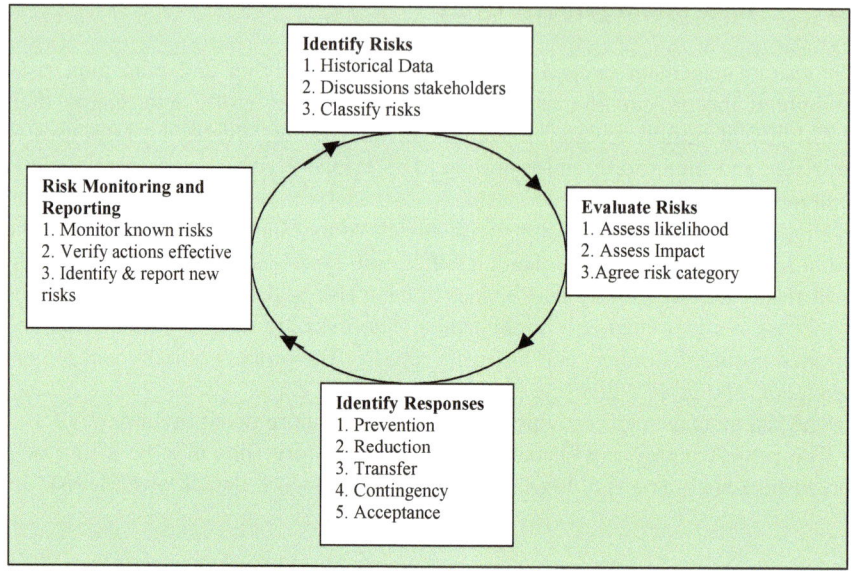

Fig. 7.3 Continuous risk management cycle

type and description, its owner, its likelihood of occurrence, and its impact should it occur (yielding the risk category), as well as the response to the risk.

7.2.1 Risk Identification

Risk identification is the process of determining risks that could prevent the project from achieving its objectives, and the risks are recorded in a risk log (or risk management tool). Each entry in the risk log includes a description of the risk, an assessment, an owner, and status. Risk identification commences early in the project and is an ongoing process throughout the project lifecycle.

Historical risks and issues from previous projects may be examined to determine if any of these are relevant to the current project. The project manager will also identify risks from discussions with the stakeholders and the project team. Often the project manager will discuss risks at the weekly project meeting, and as the project proceeds further risks will be identified, analysed, and recorded in the risk log. It is important to consider risk whenever changes occur in the project, as often changes affect current risks and lead to new risks.

For example, risks may arise whenever there are changes to the requirements, or issues with a software supplier, or the resignation of a team member. Other techniques for identifying risks include brainstorming with the project team and checklists. Risks may be broadly classified into the following types:

Business (e.g., risk of collapse of subcontractors).
Legal and regulatory (e.g., introduction of new regulations).

Table 7.1 Risk management activities

Activity	Description
Risk management strategy	This defines how the risks will be identified, monitored, reviewed, and reported during the project, as well as the frequency of monitoring and reporting
Risk identification	This involves identifying the risks to the project and recording them in a risk repository (e.g., a Risk Log or tool). Prince 2 classifies risks into: – *Business* (e.g., collapse of subcontractors) – *Legal and Regulatory* (e.g., new legislation or regulatory control of the industry) – *Organizational* (e.g., project team issues such as availability of resources, un-trained staff, weak management, personality clashes). – *Technical* (e.g., scope creep, new technology, architectural uncertainties, inadequate design) – *Environmental* (e.g., flooding, fires, or earthquakes)
Evaluating the risks	This involves assessing the likelihood of occurrence of a particular risk and its impact (on cost, schedule, etc.) should it materialize. These two parameters determine the risk category.
Identifying risk responses and selection	Project manager/stakeholders determine the appropriate response to a risk (e.g., reducing the probability of its occurrence or its impact should it occur). The risk responses include – *Prevention* which aims to prevent it from occurring – *Reduction* aims to reduce the probability of its occurrence or its impact should it occur – *Transfer* aims to transfer the risk to a third party – *Acceptance* is when nothing can be done about it – *Contingency* are actions that are carried out should the risk materialize
Risk monitoring and reporting	Monitoring existing risks to verify that the actions taken to manage the risks are effective, as well as identifying new risks. Acts as an early warning that a risk is going to materialize, and *a risk that materializes is a new project issue*
Lessons learned	Determining the effectiveness of risk management during the project, and to learning any lessons for future projects

Organizational (e.g., availability and skill of resources and management).
Technical (e.g., scope creep, architecture, design, etc.).
Environmental (e.g., flooding or fires).

7.2.2   Risk Evaluation and Prioritization

The identified risks are analysed by the project manager and relevant stakeholders to determine their likelihood of their occurrence and impact should they materialize. The importance of the risks may then be determined and appropriate mitigation plans defined. The likelihood and impact parameters below may be classified as low, medium, or high, and the impact as its effect on the project tolerance (another approach might be to define the impact in terms of a monetary value). Table 7.2 is one approach to likelihood and impact risk parameters.

The risk category (or risk criticality) may be determined from the likelihood and impact parameters. For example, one approach to defining the risk category is described in Table 7.3.

Risk category 1 is the most serious risk category, and these risks have a high probability of occurrence and a high impact should they occur. These need careful monitoring and management. Risk category 5 is the least serious and these risks have a low probability of occurrence and a low impact should they occur. However, all risks need to be carefully monitored during the project as their risk category could change during project execution.

The project's overall risk profile may be summarized in an easy-to-read diagram, which provides a crisp summary of the information in the risk log (Fig. 7.4). For example, there is one category 1 risk (i.e., risk 9), and two category 2 risks (i.e., risks 4 and 8). Risk categories 1 and 2 are potentially very serious, and the project manager will wish to mitigate risks in these categories. The risk profile

Table 7.2 Risk parameters

Likelihood	Probability	Impact	Description
Low	<20%	Low	Negligible impact on project tolerances
Medium	21–50%	Medium	Puts project tolerances at risk
High	51–100%	High	Places project outside tolerances

Table 7.3 Risk category

Risk category	Likelihood	Impact
1	High	High
2	High	Medium
2	Medium	High
3	Medium	Medium
3	High	Low
3	Low	High
4	Medium	Low
4	Low	Medium
5	Low	Low

		Impact		
		Low	Medium	High
Likelihood	Low	1,2		7
	Medium	5	6	8
	High	3	4	9

Fig. 7.4 Risk management profile

needs to be updated regularly during the project, and changes to the probability or impact of a risk result in updates to the risk profile diagram.

7.2.3 Risk Responses and Selection

The response to a risk involves identifying and evaluating a range of options for controlling the risk, and preparing and implementing a risk management plan. The actions put in place to control the risk should be proportional to the severity of the risk, as often there are costs associated with the control measures.

The project manager and other relevant stakeholders will devise an appropriate response to a risk in line with its criticality. The response may be to reduce the probability of occurrence of the risk and/or its impact should it occur. The responses could be

Prevention which aims to prevent the risk from materializing.
Reduction of probability of occurrence or its impact should it occur.
Transfer of risk (e.g., insurance).
Acceptance of risk.
Contingency actions.

The countermeasures for prevention either stop the risk from occurring or having any impact should it occur. This may involve doing things differently in the project where it is feasible to do so. The countermeasures for reduction involve actions that either reduce the likelihood of occurrence of the risk or limit its impact to acceptable levels should it occur.

The countermeasures for transfer involve actions to transfer the risk to a third party such as an insurance company such that the impact of the risk is no longer an issue for the project. Acceptance is where the risk is tolerated, as it may be that nothing can be done at a reasonable cost to mitigate the risk, or the likelihood of its occurrence is at an acceptable level. Contingency are planned actions that are carried out should the risk materialize.

There are costs associated with the actions and so there is a need to balance the cost of taking that action with the impact of the risk should it materialize. The implementation of the selected response requires planning including the budget, effort, and resources required to carry out the actions. Each action will have an owner who has overall responsibility for the implementation of the action.

7.2.4 Risk Monitoring and Reporting

Risk management takes place throughout the project lifecycle as a risk may occur at any time. It is essential that the risks are actively monitored by the project manager and reported regularly to the stakeholders during the project. It is important to check that the risk mitigation actions are being implemented and are having the desired effect, as well as watching for warning signs that a risk may be about to occur.

The project manager may present a summary of the risks in an easy-to-read diagram to the various stakeholders regularly during the project, and this may include weekly project reports and reports to the project board (Fig. 7.4).

7.2.5 Risk Log

The project manager may use a risk log to record the project risks, their likelihood of occurrence and impact, responses and the countermeasures (Fig. 7.5).

7.2.6 Risk Management Checklist

Checklists are a useful way of ensuring that an activity has been completed successfully, and that all of the required steps have been carried out. A sample checklist for risk management is given in Table 7.4.

7.3 Risk Management Case Study

The COVID-19 pandemic (also known as the coronavirus pandemic) was first identified in Wuhan, China in December 2019, and it was declared a pandemic in March 2020. There were over 8 million cases reported by June 2020 with over 400,000 deaths; this had reached over 22 million reported cases with 800,000 deaths by August 2020; over 45 million reported cases with 1.2 million deaths by November 2020; and 542 million cases with 6.3 million deaths by June 2022.

The virus was mainly transmitted between people during close contact, and transmission usually occurred as a result of the small droplets produced by coughing, sneezing, and speaking being inhaled by an individual in close proximity to the infected person (i.e., breathing in the virus as in Fig. 7.6). The droplets fall on the floor or on a surface, and an individual may also become infected by touching a contaminated surface and then touching their face. The virus was most contagious during the first 3 days after the onset of symptoms, but was also spread before

Project: CMMI L2 Improvement Programme — **Risk Log**

Risk No.	Risk Type	Raiser	Date Raised	Description	Likelihood	Impact	Category	Response Type	Countermeasure	Allocated To	Status	Last Update
1	Organization and Human	GOR	23.01.20	It is assumed that staff will be 100% available for the duration of the project.	High	High	1	Prevention	Achieve commitment from Project Board on Staff availability.	G. O'Regan	Monitored	23.01.20
2	Organization and Human	GOR	27.1.20	It is assumed that Senior Management will be fully committed throughout the project	Low	High	3	Prevention	Keep Senior Management informed on progress and results of Improvement Programme	G. O'Regan	Monitored	27.1.20
3	Organization and Human	GOR	27.1.20	It is assumed that other areas (e.g., Business / infrastructure) will provide support for the programme as a new process may potentially affect other areas	Medium	High	2	Prevention	Keep IT Mgrs / Business informed of progress during programme and stress importance in working together on improvements	G. O'Regan	Monitored	27.1.20
4	Organization and Human	GOR	27.1.20	It is assumed that Staff members will be fully committed to participation in the improvement activities. Lack of staff commitment would adversely affect the programme	Low	High	3	Prevention	Motivate staff on benefits at Kick Off meeting. Keep staff motivated throughout by emphasising that improvements will make their job easier.	G. O'Regan	Monitored	27.1.20
5	Organization and Human	GOR	27.1.20	It is assumed that external consulting company will be available at the required dates throughout the programme.	Low	High	3	Prevention	Communicate with the consulting company well in advance as to when they will be required and keep informed of progress. Adjust schedule where required.	G. O'Regan	Monitored	27.1.20
6	Organization and Human	GOR	06.04.20	A team member goes on maternity leave in May. There is a risk to the success of the programme given the loss of such a key player.	Medium	High	2	Reduction	Interviews being conducted for replacement. Keep teams focused and committed	G. O'Regan	Monitored	06.04.20

Fig. 7.5 Risk log

Table 7.4 Risk management checklist

No.	Item to check
1.	Has the initial risk analysis been performed?
2.	Is the likelihood of each risk identified?
3.	Is the impact of each risk identified?
4.	Has the risk category of each risk been determined?
5.	Has an appropriate response for each risk been identified?
6.	Is the response/countermeasure for each risk effective?
7.	Is a risk owner assigned for each risk?
8.	Is the status of each risk recorded?
9.	Have new risks been considered after changes in the project?
10.	Are risks regularly reported during the project?
11.	Are risks regularly monitored and managed during the project?
12.	Have lessons been learned from the risk management activities?

Fig. 7.6 Respiratory droplets when a man sneezes. Public domain

symptoms appear and also by asymptomatic individuals (i.e., people who did not show any symptoms).

COVID-19 was a new respiratory illness and so at the outbreak of the pandemic there was no vaccination available to provide immunity, and no recommended medication to treat the disease. There was a phenomenal response from the scientific and pharmaceutical industry to the development of vaccinations and treatments to deal with the disease (the typical length of time to produce a new vaccine is 5–10 years, but several vaccines were going through final stage 3 trials in late 2020 in an unprecedented research and development race for a first to market product).

However, the disease remained a major threat (especially to the elderly and medically vulnerable) until those vaccines and treatments were commercially available. Once vaccines became commercially available there was also the extraordinary response of a section of the population who refused to take the vaccine (who interpreted the COVID-19 virus as a conspiracy), when the vaccine was a way to save both their own lives and those who they were close to.

The common symptoms of COVID-19 included a fever, a cough, shortness of breath, fatigue and loss of smell, and the incubation period was from 1 to 14 days with some infected individuals having no symptoms. It affected the lungs and airways, but most infected people developed mild-to-moderate illness, and recovered without hospitalization, whereas the most serious cases required hospitalization including intensive care and ventilator support.

The pandemic caused global social and economic disruption, and it led to massive cancellation of sporting and cultural events, the closing of schools and universities, a massive reduction in international travel, and the temporary closure of businesses and shops.

We consider a hypothetical example of the National Health Service of an arbitrary country (not the NHS of the UK or any particular country) at an early stage of the pandemic wishing to manage the COVID-19 outbreak, and aiming to ensure that its health service is not overwhelmed by the pandemic. It will wish to control the virus by ensuring that any outbreaks are brought quickly under control by contingency measures, and its preventive measures will aim to reduce the risk of individuals becoming infected with the virus, and to limit the impact should they become infected. It may include activities which are given in Table 7.5.

7.3.1 Risk Monitoring and Control (COVID-19)

The health service will communicate the status of the pandemic on a daily basis to the government of the day, and will provide medical advice to political decision-makers based on their medical analysis. The daily briefing will include quantitative data such as

Number of new cases per day
New Clusters and Location
Number of fatalities per day
The R Rate (measurement of number of people infected by one person)
The 14-rolling day average of virus cases per 100,000 of population
The percentage increase/decrease in the virus

The medical advice and recommendations will be considered by the government of the day (cabinet subcommittee), and the response from the government may include:

Impose restrictions (e.g., on bars/restaurants/sporting events)

Table 7.5 Risk management for COVID-19

Activity	Description		
Risk identification	Risk of many individuals contracting COVID-19 and the health service being overwhelmed by coronavirus		
Risk evaluation	The likelihood of the risks materializing depends on how prepared the country is for a pandemic: – Has it a best-in-class health service? – Is the health service trained for a pandemic? – Is there an effective test and trace system in place? – Can close contacts of an infected person be easily determined? – How well educated are the population? – Is it capable of controlling entry of the virus into the state? – Is it an island and able to close its borders? – Does it have the infrastructure to introduce quarantine measures for newly arrived? – Has it effectively communicated the dangers of the virus, and the preventive measures to be followed by all? – Does it have the buy in for change from its residents? The *likelihood* of catching the virus or the health service being overwhelmed may be considered medium (this may be reduced by preventive measures such as maintaining a social distance of 1–2 metres, hygiene measures such as regular hand washing, wearing face masks, avoiding crowds, and controlling entry to state with quarantine measures). The *impact* of the health service being overwhelmed or should many people catch the virus is *potentially* high (although most people who are young/middle aged and in good health with no underlying medical conditions will experience only mild symptoms or be asymptomatic). This could result in ventilators being unavailable for seriously ill patients. This means that we are dealing with a category two risk.		
	Prevention	**Reduce**	**Contingency**
Risk responses (For preventing individuals contacting COVID-19 and health service being overwhelmed)	Set up temporary hospitals	Self-isolate if symptoms are present and monitor	Cancel all leaves for healthcare workers
	Place private hospitals in temporary public ownership	Take test to confirm and trace all others potentially infected	Crisis plea to retired/ career break healthcare professionals to return
	Close borders	Take medication	Emergency hiring of overseas healthcare professionals

(continued)

Table 7.5 (continued)

	Prevention	Reduce	Contingency
	Quarantine (new arrivals)	Monitor/GP/ Hospital	Re-impose national lockdown
	Impose national lockdown	Hospital (intensive care/oxygen/ ventilator)	Impose local lockdown to deal with clusters
	Impose restrictions (e.g., restaurants/bars)	Take new vaccination	–
	Regular hand washing and disinfecting	–	–
	Maintain social distance (1–2 metres)	–	–
	Compulsory face masks	–	–
	Self-isolation if symptoms/monitor	–	–
	Tracker app for Test/ Trace	–	–
	Develop vaccination	–	–
	Develop treatments	–	–
	Get vaccinations	–	–
Risk monitoring and reporting	The health service will communicate the status of the outbreak on a daily basis including key metrics such as – Arrival rate of infections per day – Number of deaths from the virus per day – 14-day rolling average of virus cases per 100,000 population – R rate (the average number of people that one person infects) – % increase or decrease of virus Based on analysis of the metrics action is taken to control and live with the outbreak		

Impose wearing of facemasks in shops/public transport.
Suspend international travel
Impose local lockdowns to deal with outbreaks in clusters

7.4 Review Questions

1. What is a risk?
2. Explain the difference between a risk and an issue.

3. Explain how a risk is evaluated in terms of its likelihood and impact.
4. What is the role of the project manager in risk management?
5. What is the role of the project board in risk management?
6. What is the purpose of the risk profile summary?
7. What are the possible responses to a risk?
8. Why is it important to monitor and manage risks?
9. What is a risk mitigation plan and when should it be employed?
10. What is a contingency plan and when should it be used?
11. What is the purpose of a risk log?

7.5   Summary

The effective management of risk is an important part of project management, as it is essential that the project be well prepared for any unanticipated events that may arise during project execution. Otherwise, there is a danger of major impacts on the project schedule or significant additional costs to the project.

A risk that materializes is a project issue that needs to be dealt with, and the project should have effective risk mitigation and contingency plans prepared for the most serious project risks. The project manager needs to be proactive in identifying risks that may occur during the project to ensure that they can be controlled and dealt with effectively.

Risks arise due to uncertainty, and risk management is concerned with managing uncertainty. A risk is an undesirable event that may occur during the project, and it has a measurable impact on the project. Some risks have a very low probability of occurring, but others may have a very high impact.

Once the initial set of risks to the project has been identified, they are analysed to determine their likelihood of occurrence and their impact. Countermeasures are defined to reduce the likelihood of occurrence and impact of the risks, and contingency plans are prepared to deal with the situation of the risk actually occurring. Additional risks may arise during the project, and the project manager needs to be proactive in their identification and management.

Risks need to be reviewed regularly especially following changes to the project. Events that occur may affect existing risks (including the probability of their occurrence and their impact), and may lead to new risks.

Reference

1. Office of Government Commerce, *Managing Successful Projects with PRINCE2*, (2004)

Quality Management of Software Projects

8

Key Topics

Software inspections
Software testing
Software process improvement
Problem-solving
ISO 9001
CMMI
Auditor

8.1 Introduction

The success of business is highly influenced by the quality of software, and it is essential that the software is safe, reliable, of a high quality, and fit for purpose. Companies may develop their own software internally, or they may acquire software solutions off-the-shelf or from bespoke software development. Software development companies need to deliver high-quality and reliable software consistently on time to their customers.

The development of software involves many processes such as those for defining requirements; processes for project estimation and project planning; processes for design, implementation, testing, and so on.

It is important that the processes themselves are fit for purpose, and a key premise in the software quality field is that the quality of the resulting software is influenced by the quality and maturity of the underlying processes, and compliance with them. Therefore, it is necessary to focus on the quality of the processes as well as on the quality of the resulting software.

Watts Humphrey is considered the *father of software quality*. Humphrey was an American software engineer and vice president of technical development at

IBM, and he dedicated much of his career to addressing the problems of software development such as schedule delays, cost overruns, software quality, and productivity. He joined IBM in 1959 initially as a hardware architect, but most of his IBM career was in management. He was vice president of technical development, where he oversaw 4,000 engineers in 15 development centres in over 7 countries. He was influenced by others at IBM including Fred Brooks who was the project manager of the IBM System/360 project (see Chap. 8 of [1]); Michael Fagan who developed the Fagan Inspection Methodology (see Chap. 7 of [2]); and Harlan Mills who developed the Cleanroom methodology (see Chap. 2 of [3]). Humphries ran the software quality and process group at IBM towards the end of his IBM career, and he became very interested in software quality.

He retired from IBM in 1986 and joined the newly formed Software Engineering Institute (SEI) at Carnegie Mellon University. He made a commitment to change the software engineering world by developing sound management principles for the software industry [4]. The SEI has largely fulfilled this commitment, and it has played an important role in enhancing the capability of software organizations throughout the world.

Humphries established the software process program at the SEI, and this led to the development of the software Capability Maturity Model (CMM) and its successors. Humphries asked questions such as:

How good is the current software process?

What must I do to improve it?

Where do I start?

The CMM is a framework to help an organization to understand its current process maturity and to prioritize improvements. The SEI introduced software process assessment and software capability evaluation methods in the early 1990s with the original CMM, and these include the CBA/IPI and CBA/SCE methodologies. The CMM model and the associated assessment methods were widely adopted by organizations around the world, and their successors are the CMMI Model and the SCAMPI appraisal methodology.

Humphries focused his later efforts to developing the Personal Software Process (PSP) and the Team Software Process (TSP). These are approaches that teach engineers the skills they need to make and track plans, and to produce high-quality software with zero defects. The PSP helps the individual engineer to collect relevant data for statistical process control, whereas the TSP focuses on teams, and its goal is to assist teams to improve the productivity and quality of their work.

8.1.1   What is Software Quality?

There are various definitions of quality such as the definition proposed by Philip Crosby as "*conformance to the requirements*". This definition does not take the

Table 8.1 ISO 9126-quality characteristics

Characteristic	Description
Functionality	This indicates the extent to which the required functionality is available in the software.
Reliability	This indicates the extent to which the software is reliable.
Usability	This indicates the extent to which the users of the software judge it to be easy to use.
Efficiency	This characteristic indicates the efficiency of the software.
Maintainability	This indicates the extent to which the software product is easy to modify and maintain.
Portability	This indicates the ease of transferring the software to a different environment.

intrinsic difference in the quality of products into account in judging the quality of the product. For example, this definition might suggest that a *Mercedes* car is of the same quality as a *Lada* car.[1] Further, the definition does not consider whether the requirements are actually appropriate for the product.

Juran defines quality as "*fitness for use*" and this is a better definition, although it does not provide a mechanism to judge better quality when two products are equally fit to be used. The ISO 9126 standard[2] for information technology [IS0:91] is a framework for the evaluation of software product quality. It defines six product quality characteristics (Table 8.1), which indicate the extent to which a software product may be judged to be of high quality by the customers. These include.

8.2   A Short History of Quality

In the Middle Ages, a craftsman was responsible for the complete development of a product from its conception to delivery to the customer. This led to a strong sense of pride and ownership in the quality of the product, and apprentices joined craftsmen to learn the skills of the trade.

The industrial revolution led to a change to this traditional paradigm, and labour became highly organized with workers responsible for a particular part of the manufacturing process. The sense of ownership and the pride of workmanship in the product were diluted, as workers were now responsible only for their portion of the product, and not the quality of the product as a whole.

This led to a requirement for more stringent management practices, including planning, organizing, implementation, and control. It inevitably led to a hierarchy of labour with various functions identified, and a reporting structure for the various

---

[1] Most people would judge the Mercedes to be of superior quality.

[2] This has been superseded by the ISO/IEC 25,010:2011 standard which has eight product quality characteristics.

Fig. 8.1 Shewhart's PDCA
cycle

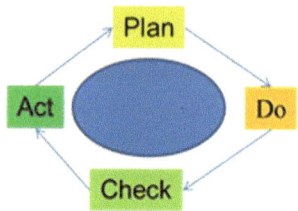

functions. Supervisor controls were needed to ensure that quality and productivity issues were addressed.

Walter Shewhart was a statistician at AT&T Bell Laboratories (or Western Electric Co. as it was known in the 1920s). He is regarded as the founder of statistical process control (SPC), which remains important today for monitoring and controlling a process. He developed a control chart, which is a tool that can be used to control the process, with upper and lower limits for process performance specified. The process is under control if it is performing within these limits (see Fig. 8.12).

The Shewhart model is a systematic approach to problem-solving and process control. It consists of four steps which are used for continuous process improvement, and these are plan, do, check, act, and it is known as the *"PDCA Model"* or Shewhart's model (Fig. 8.1).

Shewhart argued that quality and productivity improve as process variability is reduced. His influential book, *The Economic control of quality of manufactured product* [5] outlines the methods of statistical process control to reduce process variability. The book predicted that productivity would improve as process variability was reduced, and Japanese engineers verified this in the 1950s.

W. Edwards Deming was a major figure in the quality movement. He was influenced by Shewhart's work on statistical process control, and Deming's ideas on quality were adopted in post Second World War Japan and played an important role in transforming Japan's industry (Fig. 8.2).

Deming argued that it is not sufficient for everyone in the organization to be doing one's best: instead, what is required is that there be a consistent purpose and direction in the organization. That is, it is first necessary that people know what to do, and there must be a *constancy of purpose* from all individuals to ensure success.

He argued that there is a very strong case for improving quality, as costs will decrease due to less rework of defective products, and productivity will increase as less time is spent in reworking. This will enable the company to increase its market share, with better quality and lower prices, and to stay in business. Conversely, companies that fail to address quality issues will lose market share, and go out of business. Deming was highly critical of the then American approach to quality, and the lack of vision of American management to quality management.

Deming's influential book *"Out of the Crisis"* [6] proposed 14 principles to transform the Western style of management of an organization to a quality and

Fig. 8.2   W. Edwards Deming. Public Domain

customer focused organization. The implementation of his approach helps an organization to produce high-quality products. It includes:

- Constancy of purpose
- Quality built into the product
- Continuous improvement culture

Joseph Juran (Fig. 8.3) was a major figure in the quality movement, and he argued for a top down approach to quality. He defined quality as *"fitness for use"*, and he argued that quality issues are the direct responsibility of management. Management must ensure that quality is planned, controlled, and improved.

The trilogy of *quality planning*, *control*, and *improvement* is known as the *"Juran Trilogy"*, and is usually described by a diagram with time on the horizontal axis and the cost of poor quality on the vertical axis (Fig. 14.31).

Quality planning consists of setting quality goals, developing plans and determining the resources required to meet the goals. Quality control consists of evaluating performance, setting new goals, and taking action. Quality improvement consists of improving delivery, eliminating wastage and improving customer satisfaction. Juran's 10 step program is defined in [7].

Juran defined an approach to achieve a new quality performance level termed *"Breakthrough and Control"*. It is described pictorially by a control chart showing the old performance level with occasional spikes or random events; what is needed is a breakthrough to a new and more consistent quality performance, i.e., a new performance level with performance achieved at that level.

Fig. 8.3 Joseph Juran

The example in Fig. 8.12 presents the breakthrough in developing a more accurate estimation process. Initially, the variation in estimation accuracy is quite large, but as an improved estimation process is put in place, the control limits are narrowed and more consistent estimation accuracy is achieved. The breakthrough is achieved by a sustained and coordinated effort, and the old performance standard becomes obsolete. The difference between the old and the new performance level is known as the *"chronic disease"* which must be diagnosed and cured.

Philip Crosby was a key figure in the quality movement, and his quality improvement grid influenced the Capability Maturity Model (CMM) developed by the Software Engineering Institute. His influential book *Quality is Free* [8] outlines his philosophy of *doing things right the first time*, i.e., the *zero defects* (ZD) program. Quality is defined as *"conformance to the requirements"* and he argues that people have been conditioned to believe that error is inevitable.

Crosby argued that people in their personal lives do not accept this: for example, it would not be acceptable for nurses to drop a certain percentage of newly born babies. He further argues that the term *"Acceptable Quality Level"* is a commitment to produce imperfect material. Crosby notes that defects are due to two main reasons: *lack of knowledge* or a *lack of attention of the individual.*

He argued that lack of knowledge may be measured and addressed by training, but that lack of attention is a mind-set that requires a change of attitude by the individual. The net effect of a successful implementation of a zero defects program is higher productivity due to less reworking of defective products. Thus, *quality*, in effect, *is free.*

Crosby's defined a 14-step quality improvement program to achieve the desired quality level of zero defects. It requires management commitment to be successful, and an organization-wide quality improvement team needs to be set up. A measurement program is put in place to determine the status and cost of quality within the organization. The cost of quality is then shared with the staff and corrective actions are identified and implemented. The zero defect program is communicated to the staff, and one day every year is made a *zero defects day*, and is used to emphasize the importance of zero defects to the organization.

Crosby's Quality Management Maturity Grid measures the maturity of the current quality system with respect to several quality management categories, and highlights areas that require improvement. Six categories of quality management are considered: *management understanding and attitude towards quality, quality organization status, problem handling, the cost of quality, quality improvement actions, and summation of company quality posture.*

Each category is rated on a 1 to 5 maturity scale and this indicates the maturity of the particular category. Crosby's maturity grid was later adapted to the CMM.

There are several other important pioneers in the quality field including Shingo who developed his own version of zero defects termed *"Poka yoke"* (or *defects =* 0). This involves identifying potential error sources in the process and monitoring these for errors. Causal analysis is performed on any errors found, and the root causes are eliminated. This approach leads to the elimination of all errors likely to occur, and thus only exceptional errors should occur. These exceptional errors and their causes are then eliminated. The failure mode and effects analysis (FMEA) methodology is a variant of this. Potential failures to the system or sub-system are identified and analysed, and the causes and effects and probability of failure are documented.

Kaoru Ishikawa did work on *quality control circles* (QCC). A quality control circle is a small group of employees who do similar work and meet regularly to identify and analyse work-related problems. This involves brainstorming, recommending, and implementing solutions. The problem-solving tools employed include *Pareto analysis*, *fishbone diagrams*, *histograms*, *scatter diagrams*, and *control charts* (see Sect. 8.7). A facilitator will train the quality circle team leaders.

Armand Feigenbaum did work on *total quality control* which concerns quality assurance applied to all functions in the organization. Total quality control is concerned with controlling quality throughout, and it inspired the concept of TQM, which is a philosophy of quality management and improvement involving all staff and functions throughout the organization. There is a more detailed account of the work of the quality pioneers in [18].

8.3 Total Quality Managements

Total quality management (TQM) is a management philosophy that focuses attention on quality and in developing a culture of quality within the organization. Quality is a company-wide objective, and the organization's goal is total customer satisfaction. The organization aims to deliver products and services that totally satisfy the customer needs. It is a holistic approach and it applies to all levels and functions within the organization.

TQM employs many of the ideas of the pioneers in the quality movement. Management are required to take charge of the implementation of quality management, and all staff will need to be trained in quality improvement activities.

The implementation of TQM involves a focus on all areas within the organization, and in identifying areas for improvement. The problems in a particular area are evaluated and data is collected and analysed. An action plan is then prepared and the actions are implemented and monitored. This is repeated for continuous improvement. It involves:

- Identify improvement area(s)
- Problem evaluation
- Data collection
- Data analysis
- Action plan
- Implementation of actions
- Monitor effectiveness
- Repeat

There are four main parts of TQM (Table 8.2).

Total quality management (TQM) is a holistic approach to quality management, and this management philosophy involves customer focus, process improvement, developing a culture of quality within the organization and developing a measurement and analysis program. It emphasizes that customers have rights and quality expectations, which should be satisfied, and that everyone in the organization is both a customer and has customers.

Quality needs to be built into the product with quality addressed at every step in the process. It requires that all functions, in the organization follow high standards, with 100% commitment from the top management. All staff must be trained in quality management and participate in quality improvement. A commitment to quality must be instilled in all staff, and the focus changes within the organization changes from *firefighting* to *fire prevention*. Problem-solving is used to identify the root causes of problems, and corrective action is taken to prevent their reoccurrence.

Table 8.2 Total Quality Management

Part	Description
Customer Focus	This involves identifying internal and external customers and recognizing that all customers have expectations and rights which need to be satisfied every time. Quality must be considered in every aspect of the business, and the focus is on fire prevention
Process	This involves a focus on the process and improvement to the process via problem-solving. The objective of the improvements is to reduce waste and eliminate errors
Measurement and Analysis	This involves setting up a measurement program within the organization to enable effective analysis of the quality of the process and product
Human Factors	This involves developing a culture of quality and customer satisfaction throughout the organization. The core values of quality and customer satisfaction need to be instilled in the organization. This requires training for the employees on quality, customer satisfaction, and continuous improvement

The ISO 9000 standard is a structured approach to the implementation of TQM. Its clauses provide guidance on what needs to be done as well as the requirements to be satisfied.

8.3.1   Problem-Solving Techniques

There is a relationship between the quality of the process and the quality of the products built from the process. Defects may be due to a defect in the process itself, and so it is important to identify any systemic defects in the process.

Problem-solving teams are formed to solve a particular problem and to identify appropriate corrective actions. The team may be disbanded after the successful resolution of the problem, and the team first agrees on the problem to be solved. They collect and analyse the facts, and perform analysis to determine the appropriate solution. They use various tools such as fishbone diagrams, histograms, trend charts, Pareto diagrams, and bar charts to assist with problem-solving, and to analyse and identify appropriate corrective actions. Problem-solving techniques are discussed in more detail in Sect. 8.7.

8.4   ISO 9000 Standard

ISO 9000 is a family of standards consisting of three standards: namely ISO 9000:2015, ISO 9001:2015, and ISO 9004:2018. The ISO 9000 standard (Quality Management Systems—Fundamentals and Vocabulary) covers the fundamental concepts and principles of quality management, as well as the terms and vocabulary used in the standards.

The ISO 9001 standard (Quality Management Systems—Requirements) specifies the requirements of a quality management system and is applicable to

Fig. 8.4 ISO 9001 quality management system

manufacturing, software, and service organizations. It is based on several underlying quality management principles such as customer focus, leadership, engagement
of people, and continuous improvement. ISO 9001 is a process-oriented approach
that uses evidence-based decision-making, and relationship management (Fig. 8.4).

ISO 9001 details the requirements that the quality management system of the
organization must satisfy to be ISO 9001 compliant. There are over a million
ISO 9001 certified organizations in the world, and third-party certification bodies
provide independent confirmation that the organization meets the requirements of
the standard.

The ISO 9004 standard (Quality Management—Quality of an organization—
Guidance to achieve sustained success) provides guidance for continuous improvement. It may be used to assist the organizations in the implementation of ISO
9001, and it includes a self-assessment methodology that allows the organization
to identify areas of strengths or weaknesses and opportunities for improvement.

ISO 9000 was first published as a standard in 1987, and it was based on the
British BS5750 series of standards developed by the British Standards Institution
(BSI). BS 5750 was later proposed as an ISO standard.

ISO 9001 is a generic *quality management standard* that may be employed in
hardware, software development, or service companies, and so parts of the standard need to be interpreted to the type of organization that it is being applied. *It
is designed to apply to any product or service that an organization supplies. The
standard is customer and process focused and applies to the processes that an organization uses to create and control products and services. It emphasizes continuous
improvement* with guidance provided by the ISO 9004 standard.

The implementation of ISO 9001 involves understanding the requirements of the standard, and how the standard applies to the organization. It requires the organization to identify its quality objectives, define a quality policy, produce documented procedures, and carry out independent audits to ensure that the processes and procedures are followed.

An organization may be certified against the ISO 9001 standard to gain recognition for its commitment to quality and continuous improvement. The certification involves an independent assessment of the organization to verify that it has implemented the ISO 9001 requirements properly and that the quality management system is effective. It will also verify that the processes and procedures defined are consistently followed and that appropriate records are maintained.

8.5   Software Process Improvement with CMMI

The origins of the software process improvement field go back to Walter Shewhart's work on statistical process control in the 1930s. Shewhart's work was later refined by Deming and Juran, who argued that high-quality processes are essential to the delivery of a high-quality product. They argued that the quality of the end product is largely determined by the processes used to produce and support it and that there needs to be an emphasis on the process as well as on the product.

Watt Humphries and others at the SEI applied the work of Deming, Juran, and Crosby to the software field leading to the birth of the software process improvement field (SPI). Software process improvement is concerned with practical action to improve the software processes in the organization to ensure that business goals are achieved more effectively.

The development of high-quality software requires good software development processes to be in place for:

- Project management
- Estimation
- Supplier Selection and Management
- Risk management
- Requirements Development and Management
- Design and Development
- Software development lifecycles
- Quality assurance/management
- Software inspections
- Software testing
- Configuration management
- Customer satisfaction

Software process improvement initiatives support an organization in achieving its key business goals more effectively, where the business goals could be delivering software faster to the market, improving quality, and reducing or eliminating waste

[9]. It makes business sense and provides a return on investment. The CMMI model includes best practice for processes in software and systems engineering (Fig. 8.5).

The CMMI provides a solid engineering approach to the development of software, and it describes *what* the processes should do rather than *how* they should be done. The process model will need to be interpreted and tailored to meet the needs of the organization, which allows professional judgment to be used in the implementation [10].

The SEI adapted the process improvement principles used in the manufacturing field to the software field. They developed the original CMM model in the early 1990s, and its successor the CMMI in 2001. The CMMI states *what the organization needs to do* to mature its processes rather than *how this should be done.* This

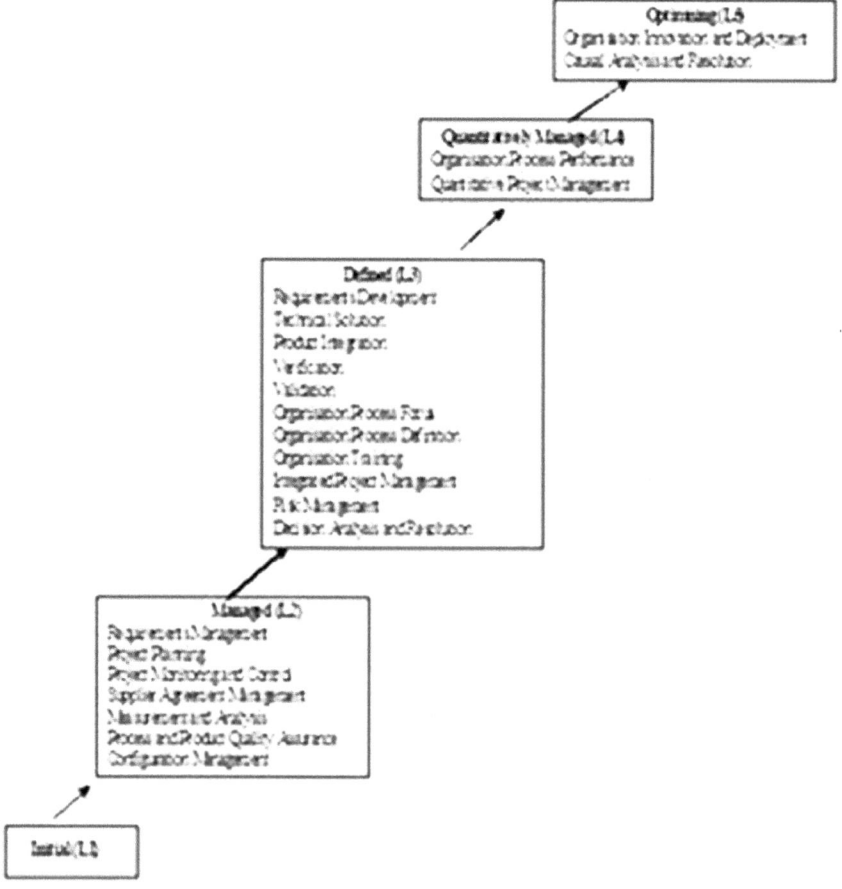

Fig. 8.5 CMMI model

gives the organization the flexibility on how it chooses to implement its processes, and the model is used by thousands of organizations worldwide.

The CMMI consists of five maturity levels with each maturity level consisting of several process areas. Each process area consists of a set of goals, which are implemented by practices related to that process area. Level two is focused on management practices; level three is focused on engineering and organization practices; level four is concerned with ensuring that key processes are performing within strict quantitative limits; and level five is concerned with continuous process improvement. CMMI v1.3 (released in 2010) supports Agile software development.[3] Table 8.3 describes the maturity levels in more detail.

The implementation of the CMMI generally starts with improvements to processes at the project level. The focus at level two is on improvements to managing projects and suppliers, and improvements are made to project management, as well as to supplier selection and management practices.

The improvements at level 3 involve a shift from the focus on projects to the organization. It involves defining standard processes for the organization, and projects may then tailor the standard process (using tailoring guidelines) to produce the project's software process. Projects are not required to do everything in the same way as the tailoring of the process allows the project's defined software process to reflect the unique characteristics of the project: i.e., a degree of variation is allowed as per the tailoring guidelines.

The implementation of level three requires defining procedures and standards for engineering activities such as design, coding, and testing. Procedures are defined for peer reviews, testing, risk management, and decision analysis.

The implementation of level four involves achieving process performance within defined quantitative limits. This involves the use of metrics and setting quantitative goals for project and process performance, and managing process performance. The implementation of level 5 is concerned with achieving a culture of continuous improvement in the company. The causes of defects are identified and resolution actions are implemented to prevent a reoccurrence.

The CMMI allows organizations to benchmark themselves against other organizations. This is done by a formal SCAMPI appraisal conducted by an authorized lead appraiser. The results of the appraisal are generally reported back to the SEI, and there is a strict qualification process to become an *authorized lead appraiser*. An appraisal is useful in verifying that an organization has improved, and it enables the organization to prioritize improvements for the next improvement cycle [11].

The CMMI (v1.3) is discussed in more detail in Chap. 20 of Ref. [2] and in Ref. [12, 13]. The reader is referred to the CMMI Institute (https://cmmiinstitute.com), which is now part of ISACA (Information Systems Audit and Control Association) for the latest developments with the CMMI.

---

[3] The CMMI has been developed further in recent years and v3.0 was released in 2023.

Table 8.3 CMMI maturity levels

Maturity level	Description
Initial	Processes are often ad hoc or chaotic with performance often unpredictable. Success is often due to the heroics of people rather than having high-quality processes in place. The defined process is often abandoned in times of crisis. It is difficult to repeat previous success, since success is due to heroic efforts of its people rather than processes. These organizations often over-commit, as they often lack an appropriate estimation process on which to base project commitments. Firefighting is a way of life in these organizations. High-quality software might be produced but at a cost including long hours, high level of rework, over budget and schedule, and unhappy customers.
Managed	The processes are defined at the project level, and there are good project management practices in place, and planning and managing of new projects is based on experience with previous projects. The process is planned, performed, and controlled, and process discipline is enforced with independent audits. The status of the work products produced by the process is visible to management at major milestones, and changes to work products are controlled. The work products are placed under appropriate configuration management control. The requirements for a project are managed and changes to the requirements are controlled. Project management practices are in place to manage the project, and a set of measures are defined for budget, schedule, and effort variance. Subcontractors are managed.
Defined	A maturity level three organization has standard processes defined that support the whole organization. These standard processes provide consistency in the way that projects are conducted. There are guidelines that allow the organization process to be tailored & applied to each project. There are standards in place for design and development and procedures defined for effective risk management and decision analysis. Level 3 processes are generally defined more rigorously than L2 processes, and the definition includes the purpose of the process, inputs, entry criteria, activities, roles, measures, verification steps, exit criteria and output. There is an organization-wide training program.
Quantitatively Managed	A level 4 organization sets quantitative goals for the performance of key processes, and these processes are controlled using statistical techniques. Software process and product quality goals are set and managed, and the processes are stable and perform within narrowly defined limits. A level 4 organization has predictable process performance, with variation in process performance identified and the causes of variation corrected.
Optimizing	A level 5 organization has a continuous process improvement culture in place, and processes are improved based on a quantitative understanding of variation. Defect prevention activities are now an integral part of the development lifecycle. New technologies are evaluated and introduced into the organization. Processes may be improved incrementally or through innovative process and technology improvements.

8.6   Software Quality Controls

Software quality controls include processes such as software inspections, testing, audits, quality reviews, learning lessons, and so on. Software inspections consist of a formal review of a deliverable by experts independent of the author, and the objective is to identify defects in the work product and to provide confidence in its correctness. Software testing is concerned with activities to ensure that the end product satisfies the functional and non-functional requirements and is fit for purpose.

Software testing consists of "*white box*" or "*black box*" testing techniques and includes *unit, system, performance*, and *acceptance testing*. The testing is quite methodical and includes a comprehensive set of manual or automated test cases. The activities involve the execution of the defined tests and the correction of any failed or blocked tests.

The cost of correction of a defect is related to the phase in which it is detected in the lifecycle. Errors detected in phase are the least expensive to correct, and defects detected out of phase become increasingly expensive to correct. The most expensive defect is that of a requirements defect identified by the customer, as its correction may involve changes to the requirements, design, and code.

It is desirable to identify defects as early as possible to minimize the effort and cost required to correct them. It is important to learn lessons from defects and to endeavour to prevent them from reoccurring. One approach to defect prevention is to hold causal analysis meetings to brainstorm and identify the root causes of problems and to identify and implement corrective actions to prevent reoccurrence.

The purpose of an audit is to verify that the processes and standards are consistently followed in the project and to identify any quality issues and improvements to the process.

The organization may conduct regular (e.g., monthly) quality reviews of the projects taking place to ensure that they are under control (e.g., on schedule and budget and with the right quality).

The purpose of the lessons learned process is to record the lessons learned during the project and to review them at the end of the project where a lessons learned report of the key lessons learned is prepared and published (see Chap. 11).

8.6.1   Software Inspections

The objective of software inspections is to build quality into the software product, rather than adding quality later. There is clear evidence that the cost of correction of a defect increases the later that it is detected, and it is therefore more cost-effective to build quality in rather than adding it later in the development cycle. Software inspections are an effective way of doing this and they provide a systematic examination of the software code or documentation without execution of the code [14]. An inspection may be conducted manually or through the use of specialized tools.

There are several types of software inspections such as code analysis, code reviews, structured walkthroughs, informal reviews, and Fagan inspections. An informal review consists of a walkthrough of the document or code by an individual other than the author. The meeting usually takes place at the author's desk (or in a meeting room), and the reviewer and author discuss the document or code informally.

The *Fagan inspection* methodology [15] includes pre-inspection activity, an inspection meeting, and post-inspection activity. It was developed by Michael Fagan at IBM and it aims to identify and remove errors in work products. The process mandates that requirement documents, design documents, source code, and test plans all be formally inspected by experts independent of the author of the deliverable.

There are various *roles* defined in the process including the *moderator* who chairs the inspection. The moderator ensures that all of the inspectors are trained and receive the appropriate materials for the inspection. S/he ensures that sufficient preparation is done and that the speed of the inspection does not exceed the recommended guidelines. The *reader* reads or paraphrases the particular deliverable; the *author* is the creator of the deliverable and has a special interest in ensuring that it is correct. The *tester* role is concerned with the test viewpoint.

Software inspections play an important role in building quality into the software, and the quality of the delivered software product is only as good as the quality at the end of each phase, so a phase should be exited only when the desired quality has been achieved. They need to be planned and included in the project schedule.

The effectiveness of an inspection is influenced by the expertise of the inspectors, adequate preparation by the inspectors, the speed in which the inspection is performed, and compliance with the inspection process. A formal inspection methodology provides guidelines on the inspection and preparation rates, and entry and exit criteria are defined for the inspection.

The inspection process will consider whether the design is correct with respect to the requirements and whether the source code is correct with respect to the design. The errors identified are classified into various types and the data are generally recorded to enable analysis to be performed on the most common types of errors to yield actions to minimize the reoccurrence of the most common defect types.

8.6.2 Software Testing

Testing is a sub-project of a project and needs to be managed as such, so good planning, monitoring, and control are required. Test planning involves defining the scope of the testing to be performed; defining the test environment; estimating the effort required to define the test cases and to perform the testing; identifying the resources needed (including people, hardware, software, and tools); assigning the resources to the tasks; defining the schedule; and identifying any risks to the testing and managing them.

Test monitoring and control involves monitoring progress and taking corrective action when progress deviates from expectations; re-planning where the scope of the testing has changed; communicating progress to the various stakeholders with test reports to provide visibility into the testing carried out; taking corrective action to ensure quality and schedule are achieved; managing risks and issues; managing the change requests that arise during the project, and providing a final test report with a recommendation to go to acceptance testing. The management of software testing involves:

- Defining the scope of the testing.
- Determine types of testing to be performed
- Estimates of time, effort, cost, resources
- Determining the start and end dates for the testing
- Define how test defects will be logged and reported
- Definition of test environment
- Scheduling the various tasks and activities
- Preparing the initial test schedule and key milestones
- Identifying the key risks to testing
- Monitoring progress, budget, schedule
- Re-planning and re-scheduling
- Communicating progress to affected stakeholders/Test Reports
- Preparing status reports and presentations
- Conducting lessons learned review to learn any lessons from the testing

The test plan for the project may be part of the project plan but it is often in a separate document. It includes the scope of the testing, the personnel involved, the resources and effort required, the key milestones, the definition of the test environment, any special hardware and test tools required, and the planned test schedule. There may be a separate test specification plan for the various types of testing, which records the test cases, including the purpose of each test case, the inputs and expected outputs, and the test procedure for the execution of the particular test case.

Several types of testing are performed during the project, including unit, integration, system, regression, performance, and user acceptance testing. The software developers perform the unit testing to verify the correctness of a module. This type of testing is termed *"white box"* testing and is based on knowledge of the internals of the software module. It involves defining and executing test cases to ensure code and branch coverage. The objective of *"black box"* testing is to verify the functionality of a module (or feature or the complete system itself), and knowledge of the internals of the software module is not required. There is detailed information on testing in [16].

8.6.3   Audits and Quality Assurance Group

There may be an independent quality assurance group that promotes quality in the organization. It provides an independent assessment of the quality of the product being built and acts as the voice of the customer, and aims to ensure that quality is considered at each step in the process.

The quality group will perform audits of various projects, groups, suppliers, and departments, and will determine the extent to which the processes are followed, and report any weaknesses in the processes and non-compliances identified. The key responsibilities of the quality group are:

- Promotes quality in organization
- Conducts audits to verify compliance
- Reports audit results to management
- Provides visibility to Management on processes followed
- Facilitate software process improvement
- Perform/participate in release sign-offs

The audit provides visibility into the work products and processes used to develop the work products. It consists of an interview with the project team, and the auditor examines the processes followed and deliverables produced by each team member, and assesses if there are any quality risks associated with the project based on the information provided. It is a systematic enquiry into the way that things are done, and audits of projects, suppliers, and departments are conducted.

The auditor relates the performed process to the defined process and writes a report detailing the findings from the audit and the recommended corrective actions with respect to any identified non-compliance with the defined process. S/he will perform a follow-up activity at a later stage to verify that the corrective actions have been carried out. The audit activities include planning activities, the audit meeting, gathering data, reporting the findings, assigning actions, and following the actions through to closure. It gives:

Visibility into the extent of compliance with the defined processes and standards.
Visibility into the processes and standards in use in the organization.
Visibility into the effectiveness of the defined processes.
Visibility into the fitness for use of the work products produced

The audits are conducted by the Quality/SQA group,[4] which is independent of the groups being audited. The auditor plans and conducts audits; reports the results to

---

[4] This group may vary from a team of auditors in a large organization to a part-time role in a small organization. It is essential that the auditor is independent of the group being audited.

Table 8.4 Auditing activities

Activity	Description
Audit planning	Select projects/areas to be audited during period Agree audit dates with affected groups Agree scope of audit and advise attendees on what needs to be brought to the meeting Book room and send invitation to the attendees Prepare/update the audit schedule
Audit meeting	Ask attendees as to their specific role (in the project), the activities performed & determine the extent to which the process is followed Employ an audit checklist as an aid Review agreed documentation Determine if processes are followed and effective
Audit reporting	Revise notes from the audit meeting and review any appropriate additional documentation Prepare audit report and record audit actions (Consider getting feedback on report prior to publication) Agree closure dates of the audit actions Circulate approved report to attendees/management
Track actions	Track audit actions to closure Record the audit action status Escalation (where appropriate) to resolve open actions
Audit closure	Once all actions are resolved the audit is closed

the affected groups; tracks the assigned audit actions to completion; and conducts follow-up audits. The auditing activities include (Table 8.4).

All involved in the audit process need to receive appropriate training. This includes the participants in the audit who receive appropriate orientation on the purpose of audits and their role in it. The auditor needs to be trained in interview techniques, including asking open and closed questions, as well as possessing effective documentation skills in report writing; in order to record the results of the audit. The auditor needs to be able to deal with any conflicts that might arise during an audit.[5] The flow of activities in a typical audit is sketched in Fig. 8.6.

---

[5] The auditor may face a situation where one or more individuals become defensive, and will need to reassure individuals that the objective of the audit is not to find fault with individuals, rather the objective is to determine any quality risks with the project as well as determining if the process is fit for purpose and to promote continuous improvement. The culture of an organization has an influence on how open individuals will be during an audit (for example, individuals may be defensive if there is a blame culture in the organization rather than an emphasis on fixing the process).

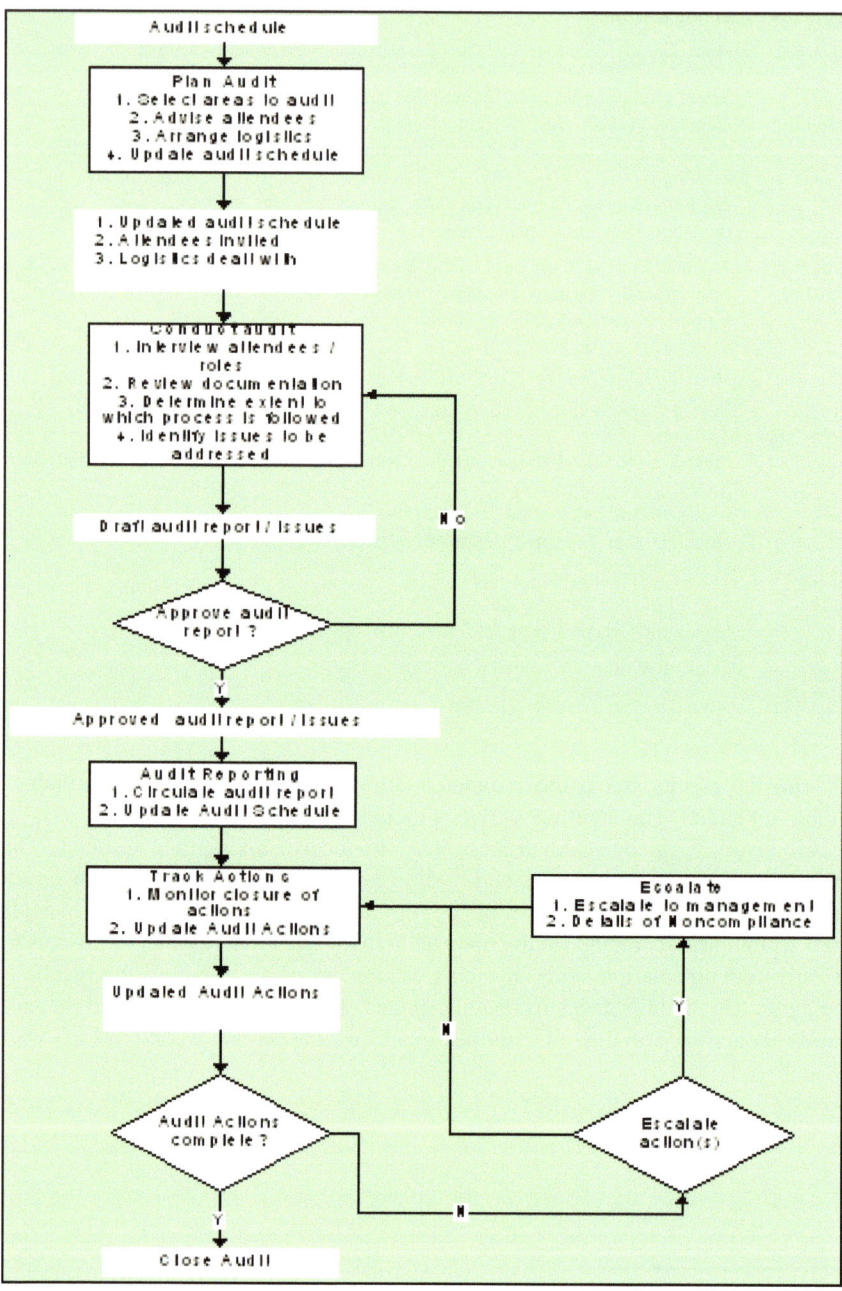

Fig. 8.6 Sample audit process

8.6.4   Quality Review of Projects

A *quality review* is a regular (often monthly) meeting in an organization where the quality of the projects in progress is reviewed by management.[6] This is usually a metrics driven meeting where the trends in project quality, as well as analysis and action plans, are presented (see Chap. 14 for discussion on software metrics).

The quality review provides visibility into the projects and allows the current quality of the projects to be clearly understood. It allows the project managers to present the actions that they are taking to address quality issues, as well as how they are dealing with the key risks and issues in the project. The project manager may present data such as the following during the quality review:

Schedule status and Variance Metric,[7]
Budget status and Variance Metric,
Effort status and Variance Metric,[8]
Functionality status and Variance Metric,
Open problem status,
Change Request status,
Milestone status,
Testing status,
Problem Arrival/Closure,
Risk Profile and Key Risks,
Key Issues.

The quality review provides appropriate visibility into project quality and its associated risks. The outcome of the quality review includes actions to be addressed by the project managers.

8.6.5   Learning Lessons in Projects

Various lessons will be learned during the project and it is important that these be recorded (e.g., in a lessons learned log spreadsheet or a tool). Agile projects conduct a retrospective review at the end of each sprint to determine what went well and not so well and to determine what needs to be done differently on future sprints (see Chap. 13) The key lessons learned are determined at the end of the

---

[6] The regular quality review may also examine the quality of other areas (apart from projects), in that it may be a regular review the quality of the entire organisation. For some organisations the quality review of a project may be done as part of the project board meeting.

[7] The Schedule Estimation Accuracy Metric is given by (Actual Calendar Days—Estimated Calendar Days)/Estimated Calendar Days * 100.

[8] The Effort Estimation Accuracy Metric is given by (Actual Effort—Estimated Effort) / Estimated Effort * 100.

project and published as a lessons learned report that is shared with the wider community (see Chap. 11).

8.7   Problem-Solving Techniques

Problem-solving is a key part of quality improvement, and a quality circle (or problem-solving team) is a group of employees who do similar work and volunteer to come together on company time to identify and analyse work-related problems. Quality circles were first proposed by Ishikawa in Japan in the 1960s.

Various tools that assist problem-solving include process mapping, trend charts, bar charts, scatter diagrams, fishbone diagrams, histograms, control charts, and Pareto charts [17]. These provide visibility into the problem and help to quantify the extent of the problem. A problem-solving team consists of:

- Group of employees who do similar work,
- Voluntarily meet regularly on company time,
- Supervisor as leader,
- Identify and analyse work-related problems,
- Recommend solutions to management,
- Implement solution where possible.

The facilitator of the quality circle coordinates the activities, ensures that the team leaders and team members receive sufficient training, and obtains specialist help where required. The quality circle facilitator has the following responsibilities:

- Focal point of quality circle activities,
- Train circle leaders/members,
- Coordinate activities of all the circle groups,
- Assist in inter-circle investigations,
- Obtain specialist help when required.

The circle leaders receive training in problem-solving techniques and are responsible for training the team members. The leader needs to keep the meeting focused and requires skills in team building. The steps in problem-solving include:

- Select the problem,
- State and restate the problem,
- Collect the facts,
- Brainstorm,
- Choose course of action,
- Present to management,
- Measurement of success.

The benefits of a successful problem-solving culture in the organization include:

- Move from fire fighting to fire prevention,
- Savings of time and money,
- Increased productivity,
- Reduced defects,
- Fire prevention culture.

Various problem-solving tools are discussed in the following sections.

8.7.1 Fishbone Diagram

This well-known problem-solving tool consists of a cause-and-effect diagram that is in the shape of the backbone of a fish. The objective is to identify the various causes of some particular problem, and then these causes are broken down into a number of sub-causes. The various causes and sub-causes are analysed to determine the root cause of the particular problem, and actions to address the root cause are then defined to prevent a reoccurrence of the effect. There are various categories of causes, and these may include people, methods and tools, and training.

The great advantage of the fishbone diagram is that it offers a crisp mechanism to summarize the collective knowledge that a team has about a particular problem, as it focuses on the causes of the problem, and facilitates the detailed exploration of the causes.

The construction of a fishbone diagram involves a clear statement of the particular problem (effect), and the effect is placed at the right-hand side of the diagram. The major categories of cause are drawn on the backbone of the fishbone diagram; brainstorming is used to identify causes; and these are then placed in the appropriate category. For each cause identified the various sub-causes may be identified by asking the question "*Why does this happen?*" This leads to a more detailed understanding of the causes and sub-causes of a particular problem.

Example 8.1 An organization wishes to determine the causes of a high number of customer-reported defects. There are various categories that may be employed such as people, training, methods, tools, and environment. In practice, the fishbone diagram in Fig. 8.7 would be more detailed than that presented. The root cause(s) are determined from detailed analysis.

This example suggests that the organization has significant work to do in several areas and that an improvement program is required. The improvements needed include the implementation of a software development process and a software test process; the provision of training to enable staff to do their jobs more effectively; and the implementation of better management practices to motivate staff and to provide a supportive environment for software development.

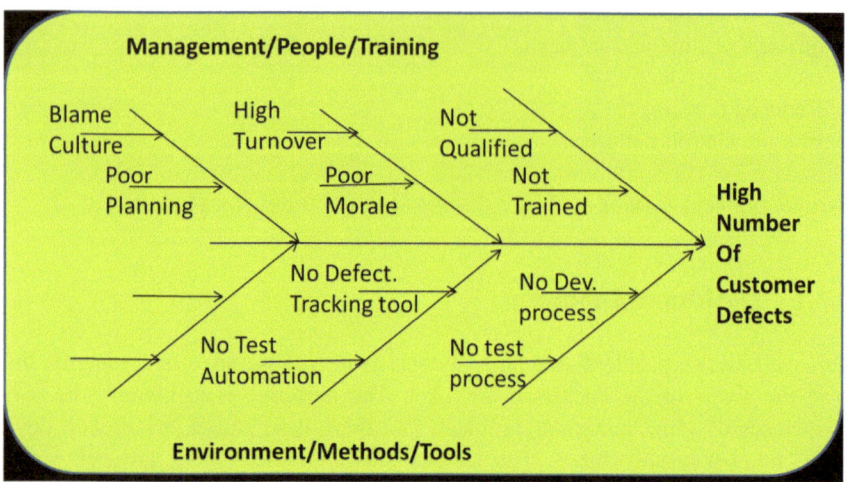

Fig. 8.7 Fishbone cause-and-effect diagram

The causes identified may be symptoms rather than actual root causes: for example, high staff turnover may be the result of poor morale and a "blame culture", rather than a cause in itself of poor-quality software. The fishbone diagram gives a better understanding of the possible causes of the high number of customer defects. A small subset of these causes is then identified as the root cause(s) of the problem following further discussion and analysis.

The root causes are then addressed by appropriate corrective actions (e.g., an appropriate software development process and test process are defined and providing training to all development staff on the new processes). The management attitude and organizational culture will need to be corrected to enable a supportive software development environment to be put in place.

8.7.2   Histograms

A histogram is a way of representing data in bar chart format, and it shows the relative frequency of various data values or ranges of data values. It is employed when there are a large number of data values, and it gives a very crisp picture of the spread of the data values, and the centring and variance from the mean.

The histogram has an associated shape; e.g., it may be a *normal distribution*, a *bimodal* or *multi-modal distribution*, or be positively or negatively skewed. The variation and centring refer to the spread of data, and the relation of the centre of the histogram to the customer requirements. The spread of the data is important as it indicates whether the process is too variable, or whether it is performing within the requirements. The histogram is termed process centred if its centre coincides with the customer requirements; otherwise, the process is too high or too low. A histogram may allow predictions of future performance to be made, assuming that the future will resemble the past.

The frequency table is constructed by dividing the data into a number of data buckets, where a bucket is a particular range of data values, and the relative frequency of each bucket is displayed in bar format. The number of class intervals or buckets is determined, and the class intervals are defined. The class intervals are mutually disjoint and span the range of the data values. Each data value belongs to exactly one class interval and the frequency of each class interval is determined. The construction of a histogram is seen in the following example.

Example 8.2 An organization wishes to characterize the behaviour of the process for the resolution of customer queries in order to achieve its customer satisfaction goal.

Goal
Resolve all customer queries within 24 h.

Question
How effective is the current customer query resolution process?

What action is required (if any) to achieve this goal?

The data class size chosen for the histogram is six hours, and the data class sizes are the same in standard histograms (they may be of unequal size for non-standard histograms). The sample mean is 19 h for this example. The histogram shown (Fig. 8.8) is based on query resolution data from 36 samples. The organization goal of customer resolution of all queries within 24 h is not met, and the goal is satisfied in (25/36 = 70% for this particular sample).

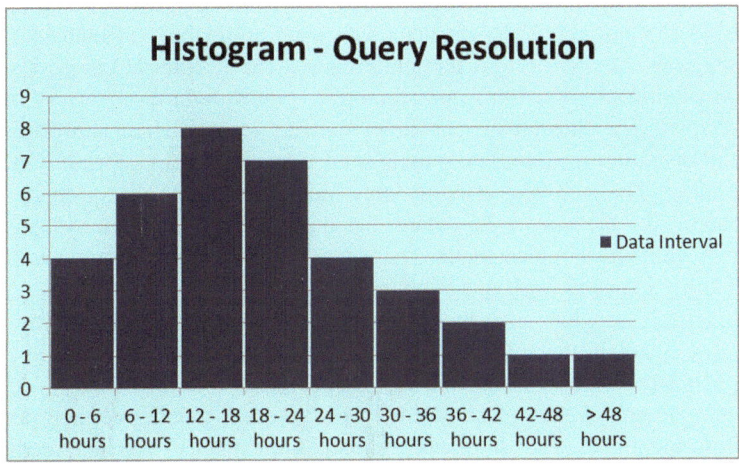

Fig. 8.8 Histogram

Further analysis is needed to determine the reasons why 30% of the query resolution is outside the target 24 h time period. It may prove to be impossible to meet the goal for all queries with the current resources, and the organization may need to hire more staff or refine the goal to state that instead all critical and major queries will be resolved within 24 h.

8.7.3   Pareto Chart

The objective of a Pareto chart is to identify and focus on the resolution of problems that have the greatest impact (as *often 20% of the causes are responsible for 80% of the problems*). The problems are classified into various categories, and the frequency of each category of problem is determined. The Pareto chart is displayed in a descending sequence of frequency, with the most significant cause presented first, and the least significant cause presented last.

A properly constructed Pareto chart will enable the organization to resolve the key causes of problems and to verify their resolution. The effectiveness of the improvements may be judged at a later stage from the analysis of new problems and the creation of a new Pareto chart. The results should show tangible improvements, with less problems arising in the category that was the major source of problems.

The construction of a Pareto chart requires the organization to decide on the problem to be investigated; to identify the causes of the problem via brainstorming; to analyse the historical or real-time data; to compute the frequency of each cause; and finally to display the frequency in descending order for each cause category.

Example 8.3 An organization wishes to understand the various causes of outages and to minimize their occurrence.

The Pareto chart (Fig. 8.9) includes data from an analysis of outages, where each outage is classified into a particular cause. The six causal categories identified are: hardware, software, operator error, power failure, an act of nature, and unknown. The three main causes of outages identified are hardware, software, and operator error, and analysis is needed to identify appropriate actions to address these. The hardware category may indicate that there are problems with the reliability of the system hardware and that existing hardware systems may need improvement or replacement. There may be a need to address availability and reliability concerns with more robust hardware solutions.

The software category may be due to the release of poor-quality software, or to usability issues in the software. This requires further investigation and it may be that better processes are required for inspections and testing. Finally, operator issues may be due to lack of knowledge or inadequate training of the operators. An improvement plan needs to be prepared and implemented, and its effectiveness will be judged by a reduction in outages and reductions of problems in the targeted categories.

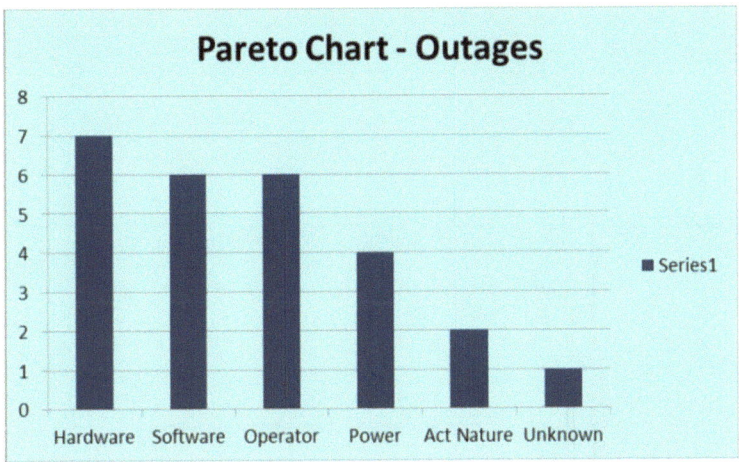

Fig. 8.9 Pareto chart outages

8.7.4 Trend Graphs

A trend graph monitors the performance of a variable over time, and it allows trends in performance to be determined, as well as allowing predictions of future performance to be made (assuming that the future resembles the past). Its construction involves deciding on the variable to measure and to gather the data points to plot the data.

Example 8.4 An organization plans to deploy an enhanced estimation process and wishes to determine if estimation is actually improving with the new process.

The estimation accuracy determines the extent to which the actual effort differs from the estimated effort. A reading of 25% indicates that the project effort was 25% more than estimated, whereas a reading of −10% indicates that the actual effort was 10% less than estimated. The trend chart (Fig. 8.10) indicates that initially estimation accuracy is very poor, but then there is a gradual improvement coinciding with the implementation of the new estimation process.

It is important to analyse the performance trends in the chart. For example, the estimation accuracy for August (17% in the chart) needs to be investigated to determine the reasons why it occurred. It could potentially indicate that a project is using the old estimation process, or that a new project manager received no training on the new process). A trend graph is useful for noting positive or negative trends in performance, with negative trends analysed and actions identified to correct performance.

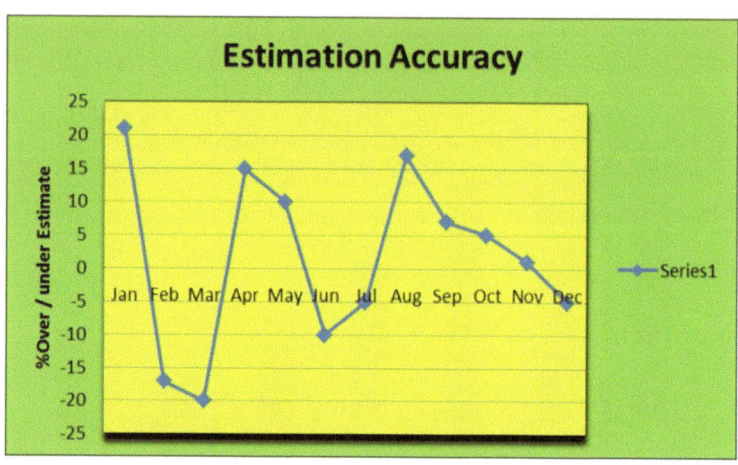

Fig. 8.10 Trend chart estimation accuracy

8.7.5 Scatter Graphs

The scatter diagram is used to determine whether there is a relationship or correlation between two variables, and, if so, to measure the relationship between them
(*correlation is not causation*). The results may be a positive correlation, negative
correlation, or no correlation. Correlation has a precise statistical definition, and
it provides a precise mathematical understanding of the extent to which the two
variables are related or unrelated.

The scatter graph provides a graphical way to determine the extent that two
variables are related, and it is often used to determine whether there is a connection
between an identified cause and the effect. The construction of a scatter diagram
requires the collection of paired samples of data, and the drawing of one variable
as the *x*-axis, and the other as the *y*-axis. The data are then plotted and interpreted.

Example 8.5 An organization wishes to determine if there is a relationship between
the inspection rate and the error density of defects identified.

The scatter graph (Fig. 8.11) provides evidence for the hypothesis that there is
a relationship between the lines of code inspected, and the error density recorded
(per KLOC). The graph suggests that the error density of defects identified during
inspections is low if the speed of inspection is too fast, and the error density is
high if the speed of inspection is below 300 lines of code per hour. A line can be
drawn through the data that indicates a linear relationship.

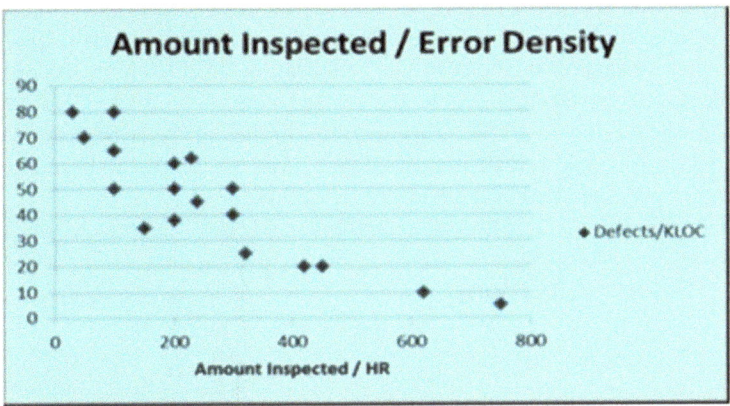

Fig. 8.11 Scatter graph amount inspected rate/error density

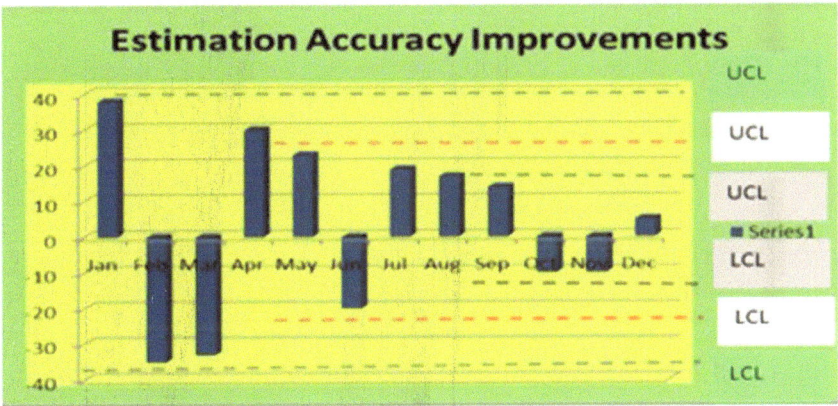

Fig. 8.12 Estimation accuracy and control charts

8.7.6 Metrics and Statistical Process Control

The principles of statistical process control (SPC) are important in the monitoring and control of a process. It involves developing a control chart, with upper and lower limits for process performance specified. The process is under control if it is performing within the lower and upper control limits.

Figure 8.12 presents an example on breakthrough in the performance of an estimation process and is adapted from [Kee:00]. The initial upper and lower control limits for estimation accuracy are set at ±40%, and the performance of the process is within the defined upper and control limits.

However, the organization will wish to improve its estimation accuracy and this leads to the organization's revising the upper and lower control limits to ±25%.

The organization will need to analyse the slippage data to determine the reasons for the wide variance in the estimation, and part of the solution will be the use of enhanced estimation methods in the organization. In this chart, the organization succeeds in performing within the revised control limit of $\pm 25\%$, and the limit is revised again to $\pm 15\%$. This requires further analysis to determine the causes for slippage and further improvement actions are needed to ensure that the organization performs within the $\pm 15\%$ control limit.

8.8   Review Questions

1. What is quality?
2. Explain the significance of Watts Humphrey in the software quality field.
3. What is total quality management?
4. Explain the significance of the ISO 9000 standard.
5. Explain the importance of software process improvement and the CMMI.
6. What are software inspections and what role do they play in delivering quality?
7. What is software testing and what role does it play in delivering quality?
8. What is the purpose of an audit?
9. Explain why the auditor needs to be independent of the area being audited.
10. Describe the activities in the audit process.
11. What happens at and after an audit meeting?
12. Describe various problem-solving techniques.
13. What is a fishbone diagram?
14. What is a histogram and describe its applications?
15. What is a scatter graph?

8.9   Summary

The development of software involves many processes, and it is important that the processes employed are fit for purpose. It is a key premise in the software quality field is that the quality of the resulting software is influenced by the quality and maturity of the underlying processes, and compliance with them. Therefore, there is a need to focus on the quality of the processes as well as on the quality of the resulting software.

There are various definitions of quality such as Crosby's definition as "conformance to the requirements". Juran defines quality as "fitness for use" and this is a better definition, although it does not provide a mechanism to judge better quality when two products are equally fit to be used.

Total quality management is a management philosophy to develop a culture of quality within the organization. It is a holistic approach and it applies to all levels and functions within the organization.

ISO 9000 is a family of quality management standards with ISO 9001 standard specifying the requirements of a quality management system. It is applicable to manufacturing, software, and service organizations, and is based on several underlying quality management principles such as customer focus, leadership, continuous improvement, and a process approach.

The CMMI provides a solid engineering approach to the development of software, and it describes what the processes should do rather than how they should be done. It needs to be tailored to meet the needs of the organization.

Software quality assurance is a systematic enquiry into the way that things are done in the organization, and it involves conducting audits of projects, suppliers, and departments. It provides visibility into the processes and standards in use, their effectiveness, and the extent of compliance with them.

Metrics play a key role in problem solving, and various problem-solving techniques such as histograms, pareto charts, trend charts and scatter graphs were discussed. The measurement data are used in the analysis to determine the root cause of a particular problem, and to verify that the actions taken to correct the problem have been effective.

References

1. G. O' Regan, *A Brief History of Computing*. 3rd Edition, (Springer, 2021)
2. G. O' Regan, *Concise Guide to Software Engineering*, 2nd Edition, (Springer, 2022)
3. G. O' Regan, *Concise Guide to Formal Methods*, (Springer, 2017)
4. W. Humphry, *Managing the Software Process*, (Addison Wesley, 1989)
5. W. Shewhart, V. Nostrand, *The Economic Control of Manufactured Products*, (1931)
6. W. Edwards Deming, *Out of Crisis*, (M.I.T. Press, 1986)
7. J. Juran, *Juran's Quality Handbook*, (McGraw Hill, 1951)
8. P. Crosby, *Quality is Free. The Art of Making Quality Certain*, (McGraw Hill, 1979)
9. I. Bhandari, A case study of software process improvement during development. IEEE Trans. Software Eng. **19**(12) 1993
10. M. B. Chrissis, M. Conrad, S. Shrum, *CMMI for Development. Guidelines for Process Integration and Product Improvement*, 3rd Edition, SEI Series in Software Engineering, (Addison Wesley, 2011)
11. CMU/SEI-2006-HB-002, *Standard CMMI Appraisal Method for Process Improvement, V1.2*, (August 2006)
12. Software Engineering Institute, *CMMI Executive Overview*. Presentation by the SEI, (2006)
13. Software Engineering Institute, *CMMI Impact. Presentation by Anita Carleton*, (August 2009)
14. F. O' Hara, *Peer Reviews—the key to cost effective quality*, (European SEPG, Amsterdam. 1998)
15. M. Fagan, *Design and code inspections to reduce errors in software development*. IBM Syst. J. **15**(3) (1976)
16. G. O' Regan, *Concise Guide to Software Testing*, (Springer, 2019)
17. M. Brassard, D. Ritter, *The Memory Jogger. A Pocket Guide of Tools for Continuous Improvement and Effective Planning*, (Goal *I* QPC. Methuen, MA, 1994)
18. G. O' Regan, *Introduction to Software Quality*, (Springer, 2014)

Project Monitoring and Control

9

Key Topics

Progress meeting
Change request
Change control
Issue
Defect
CCB
Progress report
Milestone reviews
Tolerance
Earned value analysis

9.1   Introduction

Project management is concerned with the activities involved in managing the software project, and once the authorisation and planning of the project is complete the focus then moves to the execution of the activities defined in the project plan and schedule. The resources required for the project are made available, and the project team is required to produce the project deliverables to the required quality standards within budget and time constraints.

The project may be divided into a number of lifecycle stages as defined in the project plan/schedule (with Agile projects divided into a number of sprints), with each phase having a defined start and end date, and the deliverables for the stage are produced as per with the stage plan (which may be the project plan and schedule). There may be entry criteria to be satisfied in order to commence work in a stage, and exit criteria to be satisfied to complete and exit the stage.

© The Author(s), under exclusive license to Springer Nature Switzerland AG 2025   167
G. O'Regan, *Guide to Software Project Management*, Undergraduate Topics in
Computer Science, https://doi.org/10.1007/978-3-031-80578-3_9

Fig. 9.1 Control-monitoring loop

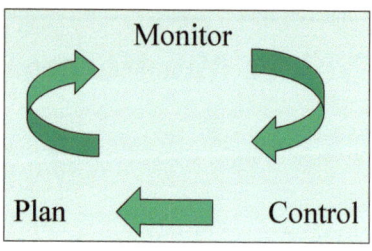

Project monitoring and control involves monitoring project execution against the plan, and taking action when progress deviates from expectations. It involves monitoring the project activities and checking that they are completed on schedule and with the required quality, and re-planning where appropriate. This is summarised in the control-monitoring loop in Fig. 9.1.

The project manager has overall responsibility for day-to-day management during project execution, and works with the project team to ensure that all work is allocated and executed. The project manager checks the progress made on a daily/weekly basis, and updates the schedule accordingly. The PM ensures that all project issues, change requests and risks that arise are recorded and managed, and that progress reports are prepared for the stakeholders. The project manager presents the status of the project to the project board regularly during the project, and acts on the direction and advice of the project board.

9.2   Monitoring and Control

Project monitoring and control is concerned with monitoring project execution, and taking corrective action when project performance deviate s from expectations. It is a continuous process where the progress of the project and the key milestones are monitored against the plan, and corrective actions taken as appropriate. The key project parameters such as budget, effort and schedule as well as risks and issues are monitored, and the status of the project is communicated regularly to the stakeholders (Fig. 9.2).

The project manager will conduct progress and milestone reviews to determine the actual progress made, with new issues and risks identified and managed. The corrective actions are defined are tracked to closure. The main focus of project monitoring and control is:

- Monitor the project plan and schedule and keep the project on track
- Conduct progress and milestone reviews to determine the actual status.
- Monitor the key project parameters
- Identify and remove roadblocks to progress and project success
- Re-plan as appropriate
- Work closely with project team to identify risks/issues as early as possible
- Monitor risks and take appropriate action.

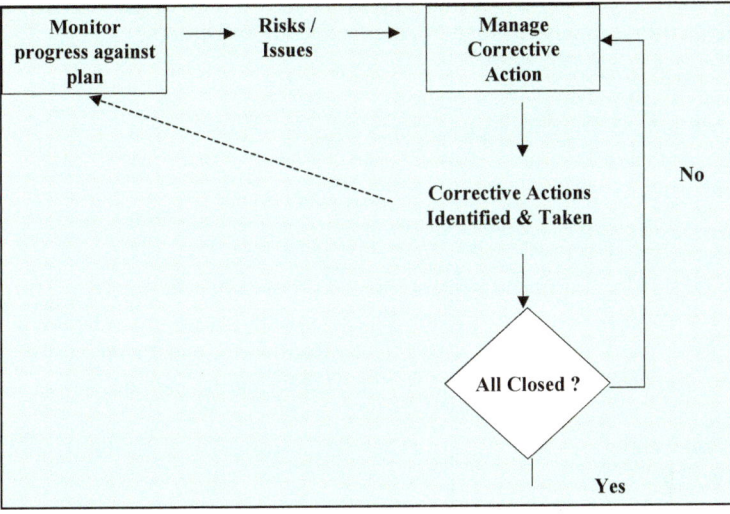

Fig. 9.2 Project monitoring and control

- Analyse issues and change requests and take appropriate action
- Track corrective action to closure
- Monitor resources and manage any resource issues.
- Report the project status to management and project board
- Present status to management and project board

9.2.1 Project Status Meetings

The project manager will conduct weekly meetings with the project team during the project to discuss progress made, and to obtain a clear status of the project. An effective project meeting needs to be well organised with a clear agenda, where the agenda is essentially the roadmap for the meeting with topics and timelines. The agenda is circulated to the attendees prior to the meeting. The team members should be well prepared and in a position to answer questions in the areas that they are responsible for in the project.

The project manager needs to keep the meeting focused and avoid going off topic, as otherwise valuable time is wasted resulting in difficulties in discussing all of the items on the agenda. This could result in a meeting that does not achieve its objectives. The project manager needs good time management skills to ensure that the time spent on the topics is appropriate and used well. The contributions from different personalities need to be balanced to ensure that the views expressed are representative of the entire project team, and this may involve asking those who are not making a contribution to the discussion.

The action items from the meeting need to be recorded, followed up and implemented in a timely manner. A sample agenda might look like:

- Actions from previous meeting
- Project updates from Project Manager
- Project updates from team
- Open issues
- New Action Items

The minutes and actions need to be published shortly after the meeting. The project manager is in a position after the meeting to update the project schedule and key project parameters with the latest project information, and to prepare a weekly report for the project stakeholders. The latest information includes:

Schedule status
Budget status
Effort status
Functionality status
Open problem status
Change Request status
Milestone status
Test status
Key Risks
Key Issues

9.2.2   Monitoring Project Deliverables

The project manager will monitor the delivery of project deliverables to ensure that work starts on the deliverables on time, and that those under development are on schedule or re-scheduled appropriately, and that those completed are completed to the right quality standards to meet customer expectations and have been approved.

The project manager will note any risks to quality and on-time delivery and will manage them appropriately, and s/he will deal with any existing issues with the project deliverables to ensure that there are minimal impacts to the project in terms of schedule/quality.

9.2.3   Monitoring Project Risks

We discussed risk management in detail in Chap. 7, and while the initial project risks are identified during project initiation further risks will become evident during project execution. Risk management takes place throughout the project life-cycle, and the existing risks must be carefully monitored and managed, and new risks identified and managed as the project proceeds. It is especially important to consider risk when there are changes in the project, such as when the scope of the project changes or when a team member resigns or when project issues arise, as often change leads to new risks.

It is important to check that the risk mitigation actions are being implemented and are having the desired effect. The project manager will monitor the actions to ensure their effectiveness, as well as watching for warning signs that a risk may be about to occur and whether the contingency plan should be invoked.

The project manager reports risks regularly to the stakeholders during the project in the regular project reports and project board reports.

9.2.4   Monitoring Project Issues

A project issue refers to an event or situation that has arisen that the project needs to deal with. For example, a stakeholder may make a request for to change the requirements; a tester may report a defect with the software; a team member might resign; and so on. These are all issues that the project needs to deal with, and clearly some issues are more serious than others. A severity (or priority) is assigned to an issue to indicate its importance (i.e., the priority of an issue relates to its impact in the project).

Project issues may be recorded in a spreadsheet (usually termed the Issue Log) or in an issue-tracking tool (e.g., JIRA). A description of the issue is recorded as well as its priority. The issue may be a change request, a defect or a more general matter that needs to be resolved. The issue needs to be investigated and an appropriate solution identified and implemented.

The project manager will monitor the open issues to ensure that they are being dealt with effectively, and that the most serious issues are dealt with promptly. The key open issues are reported regularly to the stakeholders during the project.

9.2.5   Monitoring Change Requests

A project change request (CR) is a request from a project stakeholder for a change to the requirements of the project. The request may be a major change to the scope of the project, and could have a significant cost and schedule impact, or it may be a cosmetic change with minimal impacts on the project. Change is considered to be a normal part of an Agile project and so this section is specific to traditional projects. It is desirable to minimize change towards the end of a traditional project, as it is important to keep risks to a minimum towards the end of the project.

A change request may arise at any time during the project, and its impacts (e.g., technical, risks, cost, budget, and schedule) must be carefully considered prior to its approval. A change introduces new risks to the project, and may adversely affect cost, schedule and quality.

The project manager may approve small change requests, whereas a large change request is subject to a formal evaluation by the change control board[1] (CCB) for the project. The CCB is responsible for authorising or rejecting the change request.

The project manager will monitor the change requests during the project to ensure that they their impacts on the project are determined, and that approved change requests are implemented in a timely manner.

9.2.6   Monitoring Project Defects

A defect is a flaw in the software code that causes the software to fail to perform its required function, and it arises as a result of a developer making an error that produces a defect in the code. The code where the defect is present may be on a rarely used execution path, and so the defect may not manifest itself during project execution. However, a defect that is encountered during program execution leads to a software failure, as a result of the code where the defect is present being executed and resulting in the software failing to do what it is required to do (i.e., the result is failure).

The role of the testing group is to verify the correctness of the software, and to identify the defects that are present in the software. The identified defects are logged in a spreadsheet (an Issue log or Defect Log for small projects) or in a defect-tracking tool (e.g., Bugzilla) for larger projects. The defects are scheduled for correction, assigned to developers for resolution, resolved and re-tested to verify their correctness.

The project manager and test manager will analyse various testing metrics such as the test status metric (Fig. 14.19), which indicates the amount of testing done and remaining to be done; the cumulative arrival of defects (Fig. 14.20), which is an indication of the stability of the software; the problem arrival and closure chart (Fig. 14.21), which indicates the stability of the software and the ability of the project to correct the identified problems; and the overall status of problems chart (Fig. 14.22), which shows the number of problems raised in the project and the number that remain to be resolved. These metrics provide a picture of the current quality of the software and the effort required to deal with the current quality issues.

The project manager will monitor the open defects to ensure that the most serious defects are resolved in a timely manner, and that the project meets the customer's quality expectations. The quality status of the project will be reported regularly to the stakeholders.

---

[1] The CCB is responsible for controlling change in the project, and its membership is decided during project planning.

9.2.7 Effort, Schedule and Budget Monitoring

The project manager needs to know exactly where the project is with respect to the key project parameters such as effort, schedule and budget, and so determining an up to date project status must be done on a daily/weekly basis.

Schedule and effort monitoring involves looking at the tasks in the schedule; determining those that are complete and those that are currently in progress; determining the progress made and the effort required to complete from discussions with the project team and updates from the project meetings; updating the project schedule with the latest information; and determining the impacts of the updates to the budget and schedule for the project.

The budget monitoring involves determining the amount spent on the project to date, and estimating the amount required to complete, and determining whether the project is on, over or under budget. *Earned valued analysis*, as discussed in Sect. 9.5.1, is often used to forecast cost and completion date.

The updated project parameters may lead to new project risks and issues such as the project going over budget or schedule or exceeding the project tolerance. The project manager will need to manage the situation to ensure that the project remains on track, and should project tolerances be exceeded the project manager must report the situation to the project board for resolution.

9.2.8 Business Case Monitoring

The business case is the reason for the project, and it needs to be aligned to the business strategy. It is based on the expected costs of the project, the associated risks, and the expected business benefits and savings. A project should proceed only if it has a valid business case, and the project should be terminated if its business case ceases to exist.

The project manager needs to monitor the business case throughout the project especially when changes or issues arise, as such changes may impact the business case and lead to it becoming invalid. Further, the project board may advise the project manager of changing business circumstances that could invalidate the business case resulting in the project being terminated.

9.2.9 Monitoring of Outsourcing

The project may outsource all or part of the work to a software supplier (e.g., outsourcing of development or testing or both), and so the project manager will need to monitor the subcontractor's work to ensure that it is fit for purpose and that it is completed on schedule and on budget.

The project manager needs to conduct progress and milestone reviews with the supplier, as well as monitoring the associated risks and issues, and manage them accordingly. The project manager may arrange to have an independent audit of the subcontractor's work to obtain independent visibility on the processes followed and the work products produced.

The supplier will report progress weekly to the project manager during the project, and the reports will include key data such as:

Schedule, budget and effort status
Open problem status
Change Request status
Test status
Key Risks
Key Issues

The project manager will report the progress with the supplier to the stakeholders regularly during the project.

9.2.10 Monitoring of Audits

The project may include a quality assurance role that is responsible for promoting quality in the project and for auditing various activities in the project and suppliers. The results of the audits are shared with the affected groups, and the project manager will monitor audit reports to act on any issues that could affect the successful delivery of the project.

9.2.11 Recording Lessons Learned

The project manager will set up a lessons learned log (or similar mechanism) at the start of the project where the project team can record lessons learned during the project (e.g., things that went really well and should be recommended to future projects, and things that went really poorly and should be avoided by future projects). The key lessons learned during the project are determined at project closure and communicated to the wider community (see Chap. 11).

9.2.12 Controlling the Project

Monitoring and control is like a "feedback loop" where the project manager compares actual versus planned progress and performance, and becomes aware of a situation that needs to be addressed in the project, and takes appropriate action to correct the situation.

The project manager constantly monitors the project environment during the project, and responds appropriately to keep the project on track. This includes monitoring the project deliverables to ensure that they are on schedule and delivered with the right quality, monitoring risks and issues, the business case, and so on, and taking action to manage any issues that arise.

The project manager will provide regular progress reports to the project board and the key stakeholders, to ensure that all stakeholders are kept informed on key decisions and actions taken during the project.

9.3   Managing Change Requests

The key stakeholders may request a change to the requirements at any time during a traditional project (ongoing changes to requirements are a normal part of the Agile world). The request may arise due to business or regulatory changes, or to a customer need becoming apparent at a late stage of the project when the project is nearing completion.

A request to change the requirements is termed a *change request* (CR), and it is a stakeholder request to change the scope of the project during project execution. The impacts of the change request (e.g., technical, cost, budget, and schedule) need to be carefully considered. Further, a change of scope to the project introduces new risks to the project, and it is important that these are considered to ensure that they can be managed. The introduction of change may lead to increased costs for the project as well as delays to the project schedule. It is important to consider these, and if the project will go outside its tolerance then it will need to be discussed with the project board. There could also be risks to quality should the projects stay with its original timelines, as insufficient time may be available for the testing activities, which may result in insufficient testing being performed.

Requirements management is concerned with managing changes to the requirements of the project, and in maintaining consistency between the requirements and the project plans and the associated work products. It is important that changes to the requirements are controlled, and that the impacts of the changes are fully understood prior to authorization. Once the system requirements have been approved, any proposed changes to the requirements are subject to formal change control.

The project will set up a group that is responsible for authorising changes to the requirements (usually called the *change control board* (CCB)). The CCB is responsible for analysing requests to change the requirements, and it makes an informed decision on whether to accept or reject the change request based on its impacts on the project and the associated risks. The activities involved in managing change requests are summarised in Table 9.1 below.

Following the approval of a change request the affected documents such as the system requirements, the design, software modules and test specification are modified accordingly. This is done to ensure that all of the project deliverables are kept consistent with the latest version of the requirements. Testing is carried out to verify that the changes made have been implemented correctly.

Table 9.1 Managing change requests

Activity	Change request
Log Change Request	The change request is logged and a unique reference number and priority assigned
Assess Impact	The cost, schedule, technical and quality impacts are determined and the risks identified
Decision	The CCB authorises or rejects the change request
Implement Solution	The affected project documents and software modules are identified, and modified accordingly
Verify Solution	Testing (Unit, System and UAT) are employed to verify the correctness of the solution
Close CR	The change request is closed

The objective of requirement traceability is to verify that all of the defined requirements for the project have been implemented and tested. One way to do this is to consider each requirement number and to go through every part of the design document to find where the requirement is being implemented in the design, and similarly to go through the test documents and find any reference to the requirement number to show where it is being tested. A more effective mechanism to do this is to employ a traceability matrix, which may be employed to map the user requirements to the system requirements; the system requirements to the design; the design to the unit test cases; the system test cases; and the UAT test cases. The matrix provides a crisp summary of how the requirements have been implemented and tested (Table 9.2).

Table 9.2 Sample trace matrix

Requirement No.	Sections in Design	Test cases in Test Plan
R1.1	D1.4, D1.5,D3.2	T1.2,T1.7
R1.2	D1.8, D8.3	T1.4
R1.3	D2.2	T1.3
......	......	"...."
R1.50	D20.1, D30.4	T20.1 T24.2

9.4   Managing Defects

The execution of the test cases by the testers may result in the situation where the actual results obtained differ from the expected results, and this generally results in a defect report[2] (or bug[3]) being generated. It is important to log all problems that arise during testing, and this is often done with a defect-tracking tool (it could involve a defect tracking spreadsheet for logging defects and a defect form for small projects). Each defect (bug) should be described in detail including:

- Problem number
- Severity
- Tester
- Date raised
- Status
- Description of problem and steps to reproduce
- Impacts of problem
- Responses to Problem
- Implementation and Verification

The severity of the defect indicates how serious the problem is, and there are usually several categories of severity such as:

- Critical
- Major
- Medium
- Minor

Defects are scheduled for correction in a later release of the software, and the correction involves analysis by the developers to determine the cause of the problem, and the implementation of the appropriate changes to the software to resolve the problem. The updated software needs to be retested to ensure that the defects have been resolved, and that no new defects have been introduced. Regression testing is performed to ensure that the core functionality of the system is preserved following corrections to the software.

The status of a defect indicates whether it has been resolved or not. It could be one of the following:

- Open (Defect identified by test team)
- Assigned (Defect assigned to developer for resolution)

---

[2] The difference between expected/actual results could be due to factors rather than a genuine defect such as poor test data, errors made by the tester, or invalid expected results.

[3] Grace Murray Hopper coined the term "computer bug" when she traced an error in the Harvard Mark II computer to a moth stuck in one of the relays. The bug was carefully removed and taped to a daily logbook, and the term is now ubiquitous in the computer field

- Changes Implemented (Developers have implemented changes)
- Changes Verified (Testing has been conducted to verify changes)
- Closed (Defect closed)

9.5   Milestone Reviews

Milestones are pre-planned events or specific points in time along a project time-line that allow the project manager to determine if a project is on schedule, and satisfying the stakeholder requirements. Each milestone acts as a major progress point in the project (e.g., the end of a phase in a traditional waterfall project or the end of a sprint in an Agile project), where the project needs to have completed a set of defined activities and deliverables. Each project will define its own milestones and they could include:

- Planning/Requirements complete
- Design/Development complete
- System Testing complete
- UAT Testing complete
- Deployment complete
- Project closure complete

There is a formal review of the project status at each milestone to ensure that all activities and deliverables for that milestone are complete, and that the customer's quality expectations are being satisfied. The milestone review includes participation from the project team, managers, end users, suppliers and any other relevant stakeholders.

The project manager reviews the commitments made for the project milestone to ensure that they are complete and with the right quality. The project manager will review the key project parameters such as budget and schedule status, the key risks and issues, the quality status, and so on, to determine any impacts and issues, and the results of the milestone review is a set of corrective actions and a decision on whether the project is ready to proceed to the next phase/milestone.

There may be audits of the project activities at the project milestone to ensure that the defined processes have been followed, and that the defined work products are completed to the right quality.

9.5.1   Earned Value Analysis

Earned value analysis is performed in project management to provide insight into the project health in terms of cost and on-time delivery at a particular point in time during project execution, and it allows the project manager to make adjustments to get the project back on track. It is a fast way to assess project progress by comparing the amount of work planned to be complete at a particular stage in the project, against the amount actually completed and what it has actually cost. These measurements are then used to forecast the project's total cost and completion date. These may then be compared with the project plan and schedule to determine the extent to which the project is on budget and schedule.

The earned value (EV) is the value created by the project at that point in time. It is calculated by the percentage of project completion at that point during project execution multiplied by the project budget. Similarly, the planned value (PV) at a point in time is given by the planned percentage complete of the project (as defined in the project plan/schedule) multiplied by the project budget. The difference between the planned and actual earned value leads to the schedule variance (SV) and cost variance (CV) for the project.

The schedule variance is the difference between the planned versus actual progress to date, and is usually measured in calendar weeks/months. A positive number indicates that the project is behind schedule, with a negative number indicating that the project is ahead of schedule (Fig. 9.3).

Similarly, the cost variance is given by the difference in planned versus actual spending with a positive number indicating an under-spend on the project, and a negative number indicating that the project has over-spent at this point. A negative value could indicate a danger of the project going over budget or running out of funds prior to completion.

The schedule performance index (SPI) is similar to the schedule variance, and is given by EV/PV. A value above 1 indicates that the project is ahead of schedule and a value less than 1 indicates that the project is behind schedule. SPI is useful as it offers a way to forecast the project completion date by planned duration/SPI, and enables the project manager to take early action to manage the situation of the project being behind schedule.

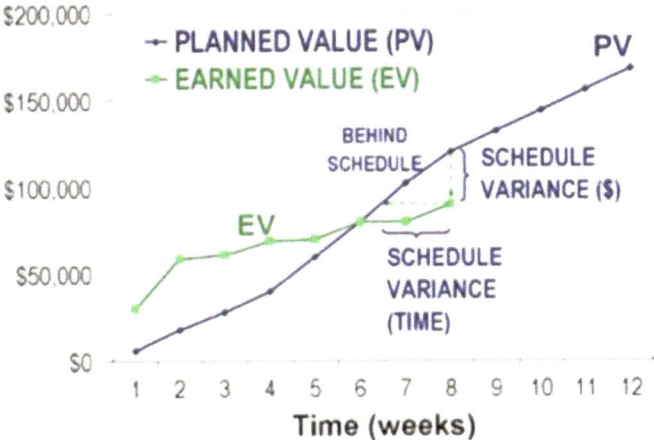

Fig. 9.3 Earned value analysis. public domain

The cost performance index (CPI) is similar to the cost variance, and is given by the planned cost divided by the actual cost (PC/AC). A value above 1 indicates that the project is under budget whereas a value under 1 indicates that the project is over budget. CPI is useful as it offers a way to forecast the project completion cost by total budget/CPI, and this allows the project manager to manage the situation of the project overspending.

For more detailed information on Earned Value Analysis see Ref. [1].

9.6   Managing Stages and Stage Boundaries

The project is generally divided into a number of phases for traditional projects (or sprints for Agile projects), and the phases are recorded in the lifecycle stages part of the project plan (see Table 6.5).

Each lifecycle phase has a defined start and end date and a defined set of deliverables to be produced during the stage (as defined in the stage plan or the project plan and schedule). There are entry criteria to be satisfied in order to commence work in a stage (e.g., planning complete and required resources available), and exit criteria to be satisfied to complete and exit the stage.

There may be a separate plan for the stage or it may be part of project plan and schedule. The schedule details the deliverables that will be produced during the stage, their start and end date, the resources involved, and the % complete.

The milestone review at the end of the stage is a formal review of the project status at the end of the stage, where it is verified that all of the planned activities and deliverables are complete and approved. In addition, the exit criteria will verify that the planning is complete for the next stage.

9.7   Progress Reporting and Project Board Reviews

Progress reporting is concerned with communicating the status of the project to the stakeholders (including the project board) during the project. The project manager will prepare regular progress reports for the key stakeholders, and the report summarises the activities that have taken place during the period.

RAG reporting may be employed in presenting the project status, where RAG stands for Red, Amber, and Green, with Red indicates serious problems with the project (e.g., project is outside tolerance), Amber indicates potentially serious problems that management needs to be aware of (e.g., danger of going outside tolerance), and where Green indicates that everything is on track (i.e., project is within tolerance). The project report includes key project information such as:

– Completed deliverables (during period)
– Schedule, Effort and Budget Status (e.g., usually RAG metrics[4])

---

[4] For example, the Budget estimation Accuracy Metric is given by (Actual Spend – Original Budget)/Original Budget * 100.

- New Risks and Issues
- Key Risks and Issues (Risk Profile)
- Test & Quality Status
- Change Request status
- Milestone status
- Activities and Deliverables planned (next period)

The project manager discusses the progress report with the project board and management, and presents the current status of the project as well as the key risks and issues. The project manager will present a recovery plan (exception report) to deal with the situation where the project/testing has fallen outside the defined project tolerance (i.e., it is significantly behind schedule or over budget).

The test status for the project could be presented as in Table 9.3, which provides a summary of the testing done and remaining in the project.

The status of quality and change requests for the project may be given by Table 9.4.

The key risks and issues affecting the project will be discussed, and the project manager will explain how these are being dealt with (Table 9.5). The risk profile could be presented in a manner similar to Fig. 7.4. The new risks and issues will be discussed, and the project board will carefully consider how the project manager plans to deal with these, and will provide appropriate support.

The milestone status may be presented in a way similar to Table 9.6.

The project board will consider the status of the project as well as input from the project manager before deciding on the course of action (which could include

Table 9.3 Test status for project

Test type	# Scripts	# Run	# Pass	# Fail	% Run	%Pass
Unit	50	50	50	0	100%	100%
System	100	80	72	8	80%	90%
Regression	50	50	50	0	100%	100%
UAT	20	–	–	–	–	–
Other	10	–	–	–	–	–

Table 9.4 Quality Status for project

Severity	Total no. of defects	No. open defects	Total no. of change requests	No. open change requests
Critical	3	1	–	–
Major	10	2	2	0
Medium	20	4	–	–
Minor	15	7	–	–

Table 9.5 Key risks for project

Risk no.	Description	Countermeasure
1.	–	–
2.	–	–

Table 9.6 Milestone status

Milestone	Planned date	Forecast/actual date
Planning/Reqs Complete	–	–
Design/Devel Complete	–	–
System Testing Complete	–	–
UAT Complete	–	–
Deployment Complete	–	–
Project Closure	–	–

the immediate termination of the project if there is no longer a business case for it).

9.8   Review Questions

1. What is project monitoring and control?
2. What should the project manager monitor during project execution.
3. What is a project issue? Describe the various types of project issues.
4. What is change control?
5. What is a change request?
6. Describe how a change request is evaluated.
7. Describe how a change request could impact the schedule?
8. Describe how a change request could impact the business case?
9. What is a defect? Explain how the severities of defects are distinguished
10. What is the purpose of a project status meeting & project reporting?

9.9   Summary

Project monitoring and control involves monitoring project execution against the plan, and taking corrective action when progress deviates from expectations. It involves monitoring the project activities and checking that they are completed on schedule and with the required quality, and re-planning where appropriate. The progress of the project and the key milestones are monitored against the plan, and corrective actions taken as appropriate.

The project manager works with the project team to ensure that all work is allocated and executed, and checks the progress made on a daily/weekly basis, noting and managing any issues and risks to the schedule. The schedule is updated regularly during the project. The PM ensures that all project issues, change requests and risks that arise are recorded and managed, and that progress reports are prepared for the stakeholders.

The project manager will conduct progress and milestone reviews to determine actual progress and to ensure that the project is on schedule. The project manager presents the status of the project to the project board regularly during the project, and acts on the direction of the project board.

Reference

1. Chance W. Reichel, *Earned value management systems (EVMS): "You too can do Earned Value Management"*, (PMI® Global Congress North America, Seattle, 2006)

Outsourcing—Supplier Selection and Management

10

Key Topics

Request for Proposal
Supplier Evaluation
Formal Agreement
Statement of Work
Ethical Outsourcing
Service Level Agreement
Acceptance of Software
Breach of Contract

10.1 Introduction

Outsourcing is a common business practice where a company contracts out business functions such as manufacturing, software development, and call centres to third-party providers. The outsourcing of a business function to a distant country is termed *offshoring*, whereas *nearshoring* is outsourcing to a nearby country, and outsourcing may also be done domestically. The benefits of outsourcing include:

- Cost savings due to reduction in business expenses
- Availability of expertise not available in house
- Allows company to focus on core business activities
- Increased efficiencies.

Outsourcing involves handing control of various business functions over to a third party, and this leads to business risks such as the quality of the service may be below expectations, the third party may go out of business, or that there may be risks to confidentiality and security. The role of the project manager is to manage the day-to-day relationship with the offshore/onshore team in possibly different time zones, and there may be differences in language and culture.

Supplier selection and management is concerned with the selection and management of a third-party software supplier. Many large projects involve total or partial outsourcing of the software development, and it is therefore essential to select a supplier that can deliver high-quality and reliable software on time and on budget.

This means that the process for supplier selection needs to be rigorous, that the capability of the supplier is clearly understood, and that the associated risks with the supplier are known prior to selection. The selection is based on objective criteria such as cost, the approach, the ability of the supplier to deliver the required solution, and the supplier capability, and while cost is an important criterion, it is just one among several other important factors.

Once the selection of the supplier is finalized a legal agreement is drawn up between the contractor and supplier, which states the terms and conditions of the contract, as well as the associated statement of work. The statement of work details the work to be carried out, the deliverables to be produced, when they will be produced, the personnel involved, their roles and responsibilities, any training to be provided, and the standards to be followed.

The supplier then commences the defined work and the project manager appropriately manages the supplier for the duration of the contract. This will involve regular progress reviews, and acceptance testing is carried out prior to accepting the software from the supplier. The following activities are generally employed for supplier selection and management (Table 10.1).

Remote project management is concerned with managing remote and hybrid teams to ensure that the project objectives are achieved. Traditional project management involves teams based in the same physical location, whereas today teams often operate in hybrid mode with some employees working in the office and other employees and teams working remotely in different physical locations. This means that remote employees often play important roles in the success of projects, and remote project management has become more important in managing hybrid and remote teams.

The management of remote teams requires modern communication including video conferencing, shared files, and documents, as well as team communication and messaging apps. The creation of the team is the easy part as it is more challenging to build a team culture with remote teams. The project manager will stay engaged with the team throughout the project with virtual meetings, and remote project management is like traditional project management except that the project is executed remotely. It is a flexible methodology that can support various approaches such as traditional software engineering and Agile.

The project manager needs to determine the remote structure that is required, and then to find the people with the appropriate skills to carry out the project. The project expectations need to be communicated clearly to the team members at project initiation, including the process to be followed, work hours, project goals, their responsibilities, the tools that will be employed for collaboration, and so on.

Table 10.1 Supplier selection and management

Activity	Description
Planning and requirements	This involves defining the approach to the procurement. It involves: • Defining the procurement requirements • Forming the evaluation team to rate each supplier against objective criteria
Identify suppliers	This involves identifying suppliers and may involve research, recommendations from colleagues, or previous working relationships. Usually, three to five potential suppliers will be identified
Prepare and issue RFP	This involves the preparation and issuing of the Request for Proposal (RFP) to potential suppliers. The RFP may include the evaluation criteria and a preliminary legal agreement
Evaluate proposals	The received proposals are evaluated, and a short list is produced. The short-listed suppliers are invited to make a presentation of their proposed solution
Select supplier	Each supplier makes a presentation followed by a Q&A session. The evaluation criteria are completed for each supplier and reference sites are checked (as appropriate). The decision on the preferred supplier is made
Define supplier agreement	A formal agreement is made with the preferred supplier. This may include Negotiations with the supplier/involvement with Legal Department Agreement may vary (Statement of Work, Service Level Agreement, Escrow, etc.) Formal Agreement signed by both parties Unsuccessful parties informed Purchase Order raised
Managing the supplier	This is concerned with monitoring progress, project risks, milestones, and issues, and taking action when progress deviates from expectations
Acceptance	This is concerned with the acceptance of the software and involves acceptance testing to ensure that the supplied software is fit for purpose
Rollout	This is concerned with the deployment of the software and support/maintenance activities

The project manager will conduct regular virtual team meetings, and the team members will check in daily with the project manager to advise on progress made.

10.2 Planning and Requirements

The potential acquisition of software arises as part of a make-or-buy analysis at project initiation. The decision is whether the project team should (or has the competence to) develop a particular software system (or component of it), or whether there is a need to outsource (or purchase off-the-shelf) the required software. The supplied software may be the complete solution to the project's requirements, or it may need to be integrated with other software produced for the project. The following tasks are involved:

The requirements are defined (these may be a subset of the overall business requirements).

The solution may be available as an off-the-shelf software package (with configuration needed to meet the requirements).

The solution may be to outsource all or part of the software development.

The solution may be a combination of the above.

Once the decision has been made to outsource or purchase an off-the-shelf solution an evaluation team is formed to identify potential suppliers, and evaluation criteria are defined to enable each supplier's solution to be objectively rated.

A plan will be prepared by the project manager detailing the approach to the procurement, defining how the evaluation will be conducted, defining the members of the evaluation team and their roles and responsibilities, and preparing a schedule of the procurement activities to be carried out.

The remainder of this chapter is focused on the selection of a supplier for the outsourcing of all (or part) of the software development, but it could be easily adapted to deal with the selection of an off-the-shelf software package.

10.3   Identifying Suppliers

A list of potential suppliers may be determined in various ways including:

Previous working relationship with suppliers
Research via the Internet/Gartner
Recommendations from colleagues or another company
Advertisements/other.

A previous working relationship with a supplier provides useful information on the capability of the supplier, and whether it would be a suitable candidate for the work to be done. Further, a supplier that is ISO 9001 certified for quality and ISO 27001 certified for Information Security has independent assessment of their capability. Companies will often maintain a list of preferred suppliers, and these are the suppliers that have worked previously with the company, and whose capability is known. The risks associated with a supplier on the preferred supplier list are known and are generally less than those of an unknown supplier. If the experience of working with the supplier is poor, then the supplier may be removed from the preferred supplier list.

There may be additional requirements for public procurement to ensure fairness in the procurement process, and often-public contracts need to be more widely advertised to allow all interested parties the opportunity to make a proposal to provide the product or service.

The list of candidate suppliers may potentially be quite large, and so short listing may be employed to reduce the list to a more manageable size of around three to five candidate suppliers.

10.4   Prepare and Issue RFP

The Request for Proposal (RFP) is prepared and issued to potential suppliers, and the suppliers are required to complete a proposal detailing the solution that they will provide, as well as the associated costs, by the closing date. The proposal will need to detail the specifics of the supplier's solution, and it needs to show how the supplier plans to implement the requirements.

The RFP details the requirements for the software and must contain sufficient information to allow the candidate supplier to provide a complete and accurate response. The completed proposal will include technical and financial information, which allows a rigorous evaluation of each received proposal to be carried out.

The RFP may include the criteria defined to evaluate the supplier, and often weightings are employed to reflect the importance of individual criteria. The evaluation criteria may include several categories such as:

Functional (related to business requirements)
Technology (related to the technologies/non-functional requirements)
Supplier capability and maturity
Delivery approach
Cost.

Once the proposals have been received further shortlisting may take place to limit the formal evaluation to around 3 suppliers.

10.5   Evaluate Proposals and Select Supplier

The evaluation team will evaluate all received proposals using an evaluation spreadsheet (or similar mechanism), and the results of the evaluation yield a short list of around three suppliers. The short-listed suppliers are then invited to make a presentation to the evaluation team, and this allows the team to question each supplier in detail to gain a better understanding of the solution that they are offering and any risks associated with the supplier and their proposed solution.

Following the presentations and Q&A sessions the evaluation team will follow up with checks on reference sites for each supplier. The evaluation spreadsheet is updated with all the information gained from the presentations, the reference site checks, and the risks associated with individual suppliers.

Finally, an evaluation report is prepared to give a summary of the evaluation, and this includes the recommendation of the preferred supplier. The project board then makes a decision to accept the recommendation; select an alternate supplier; or restart the procurement process.

10.6   Formal Agreement

The preferred supplier is informed on the outcome of the evaluation, and negotiations start on a formal legal agreement. The agreement needs to be signed by both parties, and may (depending on the type of agreement) include (Fig. 10.1).

Legal Contract
Statement of Work
Implementation Plan
Training Plan
User Guides and Manuals
Customer Support to be provided
Service Level Agreement
Escrow Agreement
Warranty Period.

The *statement of work* (SOW) is employed in bespoke software development, and it details the work to be carried out, the activities involved, the deliverables to be produced, the personnel involved, and their roles and responsibilities.

A *service level agreement* (SLA) is an agreement between the customer and service provider which specifies the service that the customer will receive as well as the response time to customer issues and problems. It will also detail the penalties should the service performance fall below the defined levels.

An *Escrow agreement* is an agreement made between two parties where an independent trusted third party acts as an intermediary between both parties. The intermediary receives money from one party and sends it to the other party when

Fig. 10.1 Legal contract

contractual obligations are satisfied. Under an Escrow agreement the trusted third party may also hold documents and source code.

10.7   Managing the Supplier

The activities involved in the management of the supplier are like the standard project management activities as discussed in Chap. 5. The supplier may be based in a different physical location (possibly in another country or it may consist of hybrid teams), and so regular communication is essential for the duration of the contract. The project manager is responsible for managing the supplier and will typically communicate with the supplier daily. The supplier will send regular status reports detailing progress made as well as any risks and issues. The activities involved include:

Monitoring progress
Managing schedule, effort, and budget
Managing risks and issues
Managing changes to the scope of the project
Obtaining weekly progress reports from the supplier
Managing project milestones
Managing quality
Reviewing the supplier's work
Performing audits of the supplier's work
Monitoring test results and correction of defects
Acceptance testing of the delivered software.

The project manager will maintain daily/weekly contact with the supplier and will monitor progress, milestones, risks, and issues. The risks associated with the supplier include the supplier delivering late or delivering poor quality, and all supplier risks need to be managed.

10.8   Acceptance of Software

Acceptance testing is carried out to ensure that the software developed by the supplier is fit for purpose. The supplied software may just be a part of the overall system, and it may need to be integrated with other software. The acceptance testing involves:

Preparation of acceptance test cases (this is the acceptance criteria)
Planning and scheduling of acceptance testing
Setting up the Test Environment
Execution of test cases (UAT testing) to verify acceptance criteria is satisfied.
Test Reporting

Communication of defects to supplier
Correction of the defects by supplier
Re-testing and Acceptance of software.

The project manager will communicate any defects with the software to the supplier, and the supplier makes the required corrections and modifications to the software. Re-testing then takes place and once all acceptance tests have successfully passed the software is accepted.

10.9   Rollout and Customer Support

This activity is concerned with the rollout of the software at the customer site, and the handover to the support and maintenance team. It involves:

Deployment of the software at customer site.
Provision of training to staff.
Handover to the Support and Maintenance Team.
On-going customer support.
On-going maintenance.

10.10   Ethical Software Outsourcing

It has become popular for Western companies to outsource software developments to countries in Asia and Eastern Europe, with India now a major player in software outsourcing, and Poland and Ukraine[1] have also become popular.

There are various motivations for outsourcing such as the desire to reduce the cost of software development, or it may be that the company may wish to focus on its core business and to outsource non-core activities, or it may that the company lacks the expertise or capacity to implement the project internally. There are various models of outsourcing including where a company may partner with a third-party supplier as a way to obtain extra IT resources for a company project, or it might outsource all or parts of the project to a third-party supplier under the company's supervision, or it may outsource with the subcontractor having full responsibility for the work from the start to the end with minimal supervision.

The costs of outsourcing may be significantly cheaper than developing the software internally, but there are risks that it could be work out more expensive where there are delays or significant rework due to poor quality. There are risks of disruption of business activities depending on the political climate of the country where the subcontractor is based. Further, there may be risks of pandemics, natural disasters, or the subcontractor becoming bankrupt. It is essential that contractors are

---

[1] This was before Putin's Russia invaded Ukraine in 2022.

qualified for the work that they are to perform, and all associated risks must be managed.

The area of corporate social responsibility (CSR) has become important in recent years, and companies have a responsibility to be good corporate citizens and to consider wider society in their actions and their impact on the world. That is, corporations are expected to behave ethically and to be conscious of their carbon footprint and the sustainability of their business in the countries in which they are operating (even at the expense of profits).

There are several ethical issues with outsourcing such as the fact that outsourcing may lead to loss of jobs in the home country of the company doing the outsourcing. It would seem reasonable to expect an ethical corporation to protect jobs in the countries where it is operating.

Ethical corporations have a responsibility to ensure that there are reasonable work practices in place at the subcontractor company and that workers receive a fair salary, have reasonable conditions of employment, and are not exploited by the subcontractor. Globalization and the outsourcing of manufacturing operations led to many sweatshops in Asia, and there is the infamous case of Foxconn, an Apple supplier of the *iPhone* based in Shenzhen in China. Several Foxconn employees committed suicide in 2010 due to their working conditions and their exploitation by the company, and this raised important questions on the responsibilities of Apple for the welfare of the employees of one of its key suppliers[2]. It is reasonable to expect a company as profitable as Apple to ensure that the staff of its suppliers is not exploited.

Advanced economies have many laws and regulations to protect the environment, and the health and safety of employees. However, the laws and regulations in Asia or wherever the subcontractor is based may not be as stringent. An ethical corporate citizen has responsibilities to the environment, and it is not sufficient for the corporation to say that it is complying fully with the laws of every country it is operating, where these laws are not fit for purpose. The corporation has ethical responsibilities for the health and safety of the subcontractor staff that are working on their projects.

There may be significant cultural differences between the home country of the corporation is based and the country where the subcontractor is based, and potentially very different values between both countries. There may be problems with the political system in the country in the subcontractor country, where an authoritarian government may maintain a strong control over its citizens. There may be problems with corruption, where bribes are paid to officials and others to get things done to remove roadblocks. There may be unethical practices over price fixing, and there may be cultural differences in the understanding of the importance and protection of proprietary information, intellectual property, and compliance

---

[2] The 2010 reports highlighted serious issues with working conditions at Foxconn in China. Unfortunately, recent information indicates that there are still serious problems at Foxconn (e.g., in Zhengzhou). See the CNN article on Foxconn from 2022 [1].

with security and privacy standards. It is important to be explicit in the software outsourcing to ensure that there is no room for misunderstanding.

An ethical corporation will wish to seek the cheapest offering, but it is also important to consider the ethical implications of outsourcing. An ethical corporation will need to check the ethical behaviour of the subcontractor on a regular basis including salary and working conditions, and one way to do this is to perform audits of suppliers. Audits provide visibility into the technical software development work being done to verify its compliance with standards and all appropriate laws and regulations, and special ethical audits could be conducted to provide insight into any work practices that could create ethical difficulties.

It is generally inappropriate to award the contract to a subcontractor just on price alone, and while price is an important criterion it is just one among many criteria, and ethical criteria should also be considered. It is best to build a stable relationship with suppliers, where there is a deep understanding of each supplier and any associated risks.

10.11 Legal Breach of Contract

The legal agreement between the company and the subcontractor specifies the terms to be satisfied and the obligations on both parties for the duration of the contract. These include the deliverables to be produced, the timelines, the responsibilities of both parties, and the financial payments to be made at agreed milestones. A contract is legally binding on both parties with both having defined obligations and should one party fail to deliver according to the terms of the agreement then they may be in breach of the contract.[3]

A *material breach* is where one party does not fulfil their obligations under the contract or delivers a significantly different result from that defined in the contract. An *anticipatory breach* is where one party has indicated that they will not be fulfilling their obligations under the contract, and while an actual breach has not yet occurred there is an intention to be in breach of the contract. Both parties will generally discuss and attempt to resolve any such breaches, and it is generally easy to resolve *minor breaches*. However, if both parties are unable to resolve their dispute over a material breach in the contract, then one party may decide to sue the other party for being in breach of contract. However, legal disputes tend to be expensive and time consuming, and it is often more economical and in the best interest of both parties to come to a resolution of their dispute without the involvement of their lawyers.

The plaintiff will bring the lawsuit to court claiming a material breach in the contract, and the plaintiff will need to show that there was a legally binding contract between the two parties, that the plaintiff fulfilled all of their obligations under the contract (unless there was a legitimate reason not to), that the defendant

---

[3] It is also possible that two parties make a verbal contract that is legally enforceable.

failed to honour the terms of the legal agreement, and that the defendant's actions led to loss being suffered by the plaintiff. That is, the breach of contract claim involves proving that:

Existence of contract
Plaintiff honoured contract
Defendant did not fulfil conditions of contract
Plaintiff suffered loss or damages.

The court will need to decide if there was a material breach of the contract and will consider the arguments made by the plaintiff and the defendant. The defence may argue that misunderstandings, misinterpretations, and errors in the terms of the contract agreed by both the plaintiff and defendant led to the breach of contract, and the judge will need to weigh up and consider all of the evidence and issue a judgment. The judgment is based on the facts of the case and the details of the contract, and it may be in favour of the defendant or the plaintiff depending on the circumstances of the case. For example, if the judge decides in favour of the plaintiff the remedy may be restitution and could potentially include:

Award of financial compensation for the breach of contract
Punitive damages to punish the wrongdoer.

There are many possible breaches that could occur such as (Table 10.2).

For more detailed information on the legal and ethical aspects of computing see [2].

10.12   Review Questions

1. What are the main activities in supplier selection and management?
2. What factors would lead an organization to seek a supplier rather than developing a software solution in-house?
3. What are the benefits of outsourcing?
4. Describe how a supplier should be selected.
5. Describe how a supplier should be managed.
6. What is a service level agreement?
7. Describe the purpose of a statement of work?
8. What is an Escrow agreement?
9. What is ethical outsourcing?
10. What is a breach of contract and how should it be managed?

Table 10.2 Possible breaches of contract

Breach	Description
Missing deliverables	This is where the supplier has failed to deliver one or more deliverables, or where they have been delivered late
Deliverables not fit for purpose	This is where one or more deliverables do not satisfy the requirements, or they may fail to adhere to the defined standards or be unusable
Missing personnel	This is where the agreed human resources for the contract have not been provided
Unskilled resources	This is where the resources provided lack the skills and experience to perform their roles effectively
Inadequate development environment	This is where the software engineering environment provided is not fit for the purpose of developing and testing the software
Intellectual property not protected	This is where the intellectual property (e.g., patents and copyright) has not been properly protected
Proprietary information not protected	This is where the confidentiality of proprietary information provided to the subcontractor has not been protected
Quality problems	This is where there are serious quality problems in testing or with the software produced, and where the software does not perform correctly under real-world conditions
Inadequate support (SLA)	This is where the support provided has been below the level agreed between the parties. It may be that the resolution of problems has not achieved the targets in the service level agreement
Bankrupt supplier	This is where the supplier has become bankrupt and is unable to fulfil their obligations

10.13   Summary

Supplier selection and management is concerned with the selection and management of a third-party software supplier. Many large projects often involve total or partial outsourcing of the software development, and it is therefore essential to select a supplier who can deliver high-quality and reliable software on time and on budget.

The process for the selection of the supplier needs to be rigorous, and the capability of the supplier including the associated risks needs to be clearly understood. The selection is based on objective criteria, and the evaluation team will rate each supplier against the criteria and recommend their preferred supplier.

Once the selection is finalized a legal agreement is drawn up (which usually includes the terms and conditions of the contract as well as a statement of work).

The supplier then commences the defined work and is appropriately managed for the duration of the contract.

The project manager is responsible for managing the supplier, and this involves communicating with the supplier daily and managing issues and risks. The software is subject to acceptance testing before it is accepted from the supplier.

References

1. Apple has a huge problem with an iPhone factory in China. CNN Article (2022). https://edition.cnn.com/2022/11/25/tech/apple-foxconn-iphone-supply-china-covid-intl-hnk/index.html
2. G. O' Regan, *Ethical and Legal Aspects of Computing* (Springer, 2024)

Project Closure

11

Key Topics

Handover to Customer
Project Closure
End Project Report
Lessons Learned Log
Lessons Learned Report

11.1 Introduction

A project is a temporary activity with a start and end, and once the project goals have been achieved and the completed project successfully handed over to the customer and customer support group, it is ready to be formally closed. The early part of the project devotes a lot of time and effort to planning and estimation, but it is also important to devote sufficient time to dot all the I's and cross all the T's to bring the project to an orderly closure.

Project closure is the final phase of the project, and there are several tasks and paperwork that need to be completed, including signatures, approvals, and final payments. Project closure involves the following activities:

- Handover to customer
- Prepare End Project Report
- Prepare Lessons Learned Report
- Completion of Paperwork
- Arrange final payments
- Archive project documentation/source code
- Disband project team
- Celebrate success.

© The Author(s), under exclusive license to Springer Nature Switzerland AG 2025
G. O'Regan, *Guide to Software Project Management*, Undergraduate Topics in Computer Science, https://doi.org/10.1007/978-3-031-80578-3_11

The project manager will prepare an end-of-project report detailing the extent to which the project has achieved its targeted objectives, and these typically include key project metrics such as quality metrics, budget and timeliness metrics, and the functionality delivered metric.

That is, the success of the project is judged on the extent to which the defined objectives have been achieved, including the extent to which the project has delivered the defined functionality on schedule, on budget, and with the right quality. This is referred to as the *project management triangle*, where the quality of the software is constrained between the scope of the project, its timelines, and its budget, and the project manager can trade between these constraints (Fig. 5.3).

The project maintains a lessons learned log to record the lessons learned during the project, and the project manager schedules a lessons learned meeting with the project team as part of the project closure activities. This is a retrospective meeting with the objective of determining the key lessons learned during the project from all the lessons that were learned during the project (Agile projects conduct a retrospective meeting at the end of each Sprint). The project manager publishes the lessons learned report, which summarizes the key lessons learned from the project, and the report is circulated to management. The objective is that project managers/teams on future projects will benefit from taking advantage of things that worked really well and avoiding the same mistakes that were made (part of continuous improvement).

The project manager presents the end project report to the project board, including any factors (e.g., change requests) that may have affected the timely delivery of the project or staying within the allocated budget. The project is then officially closed and the project team disbanded and assigned to other projects.

11.2   Handover to Customer

The customer's quality expectations are defined in the quality plan, and the project quality controls need to ensure that the desired quality is achieved throughout the project. The acceptance tests are prepared by the customer and are executed at the customer site. All problems identified by the customer are reported back to the project for resolution, and all defects identified are scheduled for correction, resolved by the project, and then verified by the customer.

The objective of the acceptance testing is to ensure that the system performs correctly under real-world conditions at the customer site and is fit for purpose. Once all customer acceptance tests have passed and all known issues resolved the customer is in a position to accept the software. The customer acceptance criteria may include criteria such as:

- All acceptance tests run and passed
- All system tests run and passed
- All performance tests run and passed
- All other tests run and passed

- Zero open critical and major defects
- Only medium and minor defects open
- All known risks can be managed
- Service Level Agreement in place
- Installations, upgrade, and rollback guides prepared and verified
- Software successfully installed at the customer site
- Customer support staff trained and ready
- Training provided to all affected customer staff.

The project manager will ensure that all committed documentation and deliverables are handed over to the customer and that all required training has been provided. The project manager will ensure that the customer care and support staff have received all appropriate documentation to support the customer and that the customer care/support is operating appropriately.

11.3   Lessons Learned Report

The project manager and team record the lessons learned during the project in the lessons learned log (an Excel spreadsheet or tool), where the lessons recorded indicate the strengths and weaknesses of processes, procedures, techniques, and tools that were identified during the project (Fig. 11.1).

The project manager schedules the lessons learned meeting as part of the project closure activities. This is a retrospective meeting that reviews the lessons learned during the project, and the key lessons learned are identified. The project manager prepares the lessons learned report, which is circulated to management and the project board, and to relevant individuals in the wider organization. The objective is to ensure that project managers and staff are informed of the key lessons that the project team has learned that might benefit future projects, and to avoid projects making similar mistakes in the future.

Lessons Learned Log					Temp v1.0
Lesson No.	Lesson Learned Type	Raiser	Date Raised	Description	Comments and Recommendations
1	Project Management	GOR	28/03/2020	The Process Mapping Approach of abstracting from the details of the actual process is extremely useful in clarifying the process flow and clarifying the deliverables produced.	Employ in other process areas going forward.
	Supplier Selection and Management				
	Requirements and Design				
	Development and Testing				
	Configuration Management				
	Training and Communication and Documentation				
	Deployment and Support				
	Infrastructure				

Fig. 11.1 Lessons learned log

11.4   End Project Report

The end project report records the extent to which the project achieved its objectives in delivering the agreed functionality on time, on budget, and with the right quality. It is a crisp summary of how the project has performed including what was done in the project and indicates how successful the project has been. It may include sections such as (Table 11.1).

The project manager presents the end project report to the project board as part of the project closure activities. The project board will review and evaluate the end project report, and make an informed decision on whether to authorize the closure of the project.

11.5   Complete Outstanding Administration

There will often be final paperwork that needs to be completed prior to project closure, and this could include signatures, approvals, and final payments. That is, all documents should be approved and signed off, and all invoices and outstanding payments made.

The project manager will verify that the project has received everything stipulated in the legal agreement/statement of work (in the case of outsourcing part of the project to a software supplier). The project manager will ensure that all contracted documents and source codes have been provided, the legal contract with the supplier will be closed, and the final payment that is due to the supplier is made.

The project manager will ensure that all the project deliverables are archived, and this includes all project documents and source code, as well as relevant project information such as notes and data that may be useful that are relevant for the project.

11.6   Celebrate Success

Once the project is closed the members of the project team are disbanded and released from the project, and assigned to other duties or projects. Any specific physical resources/equipment are released for use in other projects or within the organization.

The project manager will schedule a celebration event to reward the project team for their hard work on the project (e.g., a dinner or lunch) and to celebrate the success of the project.

Table 11.1 End project report

Item	Description
Project name	
Project manager/ board	
Objectives achieved	The objectives achieved
Objectives not achieved	The objectives not achieved and explanation/impact
Functionality delivered	Metric for actual number of requirements delivered versus planned
Functionality not delivered	The requirements not delivered and business impact
Budget	Actual spend versus estimated spend (and metric)
Schedule	Actual duration versus estimated duration (and metric)
Effort	Actual effort versus estimated effort (and metric)
Impact of change requests	<table><tr><td>No. of Approved CRs</td><td>Effort Impact</td><td>Schedule Impact</td><td>Cost Impact</td></tr><tr><td></td><td></td><td></td><td></td></tr></table>
Quality status	<table><tr><td>Severity</td><td>Total No. Defects</td><td>No. Open Defects</td></tr><tr><td>Critical</td><td></td><td></td></tr><tr><td>Major</td><td></td><td></td></tr><tr><td>Medium</td><td></td><td></td></tr><tr><td>Minor</td><td></td><td></td></tr></table>
Open risks	Description of open risks and impacts

(continued)

Table 11.1 (continued)

Item	Description
Open issues	Description of open issues and impacts
Milestone status	

Milestone	Planned Date	Actual Date
Planning & Reqs Complete		
Design and Coding Complete		
System Testing Complete		
UAT Complete		
Deployment Complete		
Project Closure		

11.7 Project Closure

A project is a temporary activity and once customer acceptance testing has been successfully completed and the software successfully deployed at the customer site, and customer support measures in place, the project is ready to be closed. The project board is responsible for authorizing project closure, and the project closure activities are summarized in Table 11.2.

11.8 Review Questions

1. Describe the main activities in project closure.
2. What is meant by a lesson that is learned in the project?
3. Describe the lessons learned process.
4. What is customer acceptance testing?
5. Explain what is meant by the project management triangle.
6. Describe the criteria to be satisfied for handover to the customer.
7. How does the project board judge if the project has been successful?
8. Why is it important to archive the project?

11.9 Summary

Project closure is the formal closure of the project and disbanding of the project team, and it takes place after the software has successfully completed customer acceptance testing and has been successfully handed over and deployed at the customer site. The project manager will prepare an end-of-project report detailing

Table 11.2 Project closure activities

Activity	Description
Handover to customer	The project manager will ensure that all project deliverables are handed over to the customer and that all required training has been provided. The project manager ensures that customer care and support employees have received all appropriate documentation and are operating effectively
Completion of paperwork	There will often be final paperwork that needs to be completed, such as signatures, approvals, and final payments. That is, all documents should be approved and signed off, and all invoices and outstanding payments need to be paid
Arrange final payments/close supplier contract	The project manager will verify that the project has received everything stipulated in the legal agreement/statement of work (e.g., documents and source code), and the legal contract with the supplier will be closed and the final payment that is due to the supplier is made
Prepare/present end project report	The project manager will prepare the end-of-project report detailing the extent to which the project achieved its objectives The success of the project is judged on the extent to which the defined objectives have been achieved The project manager presents the end project report to the project board, including any factors (e.g., change requests) that may have affected the timely delivery of the project or the allocated budget
Prepare/share lessons learned report	The project manager schedules a meeting with the project team to discuss the lessons learned during the project. These are recorded in the lessons learned log, and the key lessons learned are summarized in the lessons learned report The report is shared with the project board and relevant individuals in the organization so that future projects can benefit from the experience of the project
Archive project documentation/source code	The project manager will ensure that all documents and source code, as well as relevant project information such as notes and data that may be useful for the project is archived. Its important to have an archive to keep records/knowledge

(continued)

Table 11.2 (continued)

Activity	Description
Disband project team	The members of the project team are disbanded and assigned to other duties/projects. Any physical resources/equipment are released for use in other projects or within the organization
Celebrate success	The project manager will schedule a celebration event to reward the project team for their hard work on the project (e.g., a dinner) and to celebrate the success of the project

the extent to which the project has achieved its objectives, and these typically include key project metrics such as quality metrics and budget and timeliness metrics.

The success of the project is judged on the extent to which the project has delivered the defined functionality on schedule, on budget, and with the right quality. The lessons learned log records the lessons learned during the project, and the key lessons learned are published in the lessons learned report. The report is circulated to management, and the goal is that all project managers and project teams on future projects will be aware of the lessons learned during the project as part of continuous improvement.

The project manager presents the end project report to the project board, including any factors that may have affected the timely delivery of the project. The project is then closed and the project team disbanded and assigned to other projects.

Configuration Management

12

Key Topics

Configuration Management System
Configuration Items
Baseline
File Naming Conventions
Version Control
Change Control
Change Control Board
Configuration Management Audits

12.1 Introduction

Software configuration management (SCM) is concerned with tracking and controlling changes to the software and project deliverables, and it provides full traceability of the changes made during the project. A sound configuration management system provides a record of what has been changed, as well as who changed it, and it involves identifying the configuration items of the system; controlling changes to them; and maintaining integrity and traceability.

The origins of software configuration management go back to the early days of computing when the principles of configuration management used in the hardware design and development field were applied to software development in the 1950s. It has evolved over time to a set of procedures and tools to manage changes to software.

The configuration items are generally documents in the early part of the software development lifecycle (for non-Agile projects), whereas the focus is on source code control management and software release management in the later parts of development. Software configuration management involves:

Table 12.1 Features of good configuration management

Features of good configuration management
What is the correct version of the software module to be updated?
Where can I get a copy of R4.7 of Software System X?
What versions of Software System X are installed at the various customer sites?
What customers use R3.5 of the software system?
What changes have been introduced in the new release of software (version R4.8 from the previous release of R4.7)?
What version of the Design document corresponds to software system version R3.5?
Are there any undocumented or unapproved changes included in the released version of the software?

- Identifying what needs to be controlled
- Ensuring those items are accurately defined and documented
- Ensuring that changes are made in a controlled manner
- Ensuring that the correct version of a work product is being used
- Knowing the version and status of a configuration item at any time
- Ensuring adherence to standards
- Planning builds and releases

Software configuration management allows the orderly development of software, and it ensures that only authorized changes to the software are made. It ensures that software releases are planned and that the impacts of proposed changes are considered prior to their authorization. The integrity of the system is maintained at all times, and the constituents of the software (including their version numbers) are known at any time.

Effective configuration management allows questions such as the following (Table 12.1) to be easily answered.

The symptoms of poor configuration management include corrected defects that suddenly begin to re-appear (e.g., correction made to the wrong version of the source file or older versions of source files included in the release build); difficulty in or failure to locate the latest version of source code; or failure to determine the source code that corresponds to a software release.

Therefore, it is important to employ sound configuration management practices to enable high-quality software to be consistently produced. Poor configuration management practices lead to quality problems resulting in a loss of the credibility and reputation of a company. Some symptoms of poor configuration management practices are listed in Table 12.2.

Configuration management involves systematically controlling change to the configuration items in order to maintain the integrity and traceability of the configuration throughout the software development lifecycle. There is a need to manage and control changes to documents and source code, including the project plan, the requirements document, design documents, code, and test plans.

Table 12.2 Symptoms of poor configuration management

Symptoms of poor configuration management
Defects corrected suddenly begin to re-appear
Cannot find the latest version of the source code
Unable to match the source code and object code
Wrong version of software sent to the customer
Wrong software code tested
Cannot replicate previously released code
Simultaneous changes to same source component by multiple developers with some changes lost

A key concept in configuration management is that of a "*baseline*", which is *a set of work products that have been formally reviewed and agreed upon, and serves as the foundation for future development work.*

A baseline can only be changed through formal change control procedures, which leads to a new baseline. It provides a stable basis for the continuing evolution of the configuration items, and all approved changes move forward from the current baseline leading to the creation of a new baseline. The change control board (CCB) or a similar mechanism authorizes the release of baselines, and the content of each baseline is documented. All configuration items must be approved before they are entered into the released baselines.

Therefore, it is necessary to identify the configuration items that need to be placed under formal change control and to maintain a history of the changes made to the baseline. There are four key parts to software configuration management (Table 12.3).

A typical set of software releases (e.g., in the telecommunications domain) consists of incremental development, where the software to be released consists of a number of release builds with the early builds consisting mainly of new functionality, and the later builds consisting mainly of fix releases.

Software configuration management is planned for the project, and each project will typically have a configuration management plan which will detail the planned delivery of functionality and fix releases for the project (Table 12.4).

Each of the R.1.0.O.*k* baselines is termed release builds, and they consist of new functionality and fixes to the identified problems. The content of each release build is known; i.e., the project team and manager will target specific functionality and fixes for each build, and the actual content of the particular release baseline is documented. Each release build can be replicated, as the version of the source code used to create the build is known, and the source code is under control management.

There are various tools employed for software configuration management activities such as Clearcase, PVCS, and Visual Source Safe (VSS) for source code control management. The PV tracker tool and ClearQuest may be used for tracking defects and change requests. A defect-tracking tool will list all of the open defects against the software, and a defect may require several change requests to correct the software (as a problem may affect different parts of the software

Table 12.3 Software Configuration Management Activities

Area	Description
Configuration identification	This requires identifying the configuration items to be controlled and implementing a sound configuration management system, including a repository where documents and source code are placed under controlled access. It includes a mechanism for releasing documents or code, a file naming convention, a version numbering system for documents and code, and baseline/release planning. The version and status of each configuration item should be known
Configuration control	This involves tracking and controlling change requests, and controlling changes to the configuration items. Any changes to the work products are controlled, and authorized by a change control board or similar mechanism. Problems or defects reported by the test groups or customer are analysed, and any changes made are subject to change control. The version of the work product is known, and the constituents of a particular release are known and controlled. The previous versions of releases can be recreated, as the source code constituents are fully known and available
Configuration auditing	This includes audits of the configuration management system to verify the integrity of the baseline, and that the standards and procedures are followed. The results of the audits are communicated to the affected groups, and corrective action taken to address the findings
Status accounting	This involves data collection and report generation including the software baseline status, the summary of changes to the software baseline, problem report summaries, and change request summaries

Table 12.4 Software release delivery for project

Release baseline	Contents	Date
R 1.0.0.0	F_4, F_5, F_7	31.01.25
R. 1.0.0.1	F_1, F_2, F_6 + fixes	15.02.25
R. 1.0.0.2	F_3 + fixes	28.02.25
R. 1.0.0.3	F_8 + fixes (functionality freeze)	07.03.25
R. 1.0.0.4	Fixes	14.03.25
R. 1.0.0.5	Fixes	21.03.25
R. 1.0.0.6	Official release	31.03.25

product as well as different versions of the product, and a change request may be necessary for each part). The tool will generally link the change requests to the problem report. The current status of the problem report can be determined, and the targeted release build for the problem identified.

The CMMI (see Chap. 8) provides guidance on practices to be implemented for sound configuration management (Table 12.5).

The CMMI requirements are concerned with establishing a configuration management system; identifying the work products that need to be subject to change control; controlling changes to these work products over time; controlling releases

Table 12.5 CMMI requirements for configuration management

Specific goal	Specific practice	Description of specific practice/goal
SG 1		*Establish baselines*
	SP 1.1	Identify configuration items
	SP 1.2	Establish a configuration management system
	SP 1.3	Create or release baselines
SG 2		*Track and control changes*
	SP 2.1	Track change requests
	SP 2.2	Control configuration items
SG 3		*Establish integrity*
	SP 3.1	Establish configuration management records
	SP 3.2	Perform configuration audits

of work products; creating baselines; maintaining the integrity of baselines; providing accurate configuration data to stakeholders; recording and reporting the status of configuration items and change requests; and verifying the correctness and completeness of configuration items with configuration audits. We will discuss the key parts of configuration management in the following sections.

12.2   Configuration Management System

The configuration management system enables the controlled evolution of the documents and the software modules produced during the project. It includes.

- Configuration management planning
- A document repository with check in/check out features
- A source code repository with check in/check out features
- A configuration manager (may be a part-time role)
- File naming convention for documents and source code
- Project directory structure
- Version Numbering System for documents
- Standard templates for documents
- Facility to create a baseline
- A release procedure
- A group (change control board) to approve changes to baseline
- A change control procedure
- Configuration management audits to verify the integrity of baseline.

12.2.1   Identify Configuration Items

The configuration items are the work products to be placed under configuration management control, and they include project documents, source code, and data files. They may also include compilers as well as any supporting tools employed in the project.

The project documentation will typically include project plans; the user requirements specification; the system requirements specification; the architecture and technical design documents; the test plans, etc.

The items to be placed under configuration management control are identified and documented early in the project lifecycle. Each configuration item needs to be uniquely identified and controlled. This may be done with a naming convention for the project deliverables and source code, and applying it consistently. For example, a simple approach may be to employ mnemonics labels and version numbers to uniquely identify project deliverables. A user requirements specification for project 005 in the Finance business area could, for example, be represented by

FIN_005_URS

12.2.2   Document Control Management

The project documents are stored in a document repository using a configuration management tool such as PVCS or VSS. For consistency, a standard directory structure is often employed for projects, as this makes it easier to locate particular configuration items. A single repository may be employed for both documents and software code (or a separate repository for each).

Clearly, it is undesirable for two individuals to modify the same document at the same time, and the document repository will include *check in/check out* procedures. The document must be checked out prior to its modification, and once it is checked out, another user may not modify it until it has been checked back in. An audit trail of all modifications made to a particular document is maintained, including details of the person who made the change, the date that the change was made, and the rationale for the change.

Version Numbering of Documents
A simple version numbering system may be employed to record the versions of documents: e.g., v0.1, v0.2, v0.3 is often used for draft documents, with version v1.0 being the first approved version of the document. Each time a document is modified its version number is incremented, and the document history records the reasons for modification.

- V0.1 Initial draft of document
- V0.x Revised draft ($x > 0$)

- V1.0 Approved baseline version
- V1.x Approved minor revision ($x > 0$)
- Vn.0 Approved major revision ($n > 1$)
- Vn.x Approved minor revision ($x > 0$, $n > 1$).

The document will provide information on whether it is a draft or approved, as well as the date of the last modification, the person who made the modification, and the rationale for the modification. The configuration management system will provide records of the configuration management activities, as well as the status of the configuration items and the status of the change requests. The revision history of the configuration items will be maintained.

12.2.3 Source Code Control Management

The source code and data files are stored in a source code repository using a tool such as PVCS, VSS, or Clearcase, and the repository provides an audit trail of all the changes made to the source code. An item must first be checked out for modification, the changes are made, and it is then checked back into the repository. The source code management system provides security and control of the configuration items, and the procedures include:

- Access controls
- Checking in/out configuration items
- Merging and Branching
- Labels (labelling releases)
- Reporting.

The source code configuration management tool ensures the integrity of the source code and prevents more than one person from altering the software code at the same time.

12.2.4 Configuration Management Plan

A software *configuration management plan* (it may be part of the project plan or a separate plan) is prepared early in the project, and it defines the configuration management activities for the project. It will detail the items to be placed under configuration management control, the standards for naming configuration items, the version numbering system, as well as version control and release management.[1] The CM plan is placed under configuration management control.

---

[1] These may be defined in a Configuration Management procedure and referenced in the CM plan.

The content of each software release is documented as well as installation and rollback instructions. The content includes the requirements and change requests implemented, as well as the defects corrected and the version of the new release. A list is maintained of the customer sites of where the release has been installed. All software releases are tested prior to their approval. The CM plan will include:

- Roles and responsibilities
- Configuration Items
- Naming Conventions
- Version Control
- Filing Structure for project.

The stakeholders and roles involved are identified and documented in the CM plan. Often, the role of a *software configuration manager* is employed, and this may be a full-time or part-time role.[2] The CM manager ensures that the configuration management activities are carried out correctly, and will conduct and report the results of the CM audits.

12.3   Change Control

A change request (CR) database[3] is set up to record change requests made during the project. The change requests are documented and considered by the change control board. The CCB may just consist of the project manager and the system owner for small projects, or a management and technical team for larger projects. We discussed change control and the role of the CCB in Chap. 9.

The impacts and risks of the proposed change need to be considered, and an informed decision made on whether to reject or approve the CR. The proposed change may have technical impacts, as well as introducing new project risks, and may adversely affect the schedule and budget. It is important to keep change to a minimum at the later stages of a non-Agile project in order to reduce risks.

Figure 12.1 describes a simple process for raising a change request; performing an impact assessment; deciding on whether to approve or reject the change request; and proceeding with implementation (where applicable).

The results of the CCB review of each change request (including the rationale of the decision made) will be recorded. Change requests and problem reports for all configuration items are recorded and analysed, reviewed, approved (or rejected), and tracked to closure.

A simple process map for configuration management is described in Fig. 12.2, and it shows the process for updates to configuration information following an

---

[2] This depends on the size of the organization and projects. The project manager may perform the CM manager role for small projects.

[3] This may just be a simple Excel spread sheet or a sophisticated tool.

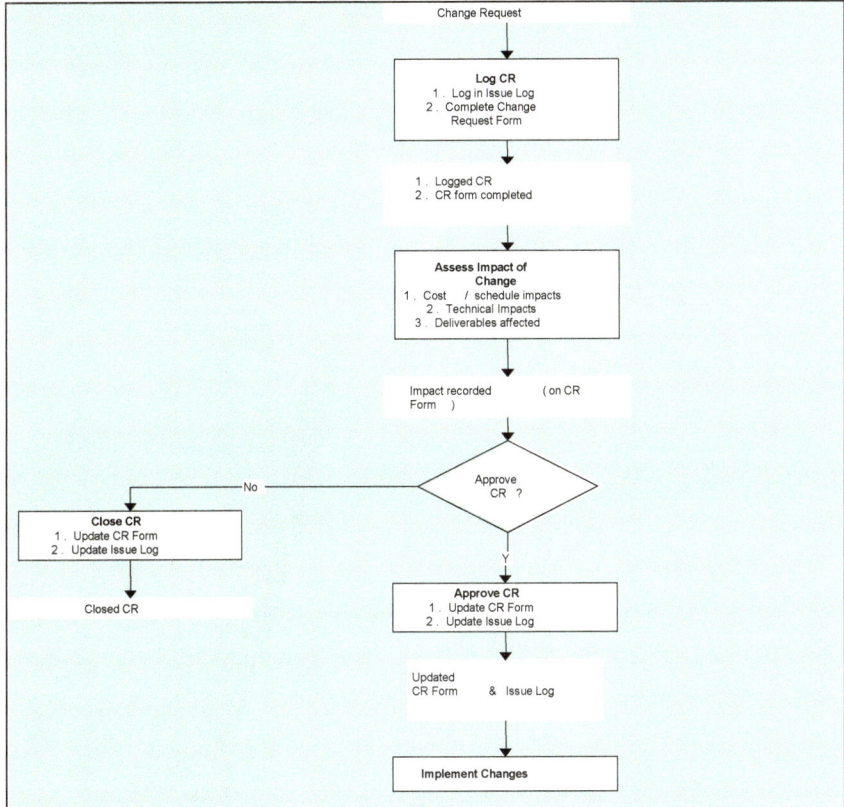

Fig. 12.1 Simple process map for change requests

approved change request. The deliverable is checked out of the repository; modifications are made and the changes approved; configuration information is updated and the deliverable is checked back into the repository.

12.4   Configuration Management Audits

Configuration management audits are conducted during the project to verify that the configuration is consistent and complete. Every project should have at least one configuration audit, and the objective is to verify the completeness and correctness of the configuration system for the project. The audit will check that the configuration records accurately reflect the configuration and that the configuration management standards and procedures have been followed. Table 12.6 presents a sample configuration management checklist.

There may also be a *librarian role* to set up the filing structure for the project, or the configuration manager may perform this role. The project manager assigns

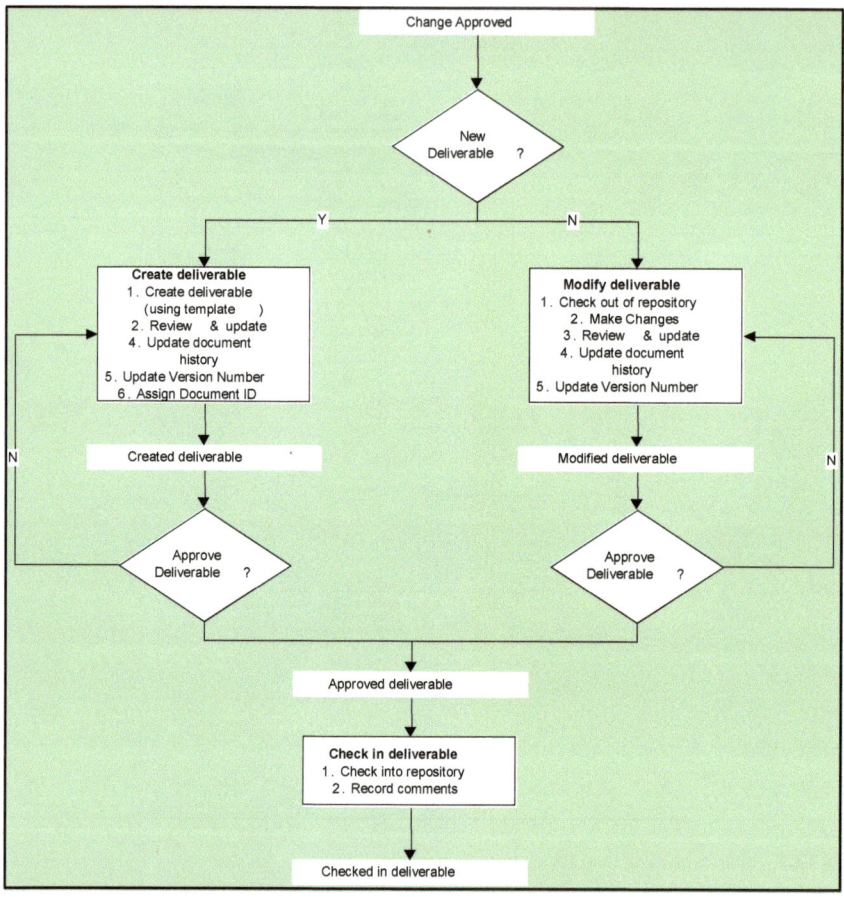

Fig. 12.2 Simple process map for configuration management

responsibilities for performing configuration management activities. All involved in the process receive appropriate training on the process.

12.5 Review Questions

1. What is software configuration management?
2. What is change control?
3. What is a baseline?
4. Explain source code control management.
5. Explain document control management.

Table 12.6 Sample configuration management audit checklist

No	Item to check
1	Is the Directory Structure set up for the project?
2	Are the configuration items identified and listed?
3	Have the latest versions of the templates been used?
4	Is a unique document Id employed for each document?
5	Is the standard version numbering system followed for the project?
6	Are all versions of documents and software modules in the document/source code repository?
7	Is the Configuration Management plan up to date?
8	Are the roles defined in the Configuration Management Plan performing their assigned responsibilities?
9	Are changes to the approved documents formally controlled?
10	Is the version number of a document incremented following an agreed change to an approved document?
11	Is there a change control board set up to approve change requests?
12	Is there a record of which releases are installed at the various customer sites?
13	Are all documents/software modules produced by vendors under appropriate configuration management control?

6. What is a configuration management audit?
7. Describe the role of the configuration manager and librarian.
8. What is a software configuration management system?

12.6   Summary

Software configuration management is concerned with the orderly development and evolution of the software. This involves tracking and controlling changes to the software and project deliverables, and it provides full traceability of the changes made during the project.

It involves identifying the configuration items that are subject to change control, controlling changes to them, and maintaining integrity and traceability throughout the software development lifecycle. There is a need for a document and source code repository, which has access controls, checking in and checking out procedures; and labelling of releases.

Configuration management ensures that the impacts of proposed changes are considered prior to authorization. It ensures that releases are planned and that only authorized changes to the software are made. A project will have a configuration management plan, and the configuration manager role is responsible for ensuring that the configuration management activities are carried out correctly during the project. Configuration audits will be conducted to verify that the CM activities have been carried out correctly. The integrity of the system is maintained, and the constituents of the software system and their version numbers are known at all times.

Project Management in the Agile World

13

Key Topics

Sprints
Stand-up meeting
Scrum
Stories
Refactoring
Pair programming
Software Testing
Test-driven development
Continuous Integration

13.1 Introduction

Agile is a popular lightweight software development methodology that aims to develop high-quality software faster than traditional approaches such as the waterfall development process. Despite the fact that it is a lightweight methodology it does not mean that anything goes, and it is, in fact, a disciplined approach to software development. It emphasizes the following features:

A collaborative style of working
Integrated teams
Frequent Deliveries
Ability to adapt to changing business needs.

Agile provides opportunities to assess the direction of a project throughout the development lifecycle. There has been a growth in interest in lightweight software development methodologies since the 1990s, and these include approaches

© The Author(s), under exclusive license to Springer Nature Switzerland AG 2025   219
G. O'Regan, *Guide to Software Project Management*, Undergraduate Topics in
Computer Science, https://doi.org/10.1007/978-3-031-80578-3_13

such as rapid application development (RAD), dynamic systems development method (DSDM), and extreme programming (XP). These approaches are referred to collectively as agile methods.

Every aspect of Agile development such as requirements and design is continuously revisited during the development, and the direction of the project is regularly evaluated. Agile focuses on rapid and frequent delivery of partial solutions developed in an iterative and incremental manner. Each partial solution is evaluated by the product owner, and feedback is provided to determine the next steps for the project. Agile is more responsive to customer needs than traditional methods such as the waterfall model, and its adherents argue that it results in:

higher quality
higher productivity
faster time to market
improved customer satisfaction.

It advocates adaptive planning, evolutionary development, early development, continuous improvement, and a rapid response to change. The term *'agile'* was coined by Kent Beck and others in the Agile Manifesto in 2001 [1]. The traditional waterfall model is similar to a wide and slow-moving value stream, and halfway through the project 100% of the requirements are typically 50% done. However, 50% of the requirements are typically 100% done halfway through an agile project (Fig. 13.1).

Fig. 13.1 Agile dog. Creative commons

Agile has a strong collaborative style of working, and ongoing changes to requirements are considered normal in the agile world. It argues that it is more realistic to change requirements regularly throughout the project, rather than attempting to define all of the requirements at the start of the project (as in the waterfall methodology). Agile includes controls to manage changes to the requirements, and good communication and regular feedback is an essential part of the process.

A *user story* may be a new feature or a modification to an existing feature. The feature is reduced to the minimum scope that can deliver business value, and a feature may give rise to several stories. Stories often build upon other stories and the entire software development lifecycle is employed for the implementation of each story. Stories are either done or not done (i.e., there is no such thing as 50% done), and the story is complete only when it passes its acceptance tests.

Scrum is an Agile method for managing iterative development, and it consists of an outline planning phase for the project, followed by a set of *sprint cycles* (where each cycle develops an increment). *Sprint planning* is performed before the start of the iteration, and stories are assigned to the iteration to fill the available time. Each scrum sprint is of a fixed length (usually 2–4 weeks), and it develops an increment of the system.

The estimates for each story (see Sect. 13.2.2) and their priority are determined, and the prioritized stories are assigned to the iteration. A short (usually 15 min) morning *stand-up meeting* is held daily during the iteration, and it is attended by the scrum master, the project manager[1], and the project team. It discusses the progress made the previous day, problem reporting and tracking, and the work planned for the day ahead. A separate meeting is held for issues that require more detailed discussion.

Once the iteration is complete the latest product increment is demonstrated to a review audience including the product owner. This is to receive feedback and to identify new requirements. The team also conducts a retrospective meeting to identify what went well and what went poorly during the sprint, as part of continuous improvement. The planning for the next sprint then commences.

The *scrum master* is a facilitator who arranges the daily meetings and ensures that the scrum process is followed. The role involves removing roadblocks to enable the team to achieve its goals and communicating with other stakeholders. Agile employs *pair programming* and a collaborative style of working with the philosophy that two heads are better than one. This allows multiple perspectives in decision-making which provides a broader understanding of the issues.

Agile employs *test-driven development* with tests written before the code. The developers write code to make a test pass with ideally developers only coding against failing tests. This approach forces the developer to write testable code, as well as ensuring that the requirements are testable. Tests are run frequently

---

[1] Agile teams are self-organizing and small teams (team size <20 people) do not usually have a project manager role, and the scrum master performs some light project management tasks.

with the goal of catching programming errors early. They are generally run on a separate build server to ensure that all the dependencies are checked. Tests are re-run before making a release. Agile employs automated testing for unit, acceptance, performance, and integration testing.

Refactoring is a design and coding practice employed in Agile, with the goal of changing how the software is written without changing what it does. It is a tool for evolutionary design, where the design is regularly evaluated and improvements are implemented as they are identified. This helps in improving the maintainability and readability of the code and in reducing complexity. The automated test suite is essential in demonstrating that the integrity of the software is maintained following refactoring.

Continuous integration allows the system to be built with every change. Early and regular integration allows early feedback to be provided and allows all of the automated tests to be run thereby identifying problems earlier. The main philosophy and features of Agile are:

- Working software is more useful than documents
- Direct interaction is preferred over documentation
- Aim is to achieve a narrow fast flowing value stream
- Rapid conversion of requirements into working functionality
- Change is accepted as a normal part of life in the Agile world
- Customer is involved throughout the project
- Demonstrates value early
- Feedback and adaptation are employed in decision-making
- User Stories and sprints are employed
- Iterative and Incremental development is employed
- A project is divided into iterations
- An iteration has a fixed length (i.e., Time boxing is employed)
- Entire software development lifecycle is employed for the implementation of the story
- Stories are either done are not done (no such thing as 50% done)
- Emphasis on Quality
- Stand-up meetings held daily
- Delivery is made as early as possible.
- Maintenance is seen as part of the development process
- Refactoring and Evolutionary Design Employed
- Continuous Integration is employed
- Short Cycle Times
- Plan regularly
- Early decision-making

Stories are prioritized based on a number of factors including:

- Business Value of Story
- Mitigation of risk
- Dependencies on other stories

13.2 Scrum Methodology

Scrum is a framework for managing an agile software development project (Fig. 13.2). It is not a prescriptive methodology as such, and it relies on a self-organizing, cross-functional team to take the feature from idea to implementation. The cross-functional team includes the *product owner* who represents the interest of the users and ensures that the right product is built; the *scrum master* who is the coach for the team, and helps the team to understand the Scrum process and to perform at the highest level, as well as performing some light project management activities such as project tracking; and the *self-organizing team* itself that decides on which person should work on which tasks, and so on.

The Scrum methodology breaks the software development for the project into a series of sprints, where each sprint is of a fixed time duration of 2–4 weeks. There is a planning meeting at the start of the sprint where the team members determine the number of items/tasks that they can commit to, and they then create a sprint backlog (*to-do list*) of the tasks to be performed during the sprint. The Scrum team takes a small set of features from ideas to coded and tested functionality that is integrated into the evolving product.

The team attends a *daily stand-up meeting* (usually for 15 min) where the progress of the previous day is discussed, as well as any obstacles to progress.

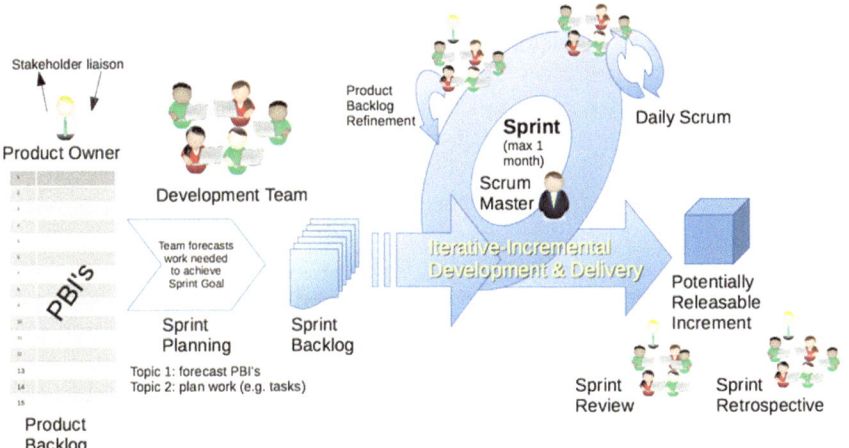

Fig. 13.2 Scrum framework. Creative commons

The new functionality is demonstrated to the product owner and any other relevant stakeholders at the end of the sprint, and this may result in changes to the delivered functionality or the addition of new items to the product backlog. There is a *sprint retrospective meeting* held at the end of the sprint to reflect on what went well and what went poorly during the sprint.

The main deliverable produced using the Scrum framework is the *product itself*, and Scrum expects to build a properly tested product increment (in a shippable state) at the end of each sprint. The *product backlog* is another deliverable and it is maintained and prioritized by the product owner. It is a complete list of the functionality (user stories) to be added to the product, and there is also the *sprint backlog* which is the list of functionality to be implemented in the sprint. Other deliverables are the *sprint burnout* and *release burnout* charts, which show the amount of work remaining in a sprint or release, and indicate the extent to which the sprint or release is on schedule.

The Scrum Master is the expert on the Agile process and acts as a coach to the team thereby helping the team to achieve a high level of performance. The role differs from that of a traditional project manager, as the Scrum Master does not assign tasks to individuals or provide day-to-day direction to the team (the team is self-organizing). However, the scrum master typically performs some light project management tasks.

Many of the traditional project managers' responsibilities such as task assignment and day-to-day project decisions revert back to the self-organizing team, and the responsibility for the scope and schedule trade-off goes to the product owner. The product owner creates and communicates a solid vision of the product, and shares the vision through the product backlog. Larger Agile projects (team size > 20) will often have a dedicated project manager.

13.2.1 User Stories

A *user story* is a short simple description of a feature written from the viewpoint of the user of the system. They are often written on index cards or sticky notes and arranged on walls or tables to facilitate discussion. This approach facilitates the discussion of the functionality rather than the written text.

A user story may be written at varying levels of detail, and a large detailed user story is known as an *epic*. An epic story is often too large to be implemented in one sprint and is often split into several smaller user stories.

It is the product owner's responsibility to ensure that a product backlog of user stories exists, but the product owner is not required to write all stories. In fact, anyone can write a user story, and each team member usually writes a user story during an Agile project. A user story-writing workshop is held at the start of the project so that the project team members are familiar with the process. User stories are written throughout an Agile project (Fig. 13.3).

The set of user stories leads to the product backlog that describes the functionality to be added during the project. Some of these will be epics that need to be

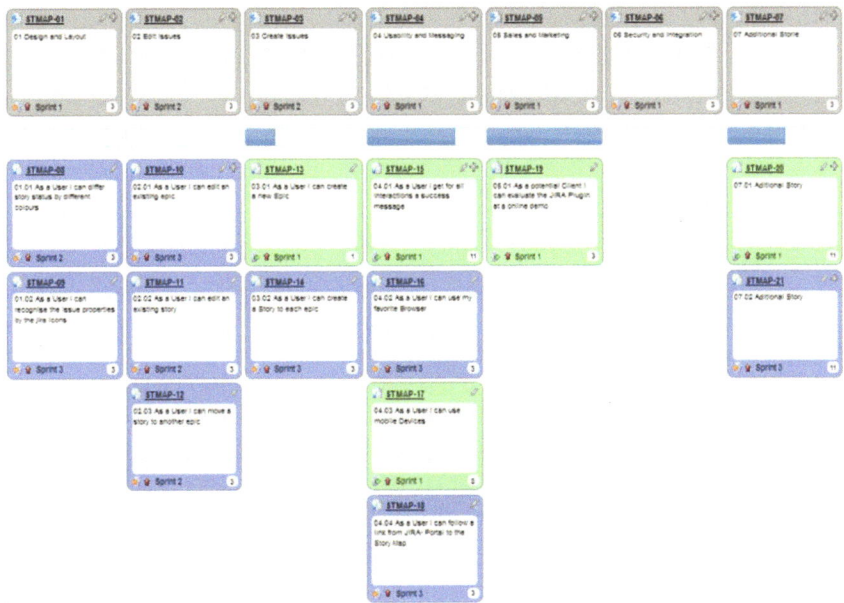

Fig. 13.3 User story map. Creative commons

decomposed into smaller stories that will fit into the time-boxed sprint. New user stories may be written at any time and added to the product backlog (the user story map in Fig. 13.3 is a two-dimensional representation of the product backlog).

There is no requirements document as such in Agile, and the product back-log (i.e., the prioritized list of the functionality of the product to be developed) is closest to the idea of a requirements document used in a traditional project. However, the written part of a user story in Agile is incomplete until the discussion of that story takes place. It is often useful to think of the written part of a story as a pointer to the real requirement, such as a diagram showing a workflow or the formula for a calculation.

13.2.2 Estimation in Agile

Planning poker is a popular consensus-based estimation technique often used in Agile, and it is used to estimate the effort required to implement a user story. The planning session starts with the product owner reading the user story, or describing a feature to the estimators.

Each estimator holds a deck of planning poker cards with values like 0, 1, 2, 3, 5, 8, 13, 20, 40 and 100, where the values represent the units in which the team estimates. The estimators discuss the feature with the product owner, and when the discussion is fully complete and all questions answered, each estimator privately selects a card to reflect his or her estimate.

All cards are then revealed and if all values are the same then that value is chosen as the estimate. Otherwise, the estimators discuss their estimates with the rationale for the highest and lowest discussed in detail. Each estimator then res-elects an estimate card, and the process continues until consensus is achieved, or if consensus cannot be achieved the estimation of the particular item is deferred until more information is available.

The initial estimation session usually takes place after the initial product back-log is written. It may take a number of days and is used to create the initial estimates of the size and scope of the project. Further estimation and planning sessions take place during the project as user stories are added to the product backlog, and these will typically take place towards the end of the current sprint.

The advantage of the Agile estimation process is that it brings multiple expert opinions from the cross-functional team, with the estimates explained in the detailed discussion. This helps to improve the estimation accuracy of the project.

13.2.3 Pair Programming

Pair programming is an agile technique where two programmers work together on one computer. The author of the code is termed the *driver*, and the other pro-grammer is termed the *observer* (or *navigator*) and is responsible for reviewing each line of written code. The observer also considers the strategic direction of the coding, proposes improvement suggestions, and identifies potential problems that may need to be addressed. The driver can focus on the implementation of the current task, and use the observer as a safety net. The two programmers switch roles regularly during the development of the new functionality (Fig. 13.4).

Pair programming requires more programming effort compared to programmers working in isolation. However, the resulting code is generally of higher quality, with fewer defects and a reduction in the cost of maintenance. Further, pair pro-gramming enables a better design solution to be created as more design alternatives are considered.

This is because two programmers are bringing different experiences to the prob-lem, and they may have different ways of solving the problem. This leads them to explore a larger number of ways of solving the problem than an individual pro-grammer. Finally, pair programming is good for knowledge sharing and learning, including knowledge of programming practice and design, and knowledge about the system among the team.

The *Jira tool* is often used in Agile projects for development sprints, daily work, and progress reporting. It allows Agile projects to track and manage issues and to show their resolution through the workflow. An issue could be a user story that needs to be implemented in the sprint, software defects, or new features or requirements.

Fig. 13.4   Pair programming. Creative commons

13.3   Software Testing in Agile

Traditional software projects employ a testing phase to verify the correctness of the software, and the testing verifies that the defects identified during testing have been resolved. The developers and testers are in a sense in different silos in a traditional project, which potentially leads to an adversarial relationship between them. However, in the Agile world testing is employed from the very beginning of the project to provide regular feedback on the extent to which the product meets the business needs. The developers and testers are very much part of the one integrated team, and they work closely together in a spirit of collaboration. That is, *there is a completely different mindset to testing employed in the Agile world*.

Testing is the responsibility of the test group in a traditional project, whereas testing is the responsibility of the entire team in an Agile project. Agile projects employ continuous testing from the start of the project, and this helps in ensuring that continuous progress is made during the sprint, and that the features have been correctly implemented.

It is fundamental in Agile that all the features be completely tested (including UAT testing) during the sprint, *as any features that have not been completely tested are considered to be not done*. This may result in the team being unable to do as much in the sprint as previously thought, and everyone tests to eliminate the bottleneck.

There is often a large gap in time between development and testing in traditional projects, and this increases the risk to the quality of the project. However, Agile teams *test early and test often*, which provides a short feedback loop on the quality of the software. That is, the team knows early whether there are problems with the software, whereas conventional projects learn about problems very late in the project. Agile's approach is to keep the code clean and defects are corrected as they are identified.

Automated tests (including unit and regression) are run frequently to provide rapid feedback, and this helps to reduce risk and rework. Manual testing (e.g., exploratory or regression) takes longer to execute and may require one or more team members to be available for several days.

Traditional projects produce a suite of comprehensive test documentation including test plans, test case specifications, test reports, and so on. However, in the Agile world lightweight test documentation is employed with Agile testers using reusable checklists to suggest tests and using lightweight documentation tools.

Agile generally employs automated testing for unit, acceptance, performance, and integration testing. Traditional projects employ a *"test-last"* approach with the requirements and design coming first, the tests derived from them, and the testing taking place at the end of the project. Agile employs a *"test-first"* approach with the tests defined with the requirements and used to drive the development effort.

That is, Agile employs *test-driven development* with tests written before the code. The developers write code to make a test pass with ideally developers only coding against failing tests. The code may then be refactored to improve its maintainability and readability and retested. Test-driven development forces the developer to write testable code, as well as ensuring that the requirements are testable. Tests are run frequently with the goal of catching programming errors early, and they may be run on a separate build server to ensure that all dependencies are checked prior to making a release.

Agile employs automated unit/integration tests which are written by the programmer, and are executed frequently especially following change. It employs automated system tests that define the externally expected behaviour of the system and these tests are executed regularly as part of continuous integration. Exploratory testing is employed as an Agile practice to learn about the software by designing and executing tests and may be used to target vulnerabilities in the system.

13.3.1 Test-Driven Development

Test-driven development (TDD) was developed by Kent Beck and others as part of their work on extreme programming (XP) in the late 1990s, and the approach involves the developers focusing on the requirements and writing test cases early (based on the requirements) before writing the code. The application is thus written with testability in mind, which means that the developers consider how to test the application in advance before writing any code. Further, it ensures that there are test cases for every feature, and writing tests early helps in gaining a deeper understanding of the requirements.

TDD is based on the transition of the requirements into a set of test cases, and the software is then written to pass the test cases. In other words, test-driven development of a new feature begins with writing a suite of test cases based on the requirements for the feature, and the code for the feature is then written to pass the test cases. *This is a paradigm shift from traditional software engineering* where unit tests are written and executed after the code is written.

The tests are written for the new feature, and initially, all of the tests fail as no code has been written. The first step is to write some code that enables the new test cases to pass, this new code may be imperfect (it will be improved later), but this is acceptable at this time as the only purpose is to pass the new test cases. The next step is to ensure that the new feature works with the existing features, and this involves executing all new and existing test cases.

This may involve modification of the source code to enable all of the tests to pass and to ensure that all features work correctly together. The final step is *refactoring* the code, and this involves cleaning up and restructuring the code, and improving its structure and readability. The test cases are re-run during the refactoring to ensure that the functionality is not altered in any way. The process repeats with the addition of each new feature.

Continuous integration allows the system to be built with every change, and this allows early feedback to be provided. It also allows all of the automated tests to be run, thereby ensuring that the new feature works with the existing functionality, and identifying problems earlier.

13.3.2 Agile Test Principles

The Agile methodology is a test-driven approach, with testing continuous rather than sequential as in the waterfall model. It is performed by the integrated team rather than by a dedicated test team (traditional projects). Continuous testing shortens the time for feedback to be provided, and the code is kept clean since all defects are corrected within the sprint. Agile uses lightweight documentation for testing (reusable checklists) to focus on the tests. The test principles are summarized in Table 13.1.

13.4 Advantages and Disadvantages of Agile

There are several advantages and disadvantages of the Agile compared to traditional software engineering. Agile is a flexible methodology with a focus on quality and continuous improvement, with the customer involved at all times throughout the software development process. The customer is involved in the decision-making process and may propose changes at any time to ensure that the final product is fit for purpose and satisfies the needs of the market. Its emphasis is on working software code rather than documentation, which allows the customer

Table 13.1 Agile test principles

Principle	Description
Testing provides feedback	Testing is used to provide feedback and visibility to move the project forward
Continuous testing	Testing is a way of life in Agile and it takes place frequently during the sprint
Testing by entire team	Both developers and testers execute tests with the whole team becoming involved to eliminate bottlenecks in testing
Short feedback loop	Agile teams test early and test often to obtain rapid feedback on how the software is behaving
Clean code	Developers fix genuine defects as they are found thereby keeping the code clean
Lightweight documentation	Testers use reusable checklists and lightweight documentation tools
Done means "Done"	A feature is not complete until it has been fully implemented and tested
Test driven	The tests are defined with the requirements and used to drive the development efforts

to give regular feedback to the project team on its fitness for purpose, thereby enabling the product to be continuously improved during the development process.

Among the disadvantages of Agile is that it is less predictable than conventional projects, which makes it more difficult to accurately estimate the time and resources required to complete an Agile project. The methodology requires a greater commitment of staff to be effective, and it takes time for a newly set up self-organizing team to master the Agile approach. Further, there is a lack of appropriate project documentation during the project, which potentially makes it difficult for new team members to become familiar with the project as well as making it more difficult to maintain the software.

13.5   Review Questions

1. What is Agile?
2. How does Agile differ from the traditional waterfall model?
3. What is a user story?
4. Explain how estimation is done in Agile.
5. What is test-driven development?
6. Describe the scrum methodology and the role of the Scrum Master.
7. Explain how testing is performed in the Agile world.
8. Explain pair programming and describe its advantages.
9. What are the strengths and weaknesses of the Agile methodology?

13.6   Summary

This chapter gave a brief introduction to project management in the Agile world. Agile is a popular lightweight software development methodology that advocates adaptive planning, evolutionary development, early development, continuous improvement, and a rapid response to change. The traditional waterfall model is similar to a wide and slow-moving value stream, and halfway through the project 100% of the requirements are typically 50% done. However, 50% of the requirements are typically 100% done halfway through an agile project.

Agile has a strong collaborative style of working, and ongoing changes to requirements are considered normal in the Agile world. It includes controls to manage changes to the requirements, and good communication and early regular feedback is an essential part of the process.

The Scrum approach is an Agile method for managing iterative development, and it consists of an outline planning phase for the project followed by a set of sprint cycles (where each cycle develops an increment). Each scrum sprint is of a fixed length, and it develops an increment of the system.

The estimates for each story and their priority are determined, and the prioritized stories are assigned to the iteration. A short (usually 15 min) morning stand-up meeting is held daily during the iteration and discusses the progress made the previous day, problem reporting and tracking, and the work planned for the day ahead.

Software testing is employed from the very beginning of an Agile project to provide regular feedback on the extent to which the product meets business needs. The developers and testers are part of one integrated team, and they work closely together in a spirit of collaboration. There is a completely different mindset to testing employed in the Agile world.

Once the iteration is complete the latest product increment is demonstrated to a review audience including the product owner. This is to receive feedback and to identify new requirements. The team also conducts a retrospective meeting to identify what went well and what went poorly during the iteration, as part of continuous improvement of future sprints.

Reference

1. K. Beck et al., Manifesto for Agile Software Development. Agile Alliance (2001). http://agilem anifesto.org/

Project Management Metrics

14

14.1 Introduction

Measurement is an essential part of mathematics and the physical sciences, and it has been successfully applied to the software engineering field. Its purpose is to establish and use quantitative measurements to manage software development activities in an organization; to assist the organization in understanding its current software engineering capability; and to provide an objective indication that software process improvements have been successful.

Measurements provide visibility into the various areas of the organization, and the quantitative data allow trends to be seen over time. The analysis of the trends leads to corrective action plans. Measurements may be employed to track the quality, timeliness, cost, schedule, and effort of software projects. The terms *"metric"* and *"measurement"* are used interchangeably in this book, and the formal definition of measurement given by Fenton [1] as:

> Measurement is the process by which numbers or symbols are assigned to attributes or entities in the real world in such a way as to describe them according to clearly defined rules.

© The Author(s), under exclusive license to Springer Nature Switzerland AG 2025
G. O'Regan, *Guide to Software Project Management*, Undergraduate Topics in
Computer Science, https://doi.org/10.1007/978-3-031-80578-3_14

Measurement plays a key role in the physical sciences: for example, calculating the distance to the planets and stars; determining the mass of objects; computing the speed of mechanical vehicles; calculating the electric current flowing through a wire; computing the rate of inflation; estimating the unemployment rate, and so on. Measurement provides a more precise understanding of the entity under study.

Often several measurements are used to provide a detailed understanding of the entity under study. For example, the cockpit of an airplane contains measurements of altitude, speed, temperature, fuel, latitude, longitude, and various devices essential to modern navigation and flight.

Metrics play a key role in problem-solving, and several problem-solving techniques were discussed in Chap. 8. For example, a telecommunications outage is measured as the elapsed time between the downtime and the subsequent uptime, and the longer the outage lasts the more serious it is. That is, measurement data are invaluable in providing a quantitative measure of the extent of the problem. It enables analysis to be performed on the root cause of a particular problem, e.g., of a telecommunications outage, and to verify that the actions taken to correct the problem have been effective.

Metrics provide an internal view of the quality of the software project, but care is needed before deducing the behaviour that will be exhibited externally from the various internal measurements. A *leading measure* is a software measure that usually precedes the attribute that is under examination; for example, the arrival rate of software problems is a leading indicator of the maintenance effort. Leading measures provide an indication of the likely behaviour of the product in the field and need to be examined closely. A *lagging indicator* is a software measure that is likely to follow the attribute being studied; for example, escaped customer defects are a lagging indicator of the quality and reliability of the software. It is important to learn from lagging indicators even if the data can have little impact on the current project.

14.2   The Goal Question Metric Paradigm

Many software metrics programs have failed because they had poorly defined, or non-existent goals and objectives, with the metrics unrelated to the achievement of the business goals. The *Goal Question Metric* (GQM) paradigm was developed by Victor Basili and others at the University of Maryland in the late 1980s [2], and it is a rigorous goal-oriented approach to measurement, in which goals, questions, and measurements are closely integrated.

The business goals are first defined, and then the relevant questions that relate to the achievement of the goal are determined. For each question, a metric that gives an objective answer to the particular question is defined. The statement of the business goal is precise, and it is related to individuals or groups. The GQM approach is a simple one, and managers and engineers proceed according to the following three stages:

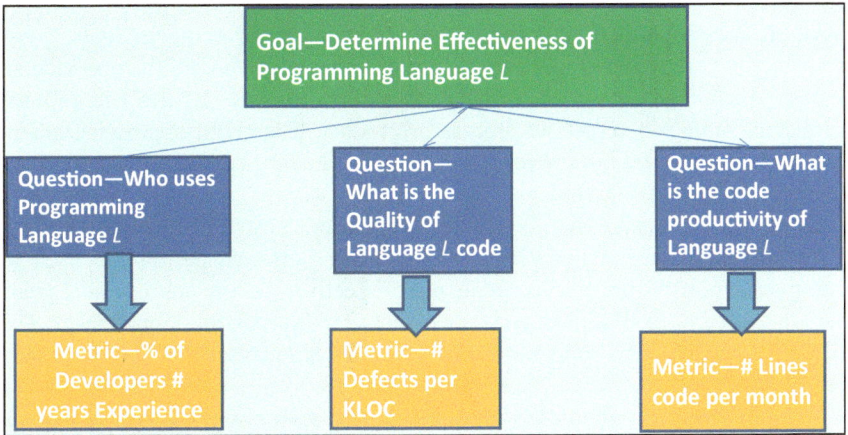

Fig. 14.1 GQM example

- Set goals specific to needs in terms of purpose, perspective, and environment
- Refine the goals into quantifiable questions
- Deduce the metrics and data to be collected (and the means for collecting them) to answer the questions.

Consider the goal of determining the effectiveness of a new programming language *L*. There are several valid questions that may be asked at this stage, including: What percentage of programmers use L?, What is their level of experience? What is the quality of software code produced with language L? What is the productivity of programmers who use language L? This leads naturally to the quality and productivity metrics as detailed in Fig. 14.1.

Goal
The focus on improvements should be closely related to the business goals, and the first step is to identify the key goals that are essential for business success. The business goals are related to the strategic direction of the organization and the problems that it is currently facing. There is little sense in directing improvement activities to areas that do not require improvement, or where there is no business need to improve, or where there will be a minimal return to the organization.

Question
These are the key questions that determine the extent to which the goal is being satisfied, and for each business goal the set of pertinent questions need to be identified. That is, the information required to determine the current status of the goal is determined from the answers to the related questions. Each question is analysed to determine the best approach to obtain an objective answer, and to define the metrics that are needed, and the data that needs to be gathered to answer the question objectively.

Metrics

These are measurements that provide a quantitative answer to the particular question, and they are closely related to the achievement of the goals. They provide an objective picture of the extent to which the goal is currently satisfied and improve the understanding of a specific process or product. The GQM approach leads to measurements that are closely related to the goal, *rather than measurement for the sake of measurement.*

GQM helps to ensure that the defined measurements will be relevant and used by the organizations to understand their current performance, and to used to improve and satisfy the business goals more effectively. Clear improvement goals that are related to the business goals are essential for successful improvement. The GQM measures may be from various viewpoints, e.g., manager viewpoint, project team viewpoint, etc.

There are two key approaches to software process improvement: i.e., *top-down* or *bottom-up* improvement. Top-down approaches are based on process improvement models and appraisals: e.g., models such as the CMMI, ISO 15504, and ISO 9000 (see Chap. 8), whereas GQM is a bottom-up approach to software process improvement, and is focused on improvements related to certain specific goals. The top-down and bottom-up approaches are often combined in practice.

14.3   The Balanced Scorecard

The balanced scorecard (BSC) (Fig. 14.2) is a management tool that is used to clarify and translate the organization vision and strategy into action. It was developed by Kaplan and Norton [3], and has been applied to many organizations. The European Software Institute (ESI) developed a tailored version of the BSC for the IT sector (the IT Balanced Scorecard).

The BSC assists in selecting appropriate measurements to indicate the success or failure of the organization's strategy. There are four perspectives in the scorecard: *customer, financial, internal process*, and *learning and growth*. Each perspective includes objectives to be accomplished for the strategy to succeed, measures to indicate the extent to which the objectives are being met, targets to be achieved in the perspective, and initiatives to achieve the targets. The balanced scorecard includes financial and non-financial measures.

The BSC is useful in selecting the key processes that the organization should focus its process improvement efforts on in order to achieve its strategy. Traditional improvement is based on improving quality; reducing costs; and improving productivity, whereas the balanced scorecard takes the future needs of the organization into account, and identifies the processes that the organization needs to excel at in the future to achieve its strategy. This results in focused process improvement, and the intention is to yield the greatest business benefit from the improvement program.

The starting point for the organization is to define its *vision* and *strategy* for the future. This often involves strategy meetings with the senior management to clarify

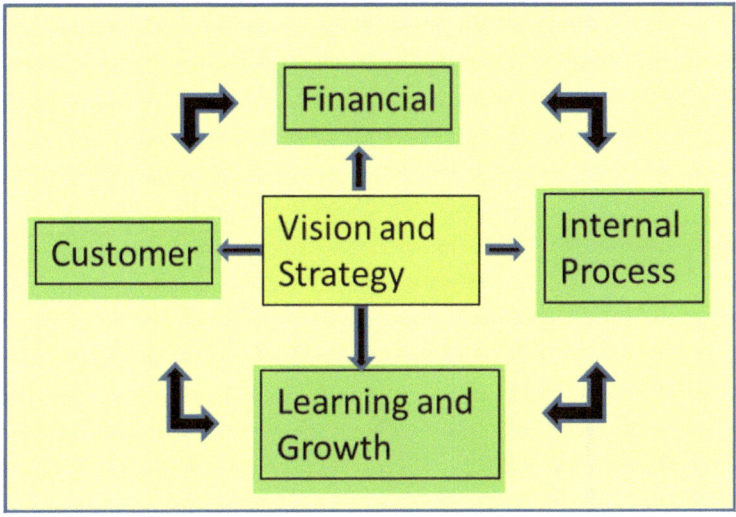

Fig. 14.2 The balanced scorecard

the vision and to achieve consensus on the strategic direction for the organization among the senior management team. The vision and strategy are then translated into *objectives* for the organization or business unit. The next step is communication, and the vision, strategy, and objectives are communicated to all employees. These critical objectives must be achieved in order for the strategy to succeed, and so all employees (with management support) will need to determine their own local objectives to support the organization strategy. Goals are set and rewards are linked to performance measures.

The financial and customer objectives are determined from the strategy, and the key business processes to be improved are then identified. These are the key processes that will lead to a breakthrough in performance for customers and shareholders of the company. It may require new processes with re-training of employees on the new processes necessary, and the balanced scorecard is very effective in driving organizational change. The financial objectives require targets to be set for customers, internal business processes, and the learning and growth perspective. The learning and growth perspective will examine the competencies and capabilities of employees and the level of employee satisfaction (Fig. 14.3).

Table 14.1 presents sample objectives and measures for the four perspectives in the BSC for an IT service organization.

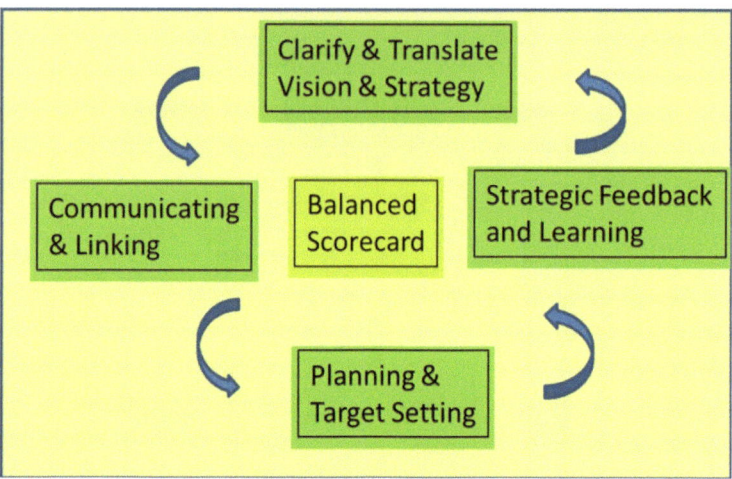

Fig. 14.3 Balanced score card and implementing strategy

Table 14.1 BSC objectives and measures for IT service organization

Financial	*Customer*
Cost of provision of services	Quality service
Cost of hardware/software	Reliability of solution
Increase revenue	Rapid response time
Reduce costs	Accurate information
Timeliness of solution	Timeliness of solution
99.999% network availability	99.999% network availability
24/7 customer support	24/7 customer support
Internal business process	*Learning and growth*
Requirements definition	Expertise of staff
Software design	Software development capability
Implementation	Project management
Testing	Customer support
Maintenance	Staff development career structure
Customer support	Objectives for staff
Security/proprietary information	Employee satisfaction
Disaster prevention and recovery	Leadership

14.4   Software Metrics for Project Management

The objective of this section is to present a set of project management metrics to provide visibility into the project and to show how metrics can facilitate improvement. The objective is to show how metrics may be employed for effective management and decision-making. Many organizations have monthly quality or operation reviews in which the presentation of metrics plays an important role.

We present sample metrics for various areas that impact software project management, including metrics for human resources, customer satisfaction, supplier quality, internal audit, as well as metrics for accuracy of the estimation of schedule and budget, and quality metrics for requirements, development, testing, and process improvement. These metrics may be presented at a regular management review and performance trends observed, and the main output from a management review is a series of improvement actions.

14.4.1   Customer Satisfaction Metrics for Project

Figure 14.4 shows the customer survey arrival rate per customer per month, and it indicates that there is a survey process in place for measuring satisfaction with the projects taking place and that the customers are surveyed throughout the year. It does not provide any information as to whether the customers are satisfied, whether any follow-up activity from the survey is required, or whether the frequency of surveys is sufficient (or excessive) for the organization.

Figure 14.5 gives the customer satisfaction measurements in several categories including quality, the ability of the project to meet the committed dates and to deliver the agreed content, the ease of use of the software, the expertise of the staff, and the value for money. The chart indicates the extent to which the customer is happy with the delivery of the project, and the customer care group needs to follow up negative feedback with the customer. Figure 14.5 is interpreted as follows:

8–10	Exceeds expectations
7	Meets Expectations
5–6	Fair
0–4	Below Expectations

Fig. 14.4 Customer survey arrivals

Fig. 14.5 Customer satisfaction measurements for project A

In other words, a score of 8 for quality indicates that the customers consider the software to be of high quality, and a score of 9 for value for money indicates that the customers consider the solution to be excellent value. It is essential that the customer feedback is analysed (with follow-up meetings held where appropriate). There may be a need to prepare an action plan to deal with customer issues and communicate the plan to the customer.

14.4.2 Process Improvement Metrics

The objective of process improvement metrics is to provide visibility into the process improvement in the organization (we discuss process improvement of project management in Chap. 16).

Figure 14.6 shows the arrival rate of improvement suggestions from the software community, and these may include suggestions to improve project management, testing, and so on. The chart indicates that the arrival rate is high initially and the closure rate low, which is consistent with the commencement of an improvement initiative. The closure rate then improves which indicates that the improvement team is active in implementing the improvement suggestions. The closure rate is low during July and August, which may be explained by the holiday period.

The chart provides no information on the effectiveness of the process improvements and the overall impact on quality and productivity. There are no measures of the cost of improvements, and this is needed for a cost benefit analysis of the benefits versus the cost of the improvements.

Figure 14.7 provides visibility into the status of the improvement suggestions for project management, and the number of raised, open, and closed suggestions per month. The chart indicates that gradual progress has been made in the improvement program with a gradual increase in the number of suggestions that are closed.

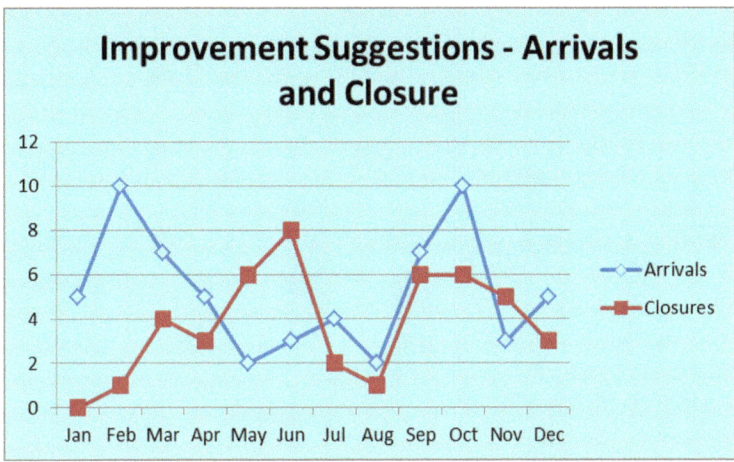

Fig. 14.6 Process improvement measurements

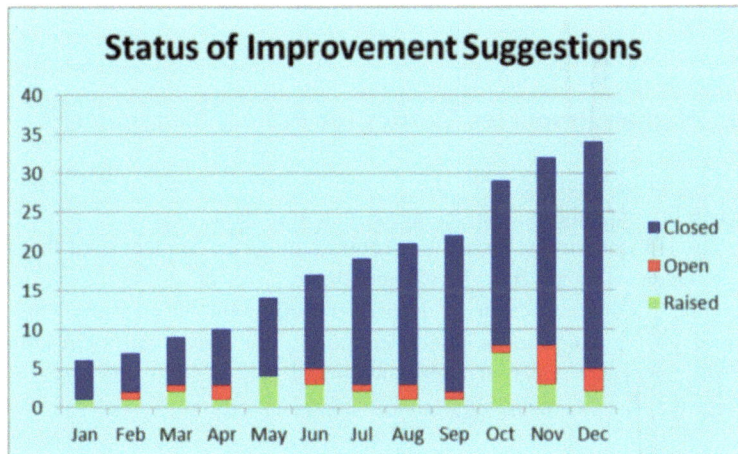

Fig. 14.7 Status of PM improvement suggestions

Figure 14.8 provides visibility into the age of the PM improvement sugges-tions, and acts as a partial measure of the productivity of the improvement team. The charts in Figs. 14.6, 14.7, and 14.8 give a more complete picture of team productivity.

There may be other charts associated with process improvement programs such as a chart to indicate the status of the implementation of a CMMI improvement program as provided in Fig. 14.30. Similarly, a chart that gives the current status of an ISO 9001 implementation could be derived from the number of actions which

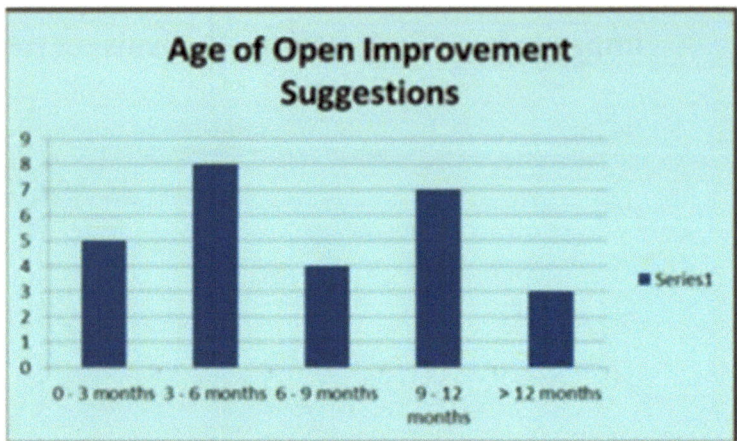

Fig. 14.8 Age of PM improvement suggestions

are required to implement ISO 9000, the number implemented, and the number outstanding.

14.4.3 Human Resources Metrics for Project Management

Figure 14.9 gives visibility into the human resources needs of the project and gives visibility into the headcount needs and the actual resources provided per month. The HR department tracks the current number of employees of the organization per calendar month (Fig. 14.10), and the turnover of staff in the organization (Fig. 14.11). The human resources department will maintain measurements of the number of job openings to be filled per month, the arrival rate of resumes per month, the average number of interviews to fill one position, the percentage of employees that have received their annual appraisal, etc.

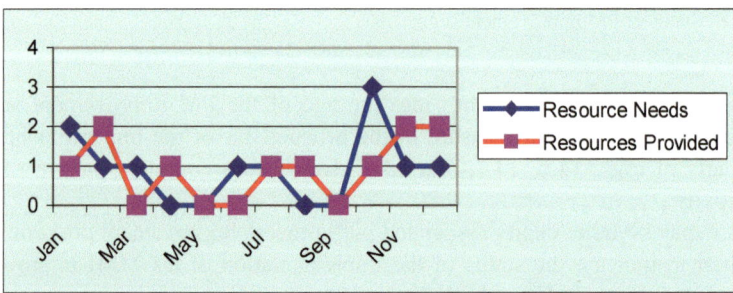

Fig. 14.9 Headcount needs and provision for project

Fig. 14.10   Headcount in organization

Fig. 14.11   Employee turnover in the current year

One of the key goals of the HR department is to attract and retain the best employees, and this breaks down into the two obvious sub-goals of attracting the best employees and retaining them. Figure 14.11 gives visibility into the turnover of staff in the project during the calendar year, and it indicates the effectiveness of staff retention in the organization.

14.4.4   Project Management Effectiveness

The success of the project manager is judged by the extent to which s/he delivers the agreed functionality for the project on time and budget, and with the right quality. The timeliness metric provides visibility into the extent to which the project has been delivered on time, and the number of months over or under schedule per project in the organization is shown. The schedule estimation metric is a lagging measure, as it indicates that the project has been delivered within a schedule or not after the event (Fig. 14.12).

The on-time delivery of a project requires that the various milestones in the project be carefully tracked and corrective actions taken to address slippage during the project. The second metric provides visibility into the effort estimation accuracy of a project. Accurate effort estimation is essential in calculating the cost of the project and in preparing the project schedule. We discussed the Standish Research data on projects in Chap. 1, which showed that the accurate effort and schedule estimation is difficult (Fig. 14.13).

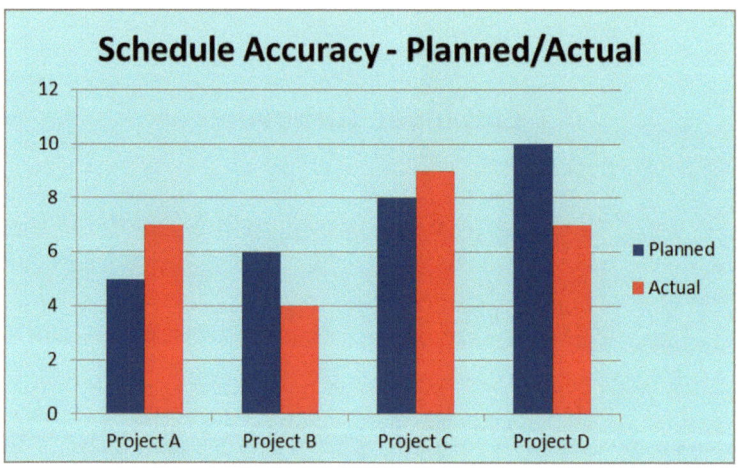

Fig. 14.12 Schedule estimation metric

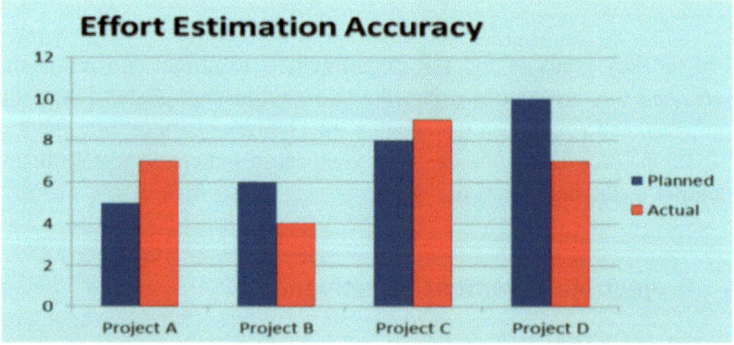

Fig. 14.13 Effort estimation metric

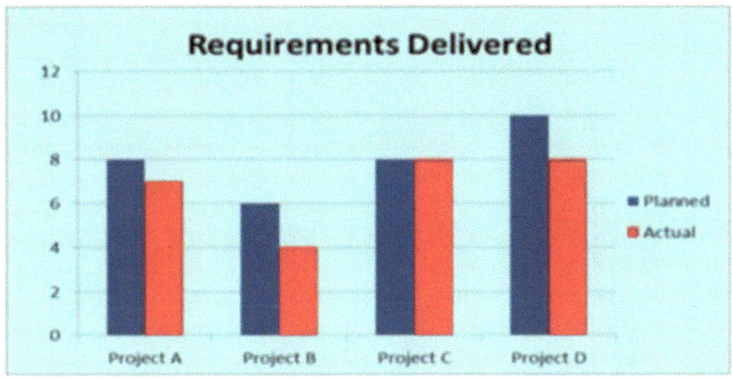

Fig. 14.14 Requirements delivered

The effort estimation chart is similar to the schedule estimation chart, except that the schedule metric is referring to elapsed calendar months, whereas the effort estimation chart refers to the planned number of person months required to carry out the work versus the actual number of person months that it actually took. Projects need an effective estimation methodology to enable them to be successful in project management, and the project manager will use metrics to determine how accurate the estimation has actually been.

The next metric is related to the commitments that are made to the customer with respect to the content of a particular release, and it indicates the effectiveness of the projects in delivering the agreed functionality to the customer (Fig. 14.14). This chart could be adapted to include enhancements or fixes promised to a customer for a particular release of a software product.

14.4.5 Development and Testing Metrics for Project

These metrics give visibility into the development and testing of the software. Figure 14.15 shows the total number of change requests and defects raised during the project (these are the project issues), as well as their severities. The presence of a large number of change requests suggests that the initial definition of the requirements for the project was incomplete and that the requirements process may need improvement.

Figure 14.16 gives the status of open issues (open change requests and defects) of the project, and is an indication of the current quality of the project, and the effort required to achieve the desired quality in the software. This chart is not used in isolation, as the project manager will need to know the arrival rate of problems (see Fig. 14.18) to determine the stability of the software product.

The organization may decide to release a software product with open problems provided that the associated risks with the known problems can be managed.

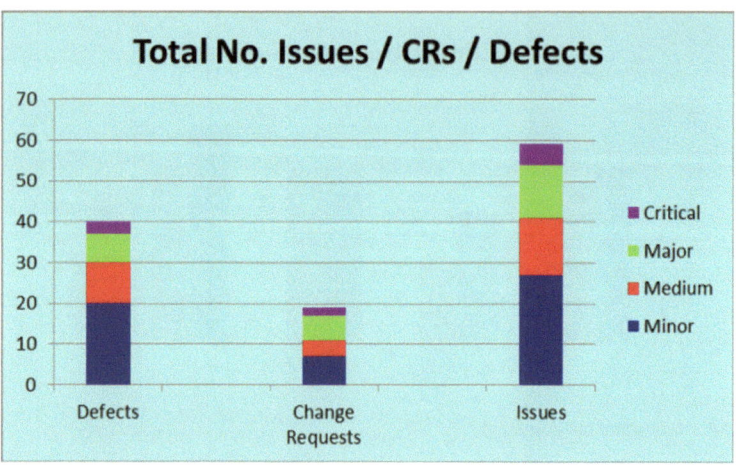

Fig. 14.15 Total number of issues in project

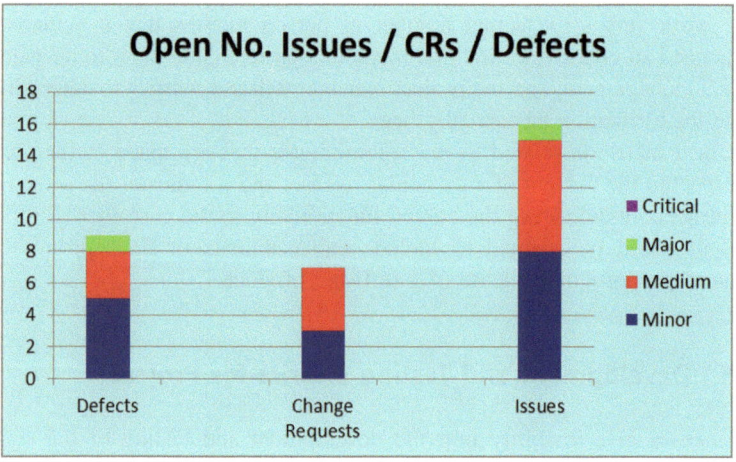

Fig. 14.16 Open issues in project

It is important to perform a risk assessment to ensure that these may be managed, and the known problems (and ways to work around the problems) should be documented in the release notes for the product.

The project manager will need to know the age of the open problems to determine the effectiveness of resolving problems in a timely manner. Figure 14.17 presents the age of the open defects, and it highlights the fact that there is one major problem that has been open for over one year. The project manager needs to prevent this situation from arising, as critical and major problems need to be swiftly resolved.

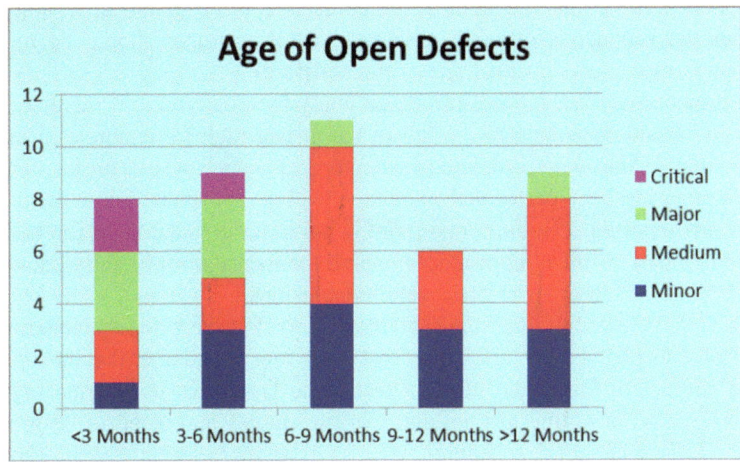

Fig. 14.17   Age of open defects in project

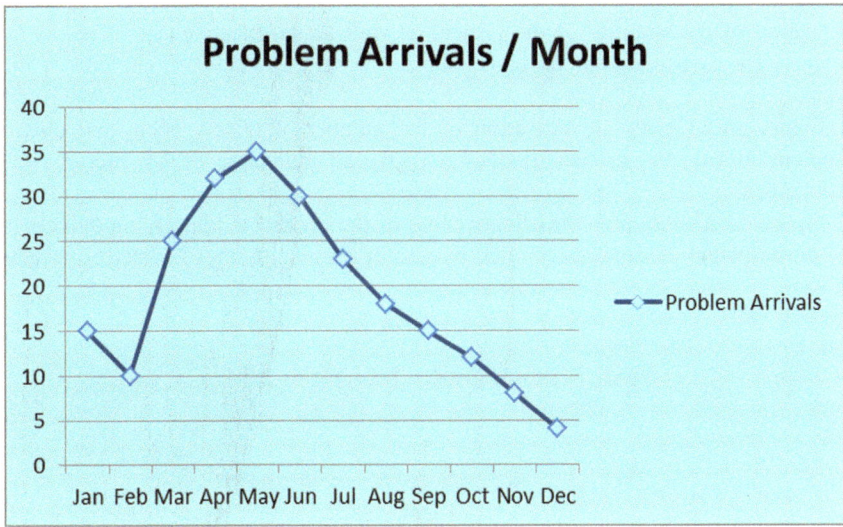

Fig. 14.18   Problem arrivals per month

The problem arrival rate enables the project manager to judge the stability of the software, and this metric (used with other metrics) helps in judging whether the software is ready for release to potential customers. Figure 14.18 presents a sample problem arrival chart, and the chart indicates positive trends with the arrival rate of problems falling to very low levels.

The objective is that the number of defects reported at the acceptance test and after the product is officially released to the customer should be minimal (preferably zero defects post-release of the software).

The project manager will need to do an analysis to determine if there are other causes that could contribute to the fall in the arrival rate; for example, it may be the case that testing was completed in September, which would mean, in effect, that no testing has been performed since then, with an inevitable fall in the number of problems reported. The important point is not to jump to a conclusion based on a particular chart, as the circumstances behind the metric must be fully known and taken into account in order to draw valid conclusions.

Figure 14.19 presents the status of the testing for the project, including the number of tests planned, the number of test cases run, the number that have passed, and the number of failed and blocked tests. The test status is reported regularly to management during the testing, and extra resources may need to be provided when the testing is behind schedule.

Figure 14.20 is the cumulative arrival rate curve and it gives an indication of the stability of the product. The expectation is that the curve will level off towards the end of testing, as most of the defects will have been identified.

Figure 14.21 describes the arrival and closure rates of problems, and gives an indication of the stability of the project as well as its effectiveness in resolving defects. The arrival rate of problems should be very low towards the end of the project.

Figure 14.22 gives an indication of the number of raised, open, and closed problems during the project. It does not give an indication of how serious the problems are.

Figure 14.23 measures the effectiveness of the project in identifying defects in the development phase, and the effectiveness of the test groups in detecting defects

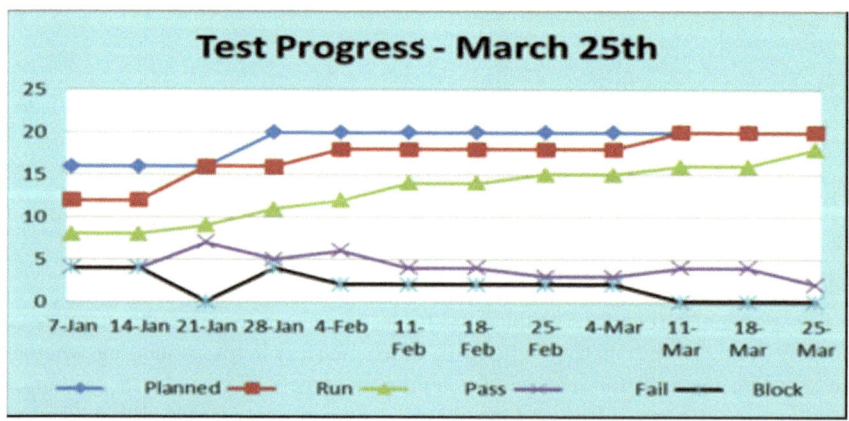

Fig. 14.19 Test progress

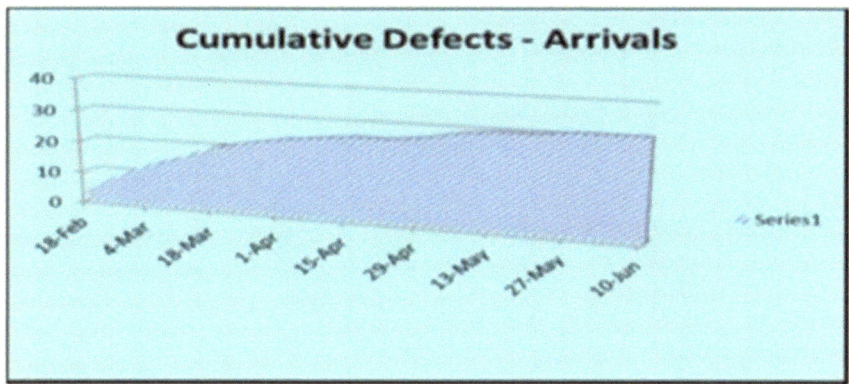

Fig. 14.20   Cumulative defects—arrivals

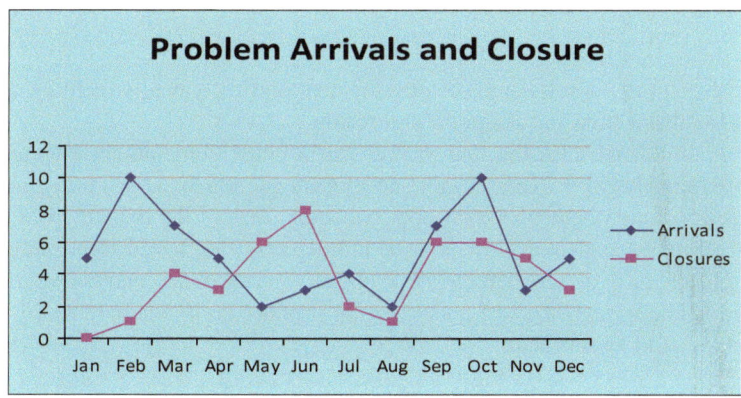

Fig. 14.21   Problem arrivals and closure

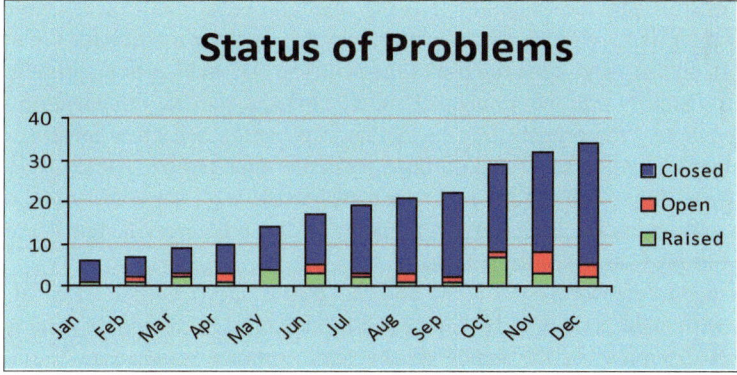

Fig. 14.22   Status of problems

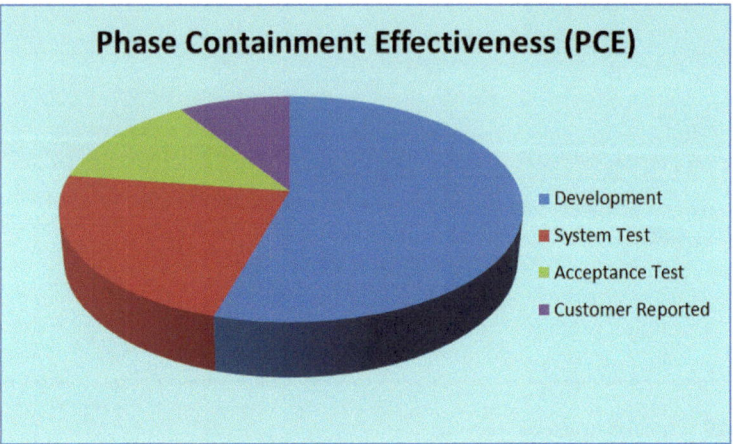

Fig. 14.23 Phase containment effectiveness

that are present in the software. The development portion typically includes defects reported on inspection forms and in unit testing.

Figure 14.23 indicates that the project had a phase containment effectiveness of approximately 54%. That is, the developers identified 54% of the defects, the system-testing phase identified approximately 23% of the defects, acceptance testing identified approximately 14% of the defects, and the customer identified approximately 9% of the defects. The objective is that the number of defects reported at the acceptance test and after the product is officially released to the customer should be minimal.

14.4.6 Quality Audit Metrics

These metrics provide visibility into the audit program for projects within the organization (if there is such a program), and they include metrics for the number of audits planned and performed and the status of the audit actions. Figure 14.24 presents visibility into the number of audits carried out in the organization.

It shows that the organization has an audit program, and gives information on the number of audits performed during a particular time period. The chart does not give a breakdown into the type of audits performed, e.g., supplier audits, project audits, and audits of particular departments in the organization, but it could be adapted to provide this information.

The auditor performs the audit and the results are documented in an audit report, with audit actions to be completed by the affected individuals and groups. Figure 14.25 presents the status of the audit actions assigned to the various projects.

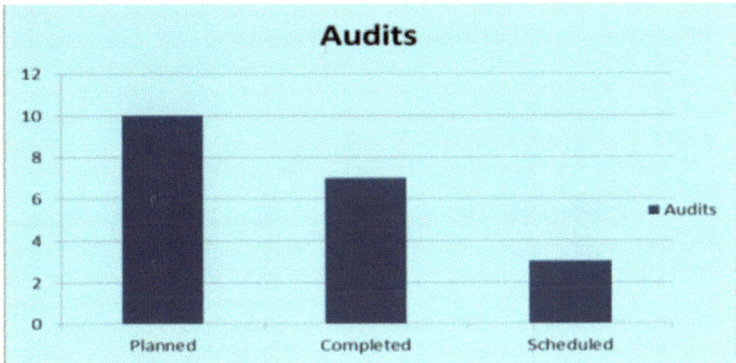

Fig. 14.24   Annual audit schedule

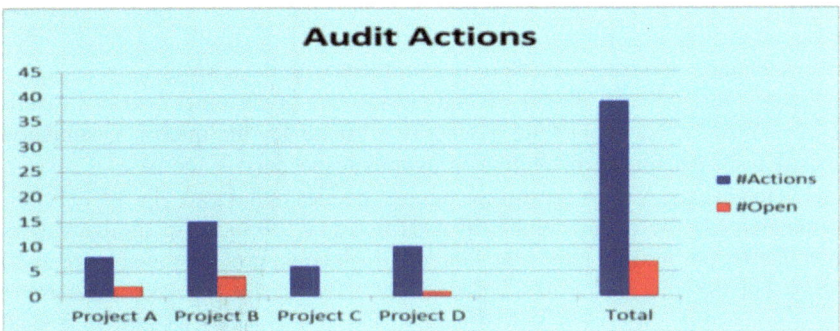

Fig. 14.25   Status of audit actions

Figure 14.26 gives visibility into the type of actions raised during a project audit. They could include entry and exit criteria, planning issues, configuration management issues, issues with compliance with the lifecycle or templates, traceability to the requirements, and so on.

14.4.7   Customer Care Metrics

The goals of the customer care group in an organization are to respond efficiently and effectively to customer problems, to ensure that the customer receives the highest standards of service from the company, and to ensure that its products function reliably at the customer's site. The work of the customer care group commences after the delivery of the project and so represents post-project activities.

The organization will need to know its efficiency in resolving customer queries, the arrival and closure rate of customer queries, the availability of its software

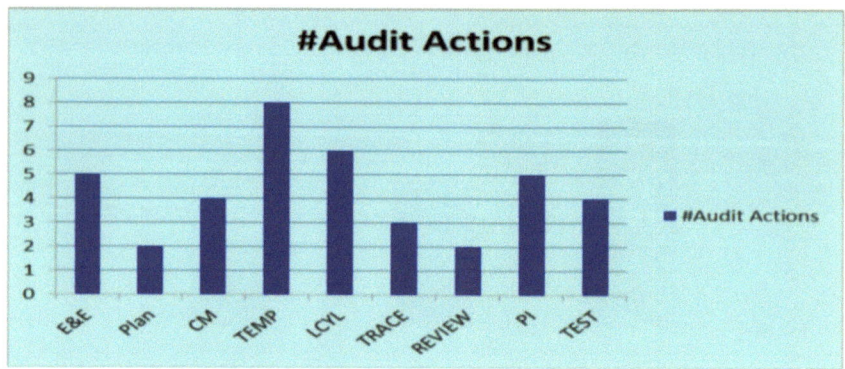

Fig. 14.26 Audit action types for project A

systems at the customer site, the duration of the outages at the various customer sites, and the age of open queries. A customer query may result in a defect report where the query indicates that there is a problem with the software.

Figure 14.27 presents the arrival and closure rate of customer queries (it could be developed further to include a severity attribute for the query). Quantitative goals may be set for the resolution of queries (especially in the case of service-level agreements). A chart for the age of open queries (similar to Fig. 14.17) could be maintained. The organization will need to know the status of the backlog of open queries per month, and a simple trend graph could provide this. Figure 14.27 shows that the arrival rate of queries in the early part of the year exceeds the closure rate of queries per month. This indicates an increasing backlog that needs to be addressed.

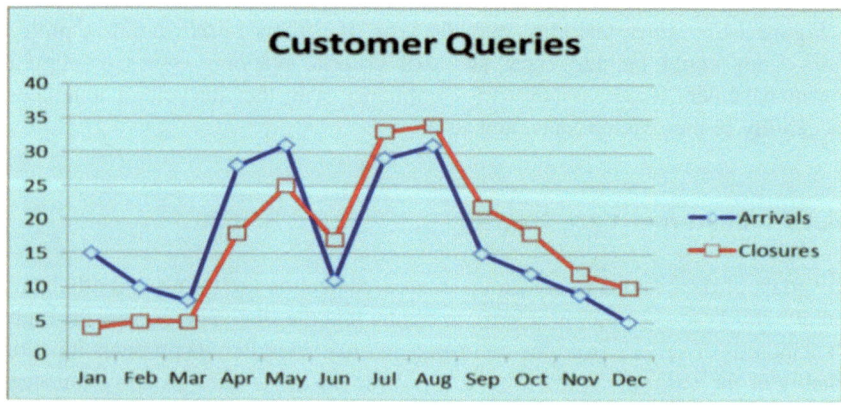

Fig. 14.27 Customer queries (arrivals/closures)

The customer care department responds to any outages and ensures that the outage time is kept to a minimum. The "*five nines initiative*" has the objective of developing systems that are available 99.999% of the time, i.e., approximately five minutes of downtime per year. The calculation of availability is given by

$$Availability = \frac{MTBF}{MTBF + MTTR}$$

where the mean time between failure (MTBF) is the average length of time between outages.

$$MTBF = \frac{Sample\ Interval\ Time}{Outages}$$

The formula for MTBF above is for a single system only, and the formula is adjusted when there are multiple systems.

$$MTBF = \frac{Sample\ Interval\ Time}{Outages} * \#Systems$$

The mean time to repair (MTTR) is the average length of time that it takes to correct the outage, i.e., the average duration of the outages that have occurred, and it is calculated from the following formula:

$$MTTR = \frac{Total\ Outage\ Time}{\#Outages}$$

Figure 14.28 presents outage information on the customers impacted by an outage during the particular month, and the extent of the impact on the customer.

The customer care department will carry out a post-mortem of an outage to ensure that lessons are learned to prevent a reoccurrence. This causal analysis identifies the root causes of the outage, and corrective actions are taken to prevent a

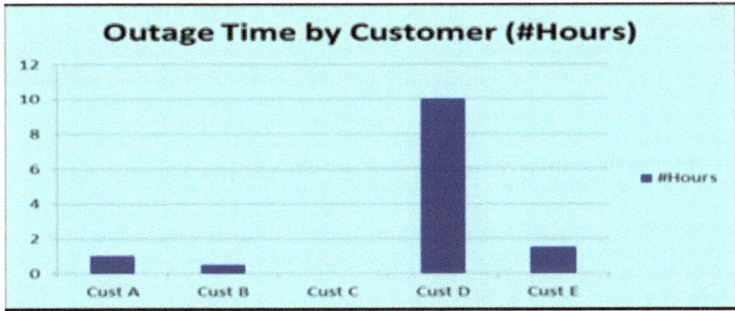

Fig. 14.28   Outage time per customer

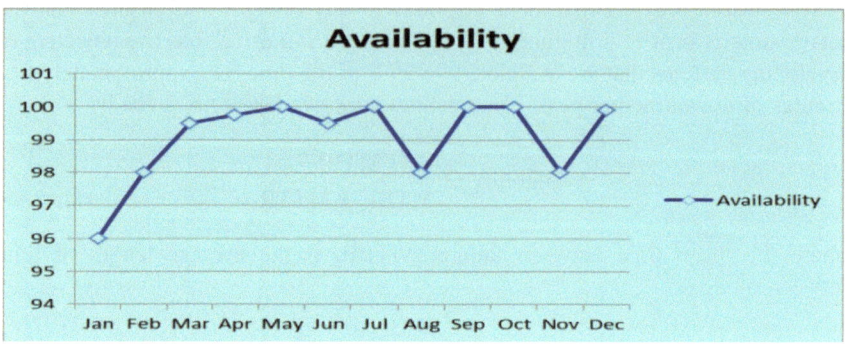

Fig. 14.29 Availability of system per month

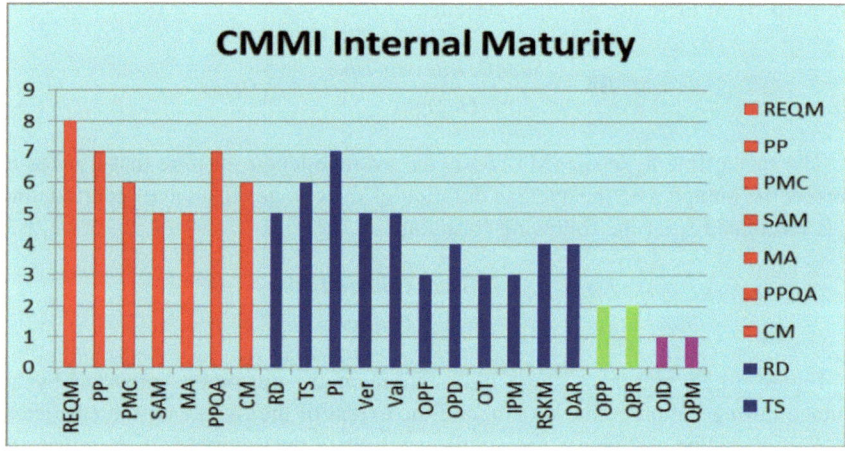

Fig. 14.30 CMMI maturity in current year

reoccurrence. The customer care group will maintain metrics of system availability and outage time per month (usually in the form of a trend graph).

Figure 14.29 provides visibility on the availability of the system at the customer sites, where organizations are designing systems that are 99.999% available.

14.4.8   Miscellaneous Metrics for an Organization

Metrics may be applied to many other areas in the organization. This section includes metrics on the CMMI maturity of an organization (where an organization is implementing the CMMI) and the cost of poor quality. Figure 14.30 gives the internal CMMI maturity of the organization, and indicates its readiness for a formal CMMI assessment. A numeric score of 1–10 is used to rate each process area, and a score of 7 or above indicates that the process area is satisfied.

Crosby argued that the most meaningful measurement of quality is the cost of poor quality [4], and that improvement activities should aim to reduce the *cost of poor quality* (COPQ). The cost of quality includes the cost of external and internal failure, the cost of providing an infrastructure to prevent the occurrence of problems, and the cost of the infrastructure to verify the correctness of the product.

The cost of quality was divided into four subcategories (Table 14.2) by Feigenbaum in the 1950s and evolved further by James Harrington of IBM.

The cost of the quality graph (Fig. 14.31) will initially show high external and internal costs and low prevention costs, and the total quality costs will be high. However, as an effective quality system is put in place and becomes fully operational, there will be a noticeable decrease in the external and internal cost of quality and a gradual increase in the cost of prevention and appraisal.

The total cost of quality will substantially decrease, as the cost of provision of the quality system is substantially below the cost of internal and external failure.

Table 14.2 Cost of quality categories

Type of cost	Description
Cost external	This includes the cost of external failure and includes engineering repair, warranties, and a customer support function
Cost internal	This includes the internal failure cost and includes the cost of reworking and re-testing of any defects found internally
Cost prevention	This includes the cost of maintaining a quality system to prevent the occurrence of problems and includes the cost of software quality assurance, the cost of training, etc.
Cost appraisal	This includes the cost of verifying the conformance of a product to the requirements and includes the cost of provision of software inspections and testing processes

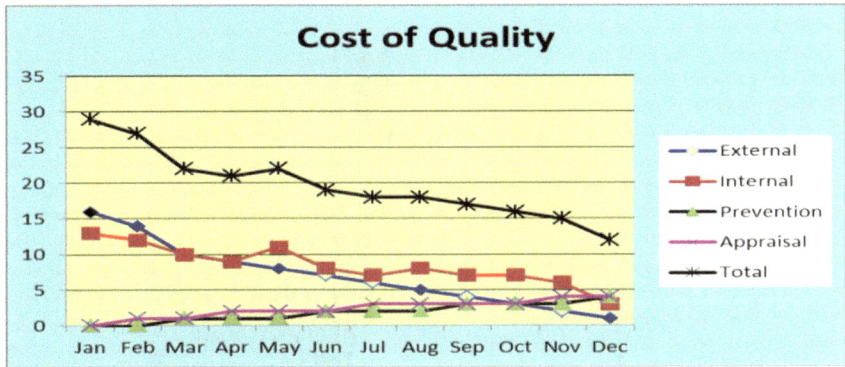

Fig. 14.31 Cost of poor quality (COPQ)

The COPQ curve will indicate where the organization is in relation to the cost of poor quality, and the organization will need to execute its improvement plan to put an effective quality management system in place to minimize the cost of poor quality.

14.5   Implementing a Metrics Program

The metrics discussed may be adapted and tailored to meet the needs of the project/ organization. The metrics are only as good as the underlying data, and so good data gathering is essential. The following are typical steps in the implementation of a metrics program (Table 14.3).

The business goals are the starting point in the implementation of a metrics program, as the metrics must be closely related to the business goals. The next step is to identify the relevant questions to determine the extent to which the business goal is being satisfied and to define metrics that provide an objective answer to the questions.

The organization defines its business goals, and each department develops specific goals to meet the organization's goals. Measurement will indicate the extent to which specific goals are being achieved, and good data gathering and recording are essential. First, the organization will need to determine which data need to be gathered, and to determine methods by which the data may be recorded. The precise data to be recorded is determined from the information required to answer the questions related to the goals. A small organization may decide to record the data manually, but often automated or semi-automated tools will be employed in larger organizations. It is essential that the data collection and extraction is efficient, as otherwise, the metrics program is likely to fail.

The roles and responsibilities of staff with respect to the implementation and day-to-day operation of the metrics program need to be defined. Training is needed to enable staff to perform their roles effectively. Finally, a regular management review is needed, where the metrics and trends are presented, and actions are identified and carried out to ensure that the business goals are achieved.

Table 14.3 Implementing metrics

Implementing metrics in organization
Define the business goals
Determine the related questions
Define the metrics
Determine tools to (semi-) automate metrics
Determine data that needs to be gathered
Identify and provide needed resources
Provide training
Gather data and prepare metrics
Communicate metrics and review monthly

Table 14.4 Goals and questions

Goal	Reduce escaped defects from each lifecycle phase by 10%
Questions	How many defects are identified within each lifecycle phase?
	How many defects are identified after each lifecycle phase is exited?
	What % of defects escaped from each lifecycle phase?

14.5.1   Data Gathering for Metrics

Metrics are only as good as the underlying data, so data gathering is a key activity in a metrics program. The data to be recorded will be closely related to the questions, and the data are used to give an objective answer to the questions. The business goals are usually expressed quantitatively for extra precision, and Table 14.4 presents an example of how the questions related to a particular goal are identified.

Table 14.5 is designed to determine the effectiveness of the software development process, and to enable the above questions to be answered. It includes a column for inspection data that records the number of *defects* recorded at the various inspections. The *defects* include the phase where the defect originated; for example, a defect identified in the coding phase may have originated in the requirements or design phase. This data is typically maintained in a spreadsheet, e.g., Excel (or a dedicated tool), and it needs to be kept up to date. It enables the phase containment effectiveness (PCE) to be calculated for the various phases.

We will distinguish between a defect that is detected *in-phase* versus a defect that is detected *out-of-phase*. An in-phase defect is a problem that is detected in the phase in which it is created (e.g., usually by a software inspection). An out-of-phase defect is detected in a later phase (e.g., a problem with the requirements may be discovered in the design or coding phase, which is a later phase from the phrase in which it was created).

Table 14.5 Phase containment effectiveness

Phase of origin								
Phase	Inspect defects	Reqs	Design	Code	Accept test	In-phase defects	Other defects	% PCE
Reqs	4		1	1		4	6	40%
Design	3					3	4	42%
Code	20					20	15	57%
Unit test		2	2	10				
System test		2	2	5				
Accept test								

The effectiveness of the requirements phase in Table 14.5 is judged by its success in identifying defects as early as possible, as the cost of correction of a requirements defect increases the later in the cycle that it is identified. The requirements PCE is calculated to be 40%, i.e., the total number of defects identified in phase divided by the total number of requirements defects identified. There were four defects identified at the inspection of the requirements, and six defects were identified outside of the requirements phase: one in the design phase, one in the coding phase, two in the unit testing phase, and two at the system-testing phase: i.e., 4/10 = 40%. Similarly, the code PCE is calculated to be 57%.

The overall PCE for the project is calculated to be the total number of defects detected in phase in the project divided by the total number of defects, i.e., 27/52 = 52%. Table 11.5 is a summary of the collected data and its construction consists of:

- Maintain inspection data of requirements, design, and code inspections
- Identify defects in each phase and determine their phase of origin
- Record the number of defects in each phase per phase of origin.

The staff who perform inspections need to record the problems identified, whether it is a defect and its phase of origin. Staff will need to be appropriately trained to do this consistently.

The above is just one example of data gathering, and in practice the organization will need to collect various data to enable it to give an objective answer to the extent that the particular goal is being satisfied.

14.6   Review Questions

1. Describe the Goal, Question, and Metric model.
2. Explain how the Balanced Scorecard may be used in the implementation of organizational strategy.
3. How is customer satisfaction measured?
4. How is the cost of poor quality measured?
5. Explain how metrics assist in project management.
6. Discuss how a metrics programme may be implemented.

14.7   Summary

Measurement is an essential part of mathematics and the physical sciences, and it has been successfully applied to the software engineering field. This chapter included a collection of sample metrics to give visibility into project management in the organization, including customer satisfaction, process improvement, project management effectiveness, HR metrics for project management, development and testing, and customer care metrics.

The balanced scorecard assists the organization in selecting appropriate measurements to indicate the success or failure of the organization's strategy. Each of the four scorecard perspectives includes objectives that need to be achieved for the strategy to succeed, and measurements indicate the extent to which the objectives are being met.

The Goal, Question, Metric paradigm is a rigorous, goal-oriented approach to measurement in which goals, questions, and measurements are closely integrated. The business goals are first defined, and then questions that relate to the achievement of the goal are identified, and for each question, a metric that gives an objective answer to the particular question is defined.

Metrics may be employed to track the quality, timeliness, cost, schedule, and effort of software projects. They provide an internal view of the quality of the software product, but care is needed before deducing the behaviour that a product will exhibit externally.

References

1. N. Fenton, *Software Metrics: A Rigorous Approach* (Thompson Computer Press, 1995)
2. V. Basili, H. Rombach, The TAME project. Towards improvement-oriented software environments. IEEE Trans. Softw. Eng. **14**(6) (1988)
3. R.S. Kaplan, D.P. Norton, *The Balanced Scorecard. Translating Strategy into Action* (Harvard Business School Press, 1996)
4. P. Crosby, *Quality is Free. The Art of Making Quality Certain* (McGraw Hill, 1979)

Tools for Project Management

15

Key Topics

Cocomo
Microsoft Project
ProjectLibre
ProjectManager
Jira
Planview
WBSPro
Crystal ball

15.1 Introduction

This chapter gives a flavour of a selection of tools[1] to support the performance of the software project management activities. The approach is to choose tools to support the process, rather than choosing a process to support the tool.[2]

Mature organizations will employ a structured approach to the introduction of new tools. First, the requirements for a new tool are specified, and the options to satisfy the requirements are identified. These may include developing a tool internally; outsourcing the development of a tool to a third-party supplier; or purchasing an off-the-shelf solution from a vendor.

---

[1] The list of tools discussed in this chapter is intended to give a flavour of what tools are available, and the inclusion of a particular tool is not intended as a recommendation of that tool. Further, the omission of a particular tool should not be interpreted as disapproval of that tool.

[2] That is, the process normally comes first then the tool rather than the other way around.

© The Author(s), under exclusive license to Springer Nature Switzerland AG 2025   261
G. O'Regan, *Guide to Software Project Management*, Undergraduate Topics in
Computer Science, https://doi.org/10.1007/978-3-031-80578-3_15

Table. 15.1 Tool evaluation table

	Tool 1	Tool 2	...	Tool k
Requirement 1	8	7		9
Requirement 2	4	6		8
...				
...				
Requirement n	3	6		8
Total	35	38	...	45

The sample tool evaluation table below (Table 15.1) lists all of the requirements vertically that the tool is to satisfy, and the candidate tools that are to be evaluated and rated against each requirement are listed horizontally. Various rating schemes may be employed, and a simple numeric mechanism is employed for the example below. The tool evaluation criteria are used to rate the effectiveness of each candidate tool and to indicate the extent to which the tool satisfies the defined requirements. The chosen tool in this example is Tool k as it is the most highly rated of the evaluated tools.

Several candidate tools are identified and considered prior to selection, and each candidate tool will be evaluated to determine the extent to which it satisfies the specified requirements. An informed decision is then made and the proposed tool may be piloted prior to its deployment. The pilot provides feedback on its suitability, and the feedback will be considered prior to a decision on full deployment, and whether any customization is required prior to roll out.

Finally, the users are trained on the tool, and the tool is rolled out throughout the organization. Support is provided for a period post-deployment. First, we consider a selection of tools for project estimation and scheduling.

15.2   Tools for Project Estimation and Scheduling

There are several tools to support project estimation and scheduling. These include tools such as Microsoft Project, which is a powerful project planning and scheduling tool that is widely used in industry. Small projects may employ a simpler tool such as Microsoft Excel, or an open source tool such as GanttProject or ProjectLibre, for their project-scheduling activities.

The Constructive Cost Model (COCOMO) is a cost prediction model developed by Barry Boehm in the late 1970s [1], and it is used to estimate effort, cost, and schedule for small and medium projects. The model was based on the waterfall model and involved a study of over 60 projects varying in size from 2000 to 100,000 lines of code, and the projects were implemented in a mixture of assembly and high-level languages.

COCOMO is based on an effort estimation equation that calculates the software development effort in person-months from the estimated project size (in thousands of *source lines of code* (SLOC[3])). The accuracy of the tool is limited, as there is a great deal of variation among teams due to differences in the expertise and experience of the personnel in the project team. COCOMO II is the successor to the original version and it was developed in the late 1990s and was designed to support other software development processes as well as addressing the move from mainframe development to desktop development. The model parameters were based on a study of over 150 projects.

There are several commercial variants of the tool including the COCOMO Basic, Intermediate, and Advanced Models. The Intermediate Model includes several cost drivers to model the project environment, and each cost driver is rated. There are over fifteen cost drivers used, and these include product complexity, reliability, and experience of personnel as well as programming language experience. The COCOMO parameters need to be calibrated to reflect the actual project development environment. The effort equation used in COCOMO is given by

$$\text{Effort} = 2.94 * \text{EAF} * (\text{KSLOC})^{\text{E}} \qquad (15.1)$$

In this equation, EAF refers to the effort adjustment factor that is derived from the cost drivers, and E is the exponent that is derived from the five scale drivers.[4] The Costar tool is a commercial tool that implements the COCOMO Model, and it may be used on small or large projects. It needs to be calibrated to reflect the particular software engineering environment, and this will enable more accurate estimates to be produced. It has been largely replaced by the System Startool, which has more features and implements more estimating models.

The effort estimates are used for scheduling the tasks and activities in a project-scheduling tool. The schedule will detail the phases in the project, the key project milestones, the activities and tasks to be performed in each phase as well as their associated duration, and the resources required to carry out each task. The project manager will update the project schedule regularly during the project to reflect the progress made, as well as adjusting the schedule whenever changes occur during the project.

We discussed various approaches to estimation in Chap. 5, including the Work Breakdown Structure, the Analogy Method, Expert Judgment, the Delphi Method, Function Points, and Planning Poker.

Microsoft Project (Fig. 5.1) is a project management tool that is used for planning, scheduling, and charting project information. It enables a realistic project schedule to be created, and the schedule is updated regularly during the project to reflect the actual progress made, and the project is re-planned as appropriate.

A project is defined as a series of steps or tasks to achieve a specific goal. The amount of time that it takes to complete a task is termed its duration, and tasks are

---

[3] SLOC includes delivered source lines of code created by project staff (excluding automated code generated and also code comments).
[4] The five scale drivers are factors contributing to duration and cost and they determine the exponent used in the Effort equation. Examples include team cohesion and process maturity.

performed in a sequence determined by the nature of the project. Resources such as people and equipment are required to perform a task. A project will typically consist of several phases such as planning and requirements; design; implementation; testing and closing the project.

The project schedule (Fig. 5.1) shows the tasks and activities to be carried out during the project; the effort and duration of each task and activity; the percentage completion of each task, and the resources needed to carry out the various tasks. The schedule shows how the project will be delivered within the key project parameters such as time, cost, and functionality without compromising quality in any way.

The project manager is responsible for managing the schedule and will take corrective action when project performance deviates from expectations. The project schedule will be updated regularly to reflect actual progress made, and the project re-planned appropriately.

GanttProject is a freely available project-scheduling software (under a GPL license) that runs under Microsoft Windows, Linux, and Mac OS X operating systems. It provides basic project-scheduling functionality such as Gantt charts for project scheduling of tasks and resource management.

ProjectLibre is a free and open source (CPAL license) project-scheduling tool that runs on Microsoft Windows, Linux, and Mac OS X operating systems. It is compatible with Microsoft Project and has been downloaded by millions of users around the world. It is the leading alternative to Microsoft Project, and there is a cloud web-based version called *ProjectLibre Cloud* (Fig. 15.1).

It has a similar user interface and functionality as Microsoft Project, and it provides a similar approach to creating a project schedule and creating a work breakdown structure with the task list and duration specified.

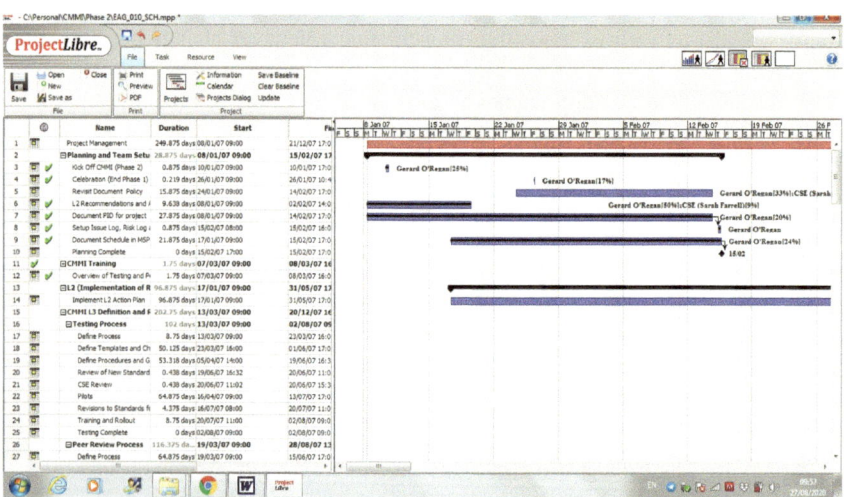

Fig. 15.1 ProjectLibre scheduling tool

WBS Schedule Pro is project management software that consists of a tool called WBS charts that is used for planning, and Network Charts that is used for scheduling. WBS Charts uses a top-down approach to create a work breakdown structure (WBS), whereas Network Charts may be employed to define the dependencies between tasks, and the critical path is automatically created. WBS Schedule Pro also includes Gantt Charts, which is a tool to create a Gantt chart from the planning data that has been entered.

15.3   Project Manager Tools

There are several project management tools that provide comprehensive functionality such as dashboard features to provide visibility into the health of the project, and where important information is kept in one central location.

The *ProjectManager* (or ProjectManager.com) tool was originally developed in New Zealand, but the company headquarters moved to the United States in 2014. It is a scaleable software-as-a-service project management tool and includes functionality that supports collaboration across teams, multiple views of the project, a "mywork space" where all the tasks assigned to a person are located, a "team space" where the team's tasks may be visualized, a timesheet feature to log hours, a customizable dashboard that provides real-time visible status of the project, and a portfolio view that gives a real-time status of all projects that are taking place in the organization (Fig. 15.2).

The dashboard is updated in real time as teams enter their progress updates, and the dashboard provides a high-level overview of the health of the project. The status indicates whether the project is on or behind schedule as well as whether it is on budget. It provides the overall status of the tasks, including whether the tasks

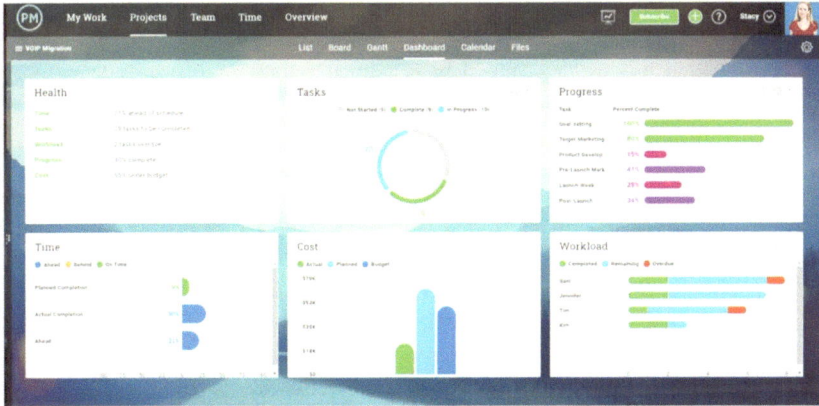

Fig. 15.2 Dashboard view in projectmanager tool

are completed, in progress, or not started, as well as showing the team members that are falling behind.

There are three versions of the tool namely the Starter version that starts with 5 users and allows them to create project plans; the Team version starts with 10 users and supports team collaboration; and the Business version that starts with 15 users and offers unlimited features and projects.

The *Scoro* tool was initially developed in Estonia, and the company headquarters are in the U.K. This business management software brings sales, projects, and reports together, and a dashboard may monitor business performance. It may be used as a project management tool to manage teams and projects, and it provides a central location where the projects may be planned, scheduled, and tracked. It allows users to create projects, allocate work, handle invoices, management meetings, and the ongoing activities to complete the project may be monitored and progress may be visualized with the Project timeline. It includes a dashboard that provides an overview of how the project is being undertaken.

The *Jira* tool was developed by Atlassian (an Australian company), and it is used for defect tracking, issue tracking and project management. It contains four packages:

Jira Core (for business and project management)
Jira Software (for project and issue tracking including Agile features)
Jira Service Desk (for IT Service Management)
Jira Align (Enterprise Agile planning).

Issues are at the heart of the Jira tool, where an issue could be simple tasks, software defects, or new features or requirements. Jira is used in the Agile world for development sprints, the daily work, and progress reporting. An issue in Agile could be a user story that needs to be implemented in the current sprint. Jira is used for issue tracking by the teams, and it shows the progress on the resolution of the issue as it moves through the workflow.

The status of an issue changes as it moves through the workflow. The status is assigned when it has been assigned to a team member for resolution, and complete when it has been completed. Jira provides traceability of the issues to code changes.

The first thing that a user sees on logging on to Jira is the dashboard, which is displayed by default on the home page. The dashboard may be tailored to meet the needs of the project or team, and it may be used to keep track of progress, workload per person, and high-risk items in an Agile project (Fig. 15.3).

Oracle Crystal Ball is a spreadsheet-based application that may be used to give insight into critical factors affecting risk and is useful when using spreadsheets to forecast uncertain results. It has functionality for Monte Carlo simulation that automatically calculates the results of thousands of different *what-if* cases, and these may be analysed to determine a range of possible outcomes and their probability of occurrence.

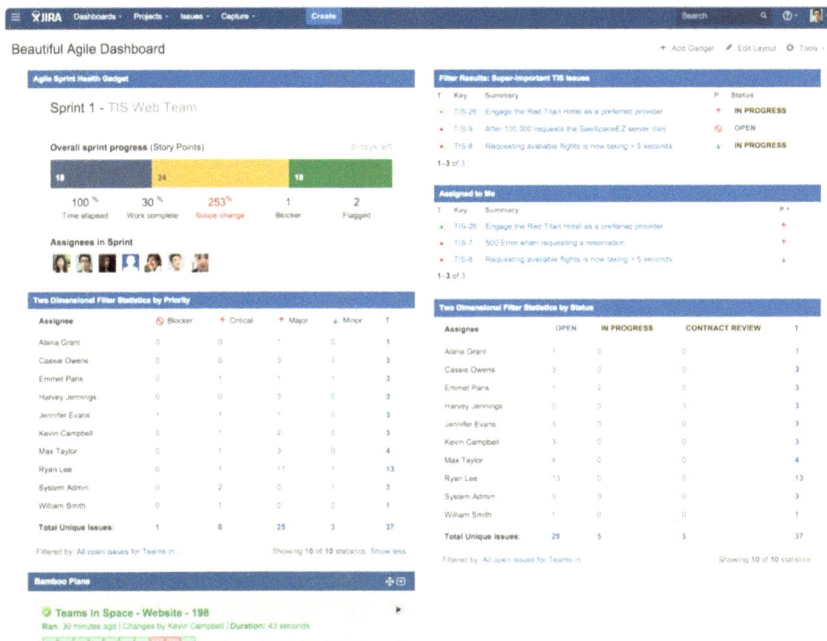

Fig. 15.3 Dashboard view of agile project in jira tool

15.4   Tools for Project Portfolio Management

Project portfolio management (PPM) is concerned with managing a portfolio of projects, and it allows the organization to choose the mix and sequencing of its projects in order to yield the greatest business benefit to the organization.

PPM tools analyse the project's total expected cost, the resources required, the schedule, the benefits that will be realized as well as interdependencies with other projects in the portfolio. This allows project investment decisions to be made methodically to deliver the greatest benefit to the organization. The approach moves away from the normal once-off analysis of an individual project proposal, to the analysis of a portfolio of projects. PPM tools aim to manage the continuous flow of projects from concept all the way to completion.

There are several commercial portfolio management tools available from vendors. These include Clarity PPM from Computer Associates; Change Point from Compuware; RPM from IBM Rational; PPM Centre from HP; and Planview Enterprise from Planview. We limit our discussion in this section to the Planview Enterprise tool.

Planview Enterprise Portfolio Management allows organizations to manage projects and resources across the enterprise, and to align their initiatives for maximum business benefit. It provides visibility into and control of project portfolios, and allows the organization to prioritize and manage its projects and resources.

This allows it to make better investment decisions, and to balance its business strategy against its available resources. Planview helps an organization to optimize its business through eight key capabilities (Table 15.2).

Planview allows key project performance indicators to be closely tracked, and these include dashboard views of variances in cost, effort, and schedule, which are used for analysis and reporting (Fig. 15.4).

Planview includes Process Builder (Fig. 15.5), which allows modelling and management of enterprise wide processes. It provides tracking, control, and audit capabilities in key process areas such as requirements management and product development, as well as satisfying key regulatory requirements.

The organization may define and model its processes in Process Builder, and this includes process adoption, compliance, and continuous improvement. The functionality includes:

- Process Design
- Process Automation
- Process Measurement
- Process Auditing

Table. 15.2 Key capabilities of planview enterprise

Capability	Description
Strategic planning	Define mission, objectives, and strategies Allocate funding/staffing for the chosen strategy Automate and manage strategic processes
Investment analysis	Devise strategic long-term plans Identify key criteria to evaluate initiatives Optimize strategic and project investments to maximize business benefit
Capacity management	Balance resources with business demands Ensure capacity supports business strategy Align top-down and bottom-up planning Forecast resource capacity
Demand management	Request work and Check status Review lifecycles
Project management	Scope, schedule, and execution of work Track/report time worked against projects Track and manage risks and issues Track/display performance and trend analysis.
Financial management	Collaborate to better forecast cost Monitor spending
Resource management	Balance portfolios/assign people efficiently Improve forecasting Keep staff productive
Change management	Determine impact of change on schedule/cost Effectively manage change

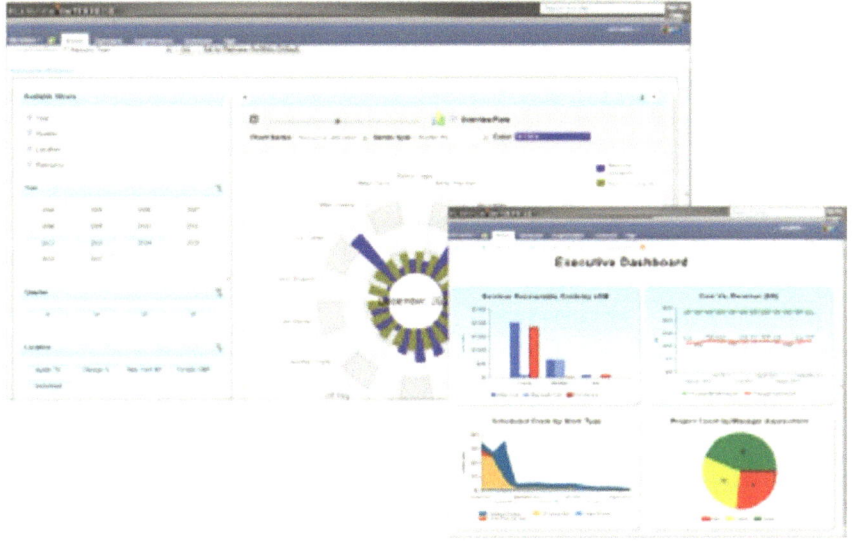

Fig. 15.4 Dashboard views in planview enterprise

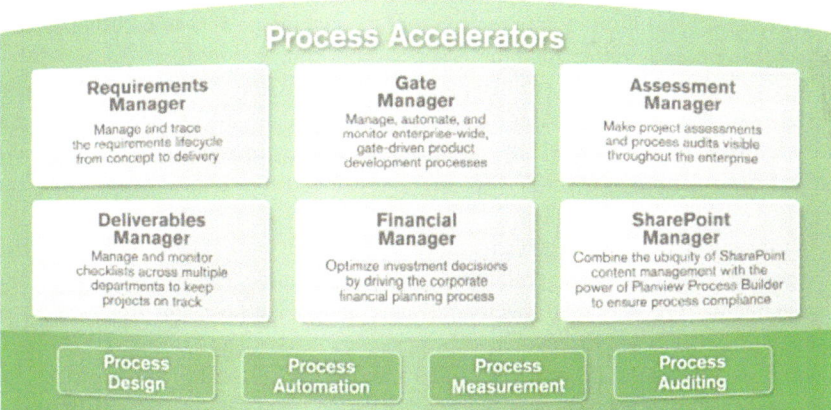

Fig. 15.5 Planview process builder

The project manager may employ tools for recording and managing risks and issues, and this may be as simple as using an Excel spreadsheet. The project manager may maintain lessons learned log to record the lessons learned during a project, and these will be analysed towards the end of a project and the lessons learned report prepared. The project reporting may be done with a tool or with a standard Microsoft Word report.

15.5   Review Questions

1. Why are tools used in project management?
2. How should a tool be selected?
3. What is the relationship between the process and the tool?
4. What tools would you recommend for project management?
5. Describe how you would go about selecting a tool for project scheduling.
6. Describe various tools that are available for estimation.
7. What tools would you recommend for project portfolio management?

15.6   Summary

The objective of this chapter was to give a flavour of various tools available to support the organization in software project management. The tools are chosen to support the process, rather than the process supporting the tool.

The project management tools included a discussion of the COCOMO Cost Model, which may be employed to estimate the cost and effort for a project; and the Microsoft Project tool, which is used extensively by project managers to schedule and track their projects. We discussed the ProjectLibre tool which is a popular alternative to Microsoft Project.

We discussed the ProjectManager tool which is a scaleable software-as-a-service tool that supports collaboration across teams The Planview Portolio Management Tool was also discussed, and this tool allows an organization to manage a portfolio of projects.

Tool selection is done in a controlled manner. First, the requirements for the tool are determined and several candidate tools are evaluated. A decision on the proposed tool is made and a pilot is conducted to ensure that it is fit for purpose. Finally, the end users are trained on the use of the tool and it is rolled out throughout the organization.

Reference

1. B. Boehm, *Software Engineering Economics* (Prentice Hall, New Jersey, 1981)

Continuous Improvement of Project Management

16

Key Topics

Software Process
Software Process Improvement
Process Mapping
Benefits of Software Process Improvement
CMMI
ISO/IEC 15504 (SPICE)
ISO 9000
PSP and TSP
Root Cause Analysis
Six Sigma

16.1 Introduction

The success of business today is highly influenced by the functionality and quality of the software, and it is essential that the software is safe, reliable, of a high quality, and fit for purpose. Companies may develop their own software internally, or they may acquire software solutions off-the-shelf or from bespoke software development. Software development companies need to deliver high-quality and reliable software consistently on time to their customers.

Cost is a key driver in most organizations and it is essential that software is produced as cheaply and efficiently as possible, and that waste is reduced or eliminated in the software development process. In a nutshell, companies need to produce software that is *better, faster, and cheaper* than their competitors in order to survive in the marketplace. In other words, they need to work smarter to improve their businesses and to deliver superior solutions to their customers.

© The Author(s), under exclusive license to Springer Nature Switzerland AG 2025   271
G. O'Regan, *Guide to Software Project Management*, Undergraduate Topics in
Computer Science, https://doi.org/10.1007/978-3-031-80578-3_16

Software process improvement initiatives are aligned with business goals and play a key role in helping companies achieve their strategic goals. It allows companies to focus on fire prevention rather than fire fighting, and to problem solve key issues to eliminate quality problems. Companies need to critically examine their current processes to determine the extent to which they meet their needs, as well as identify how the processes may be improved, and identify where waste can be minimized or eliminated.

Software process improvement (SPI) allows companies to mature their software engineering processes, and to achieve their business goals more effectively. It leads to a focus on the process and on ways to improve it. Problems are often caused by a defective process, and a focus on the process helps to avoid the blame culture that arises when blame is apportioned to individuals. This leads to a culture of openness in discussing problems and their solutions, and in instilling process ownership among the process practitioners.

The benefits of successful process improvement include the consistent delivery of high-quality software, improved financial results, and increased customer satisfaction. It has become an indispensable tool for software engineers and managers to achieve their goals and provides a return on investment.

16.2   Software Process Improvement

The origins of the software process improvement field were discussed in Chap. 8, where we discussed the work of Shewhart on statistical process control. His work was later refined by Deming and Juran, who argued that high-quality processes are essential to the delivery of a high-quality product.

Watt Humphries and others at the SEI applied Deming and Juran's approach to the software quality field leading to the birth of the software process improvement field (SPI). Software process improvement is concerned with practical action to improve the software processes in the organization to ensure that business goals are achieved more effectively (Fig. 16.1).

Definition 16.1 (*Software Process Improvement*) A program of activities designed to improve the performance and maturity of the organization's software processes.

Software process improvement initiatives support the organization in achieving its key business goals more effectively, where the business goals could be delivering software faster to the market, improving quality, and reducing or eliminating waste. The objective is to work smarter and to build software better, faster, and cheaper than competitors. It makes business sense and provides a return on investment.

There are international standards and models available to support software process improvement such as the CMMI Model, the ISO 90001 standard, and ISO 15504 (popularly known as SPICE). The CMMI model includes best practice for processes in software and systems engineering. The ISO 9001 standard is a quality

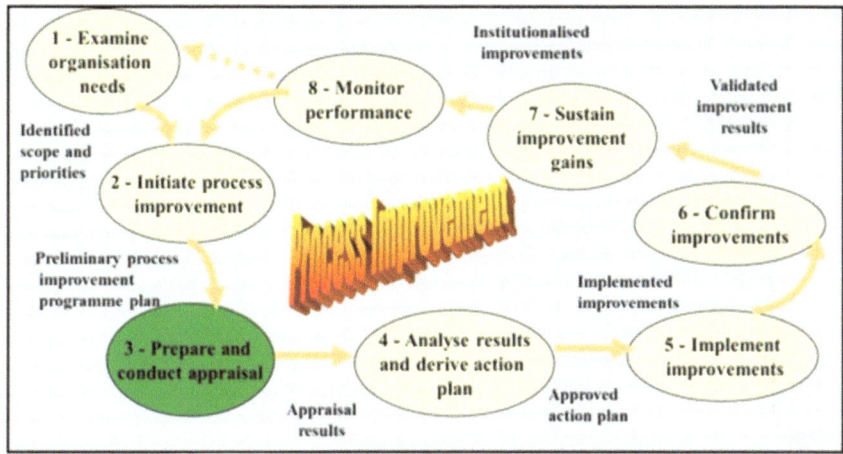

Fig. 16.1   Steps in process improvement

management system that may be employed in hardware, software development, or service companies. The ISO 15504 standard is an international standard for software process improvement and process assessment, which is popular in the automotive and medical device sectors.

Software process improvement is concerned with defining the right processes and following them consistently. It involves training all staff on the new processes, refining the processes, and continuously improving them. It enables the organization to improve and achieve its business goals more effectively.

16.2.1   What is a Software Process?

A software development process is the process used by software engineers to design and develop computer software. It may be an undocumented ad hoc process as devised by the team for a particular project, or it may be a standardized and documented process used by various teams on similar projects. The process is seen as the glue that ties people, technology, and procedures coherently together.

The processes for software development include processes to determine the requirements; processes for the design and development of the software; processes to verify that the software is fit for purpose; and processes to maintain the software.

Definition 16.2 (*Software Process*) A *process* is a set of practices or tasks performed to achieve a given purpose. It may include tools, methods, material and people.

The process is an abstraction of the way in which work is done, and it is seen as the glue that ties people, procedures, and tools together (Fig. 16.2). An organization will typically have many processes in place for doing its work, and

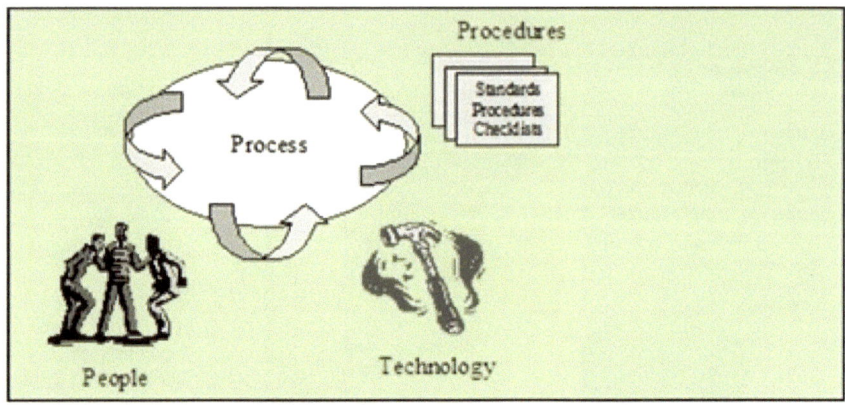

Fig. 16.2 Process as glue for people, procedures and tools

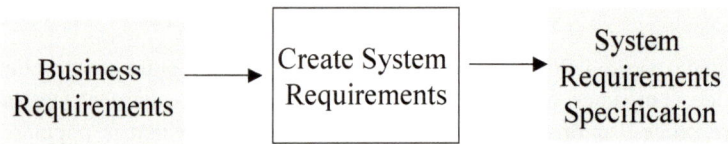

Fig. 16.3 Sample process map

the object of process improvement is to improve these to meet business goals more effectively.

The Software Engineering Institute (SEI) argues that there is a close relationship between the quality of the delivered software and the quality and maturity of the underlying processes employed to create the software.

A process is often represented by a process map which details the flow of activities and tasks. The process map will typically include the inputs to each activity as well as the output from an activity. Often, the output from one activity will become an input to the next activity. A simple example of a process map for creating the system requirements specification is described in Fig. 16.3.

As a process matures it is defined in more detail and documented. It will have clearly defined entry and exit criteria, inputs and outputs, an explicit description of the tasks, verification of the process, and consistent implementation.

16.2.2 Benefits of Software Process Improvement

The benefits of software process improvement include:

Improvements to customer satisfaction
Improvements to on-time delivery
Improved consistency in budget and schedule delivery
Improvements to quality
Reductions in the cost of poor quality
Improvements in productivity
Reductions to the cost of software development
Improvements to employee morale.

16.2.3 Software Process Improvement Models

The CMMI model (see Chap. 8) defines best practice for software processes in the organization. It describes what the processes should do rather than how they should be done, and it needs to be interpreted and tailored to meet the needs of the organization. A process model provides a common language and shared vision for improvement. Popular process models include:

Capability Maturity Model Integration (CMMI)
ISO 9001 Standard
ISO 15504
PSP and TSP.

The CMMI provides a clearly defined roadmap for improvement, and it allows the organization to improve at its own pace. Its approach is evolutionary rather than revolutionary, and it recognizes that a balance is required between project needs and process improvement needs. It allows the processes to evolve from ad hoc immature activities to disciplined mature processes. A SCAMPI appraisal determines the actual process maturity of an organization and allows the organization to benchmark itself against other organizations.

ISO 9001 is an internationally recognized quality management standard, and it is customer and process focused. It applies to the processes that an organization uses to create and control products and services, and it emphasizes continuous improvement (ISO 9004). The standard is designed to apply to any product or service that an organization supplies.

The ISO/IEC 15504 standard (popularly known as ISO SPICE) is an international standard for process assessment. It includes guidance for process improvement and process capability determination, as well as guidance for performing an assessment. It uses the international standard for software and systems lifecycle processes (ISO/IEC 12207) as its process model.

The Personal Software Process (PSP) is a disciplined data-driven process that is designed to help software engineers understand and improve their personal software process performance. It helps engineers to improve their estimation and planning skills, and to reduce the number of defects in their work.

The Team Software Process (TSP) is a structured approach to help software teams understand and improve their quality and productivity. Its focus is on building an effective software development team, and it involves establishing team goals, assigning team roles as well as other teamwork activities.

16.2.4 Process Mapping

The starting point for improving a process is to first understand the process as it is currently performed and to then determine its effectiveness. The stakeholders reach a common understanding of how the process is currently performed, and the process is then sketched pictorially, with the activities and their inputs and outputs recorded graphically. This graphical representation is termed a "*process map*", and is an abstract description of the process "*as is*".

The process map is an abstraction of the way that work is done, and it is critically examined to identify weaknesses and potential improvements. This leads to the proposed new process sketched in a process map to yield the process "*to be*".

Once the definition of the new process is agreed, the supporting templates are identified from an examination of the input and output of the various activities. There may be a need for standards to support the process (e.g., procedures and templates), which provide the details on how the process is to be carried out.

16.2.5 Process Improvement Initiatives

The need for a software process improvement initiative often arises from the realization that the organization needs to improve to achieve its business goals more effectively. The business goals may be:

Delivering high-quality products on time
Delivering products faster to the market
Reducing the cost of software development
Improving software quality.

Team members will typically be working part-time on improvements in a small organization, whereas a larger organization may assign some people full-time to the initiative. Once the business goals are defined the initiative commences with an appraisal to determine the current strengths and weaknesses of the processes; formulating a process improvement plan; implementing the plan; piloting the new

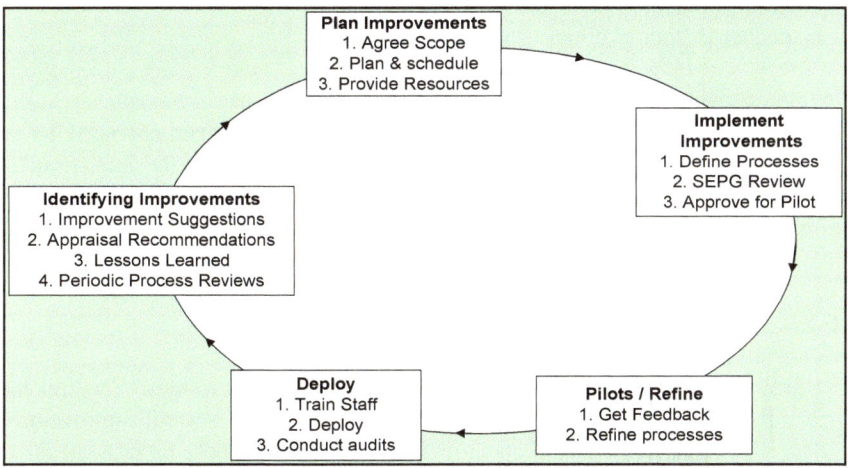

Fig. 16.4   Continuous improvement cycle

processes and verifying that they are effective; training staff and rolling out the new processes (Fig. 16.4). The software process improvement philosophy is:

- The improvement initiative is based on business needs
- Improvements are based on the strengths and weaknesses of the processes
- The improvements are prioritized (it is not possible to do everything at once)
- The improvement initiative needs to be planned and managed as a project
- The results achieved are reviewed at the end of cycle, and a new cycle started
- Organizational culture (and training) needs to be considered
- There needs to be a process champion/project manager
- Senior management need to be 100% committed to the success of the initiative
- Staff need to be involved in the improvement initiative, and there needs to be a balance between project needs and the improvement activities.

16.2.6   Barriers to Success

Some reasons for the failure of software process improvement initiatives are:

Unrealistic expectations
Trying to do too much at once
Lack of Senior Management Sponsorship
Focusing on a Maturity Level
Poor Project Management of the initiative
Insufficient involvement of staff
Insufficient time to work on improvements
Inadequate training on Software Process Improvement

Lack of pilots to validate new processes
Inadequate training/rollout of new processes.

An improvement initiative is a project and needs to be managed as such. A project manager is assigned to manage the initiative; senior management need to be 100% committed to its success and staff available to work on the improvement activities. All employees need to receive appropriate training on software process improvement.

16.2.7 Setting up an Improvement Initiative

The project manager will prepare a plan to implement the initiative within the approved schedule and budget. The project may consist of several improvement cycles, with each improvement cycle implementing one or more process areas.

One of the earliest activities carried out is an appraisal to determine the current strengths and weaknesses of the processes, as well as gaps with respect to the practices in the model. This allows management in the organization to understand its current maturity with respect to the model, and to communicate where it wants to be, as well as how it plans to get there.

The project manager then prepares a project plan and schedule. The plan will detail the scope of the initiative, the budget, the process areas to be implemented, the teams and resources required, the initial risks identified, the key milestones, and so on. The schedule will detail the deliverables to be produced, the resources required, and the associated timeline for delivery. The steps in the improvement cycle are:

Identify Improvements to be made
Plan Improvements
Implement Improvements
Pilots/Refine[1]
Deploy
Do It All Again.

16.2.8 Appraisals

An appraisal is an independent examination of the software engineering and management practices in the organization to identify the current maturity, strengths, and weaknesses in the processes and any gaps that exist with respect to the maturity model. An initial appraisal is conducted at the start of the initiative to allow the

---

[1] The result from the pilot may be that the new process is not suitable to be deployed in the organization or that it needs to be significantly revised prior to deployment.

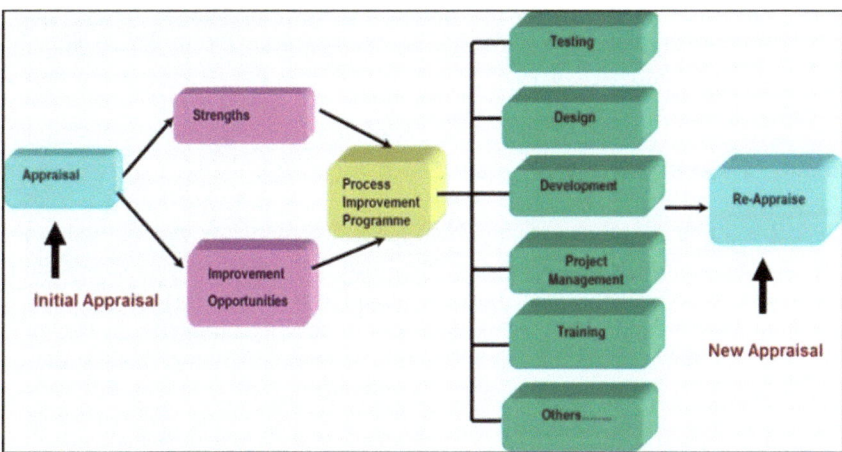

Fig. 16.5 Appraisals

organization to plan and prioritize improvements for the first improvement cycle. The improvements are then implemented, and an appraisal is conducted at the end of the cycle to confirm the progress made (Fig. 16.5).

The appraisal activities include presentations, interviews, reviews of project documentation, and detailed analysis to determine the extent to which the practices in the model have been implemented.

The appraisal leader will present the appraisal findings, which may include a presentation and an appraisal report. The appraisal output summarizes the strengths and weaknesses, and ratings of the process areas are provided (where this is part of the appraisal). The findings are used to plan the next improvement cycle, and it allows the organization to:

- Understand its current process maturity (including strengths and weaknesses)
- Relate its strengths and weaknesses to the improvement model
- Prioritize its improvements for the next improvement cycle
- Benchmark itself against other organizations (for SCAMPI Class A appraisal).

16.3   Improving Project Management

It is important to have best-in-class processes for project management and to perform periodic reviews of the processes used in the organization to ensure that they continue to meet the needs of the business. There are several well-known project management methodologies such as Prince 2 and Project Management Professional that contain best practice in project management, and an organization may improve its project management processes by tailoring some of these processes to improve its project management processes.

The CMMI provides a structured approach to software process improvement, and it contains several process areas that may be used by an organization to improve its project management processes.

16.3.1 Best Practice in Prince 2 Methodology

Prince 2 is a popular project management methodology that is widely used in the U.K. and Europe. It is a structured, process-driven approach to project management, with processes for project start up, initiating a project, controlling a stage, managing stage boundaries, closing a project, managing product delivery, planning, and directing a project. It has procedures to coordinate people and activities, as well as procedures to monitor and control project activities (Fig. 5.5).

These key processes are summarized in Table 5.5, and more detailed information on Prince 2 is in [1]. Prince 2 Agile is an extension to the original Prince 2 methodology that supports the Agile environment.

16.3.2 Best Practice in Project Manager Professional (PMP)

Project Manager Professional (PMP) is an internationally recognized project management qualification offered by the Project Management Institute (PMI). It is a process based on the work performed as processes, and it provides guidelines for managing projects, and describes the project management lifecycle and its related processes. PMP certification involves an exam based on PMI's project management body of knowledge (PMBOK).

The project management body of knowledge is a body of knowledge for project management, and the PMBOK guide is a subset of the project management body of knowledge. It was first published by the PMI in 1996 and the 6th edition provides support for Agile [2].

16.3.3 Best Practice with CMMI

The CMMI includes several process areas that are directly related to project management, and their implementation leads to an improved and more effective project management process. The first step to improving the process is to do an appraisal of the set of CMMI process areas related to project management using the continuous representation of the CMMI (Fig. 16.6).

The appraisal will lead to a capability profile of the project management process areas in the organization, and the gap between the current capability profile and the targeted capability profile of the organization needs to be addressed in an improvement program for project management (Fig. 16.7 and Table 16.1).

The CMMI processes include several level 2 process areas such as the project planning process area, which is concerned with the estimation and planning for the

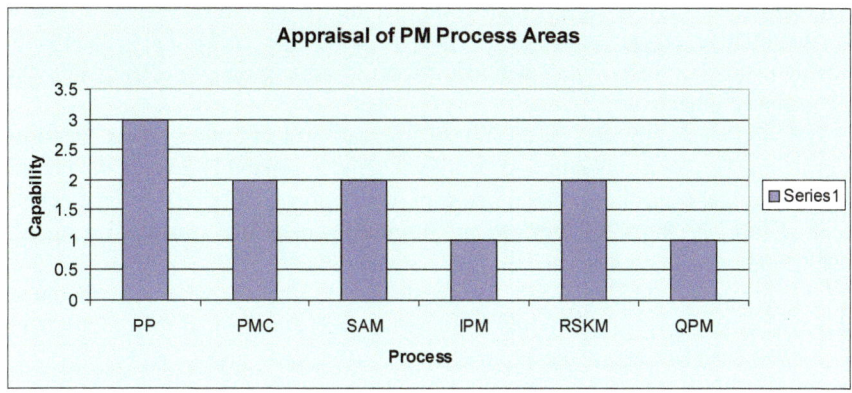

Fig. 16.6 Appraisal of PM process areas

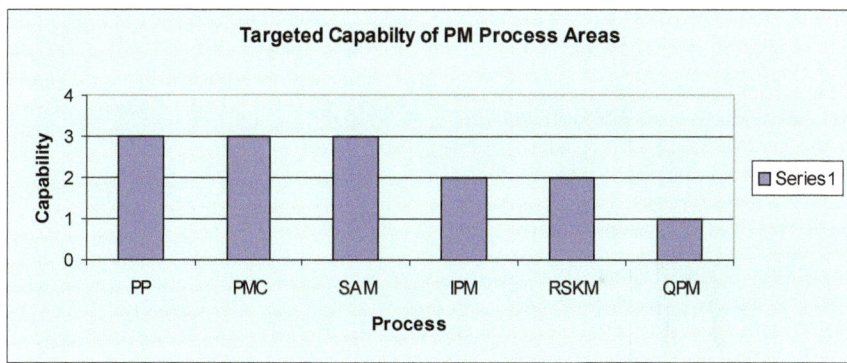

Fig. 16.7 Targeted capability profile of PM process areas

project and maintaining the plan (Table 16.2); the project monitoring and control process area is concerned with monitoring project execution and taking corrective action when progress deviates from the plan (Table 16.3); and the supplier agreement management process area is concerned with the selection and management of the supplier (Table 16.4).

There are two level 3 process areas for project management including the integrated project management process area which is concerned with tailoring the organization's set of standard processes to define the project's defined process, and the project is managed according to the project's defined process; and the risk management process area which is concerned with the identification and management of risk.

Finally, there is one level 4 process area for project management which is the quantitative project management process area. It is concerned with quantitatively managing the project's defined process to achieve the project's quality and performance objectives.

The appraisal provides a profile of current project management maturity (Fig. 16.6). The project planning capability is rated at capability level 3, the project monitoring and control, supplier agreement management, and risk management are rated at level 2, and the integrated project management and quantitative project management are rated at level 1.

The targeted capability profile for project management is where the organization wishes to be (Fig. 16.7), and the gap between current and target capability needs to be addressed in the improvement programme, and there may also be some improvement recommendations from the appraisal to be implemented. The capability levels are defined in Table 16.1.

The project monitoring and control process area, supplier agreement management, and integrated project management process need improvements to achieve the targeted capability level. This requires the implementation of the specific goals and practices and the generic goals and practices for capability level 2 for the integrated project management process area. The project monitoring and control and the supplier agreement management process area require the implementation of the generic goals and practices for capability level 3.

Table. 16.1 CMMI capability levels

Capability level	Description
Incomplete (0)	The process does not implement all of the capability level one generic and specific practices. The process is either not performed or partially performed
Performed (1)	A process that performs all of the specific practices and satisfies its specific goals. Performance may not be stable
Managed (2)	A process at this level has infrastructure to support the process. It is managed: i.e., planned and executed in accordance with policy, its users are trained; it is monitored, controlled, and audited for adherence to its process description
Defined (3)	A process at this level has a defined process: i.e., a managed process that is tailored from the organization's set of standard processes. It contributes work products, measures, and other process improvement information to the organization's process assets
Quantitatively Managed (4)	A process at this level is a quantitatively managed process: i.e., a defined process that is controlled by statistical techniques. Quantitative objectives for quality and process performance are established and used to control the process
Optimizing (5)	A process at this level is an optimizing process: i.e., a quantitatively managed process that is continually improved through incremental and innovative improvements

Table. 16.2 CMMI requirements for project planning process area

Specific goal	Specific practice	Description of specific goal/practice
SG 1		*Establish estimates*
	SP 1.1	Establish scope of project
	SP 1.2	Establish estimates of work products and task attributes
	SP 1.3	Define project life cycle
	SP 1.4	Establish estimates of effort and cost
SG 2		*Develop a project plan*
	SP 2.1	Establish the budget and schedule
	SP 2.2	Identify project risks
	SP 2.3	Plan for data management
	SP 2.4	Plan for project resources
	SP 2.5	Plan for needed knowledge and skills
	SP 2.6	Plan stakeholder involvement
	SP 2.7	Establish the project plan
SG 3		*Obtain commitment to the plan*
	SP 3.1	Review plans that affect the project
	SP 3.2	Reconcile work and resource levels
	SP 3.3	Obtain plan commitment

Table. 16.3 CMMI requirements for project monitoring and control

Specific goal	Specific practice	Description of specific practice/goal
SG 1		*Monitor project against plan*
	SP 1.1	Monitor project planning parameters
	SP 1.2	Monitor commitments
	SP 1.3	Monitor project risks
	SP 1.4	Monitor data management
	SP 1.5	Monitor stakeholder involvement
	SP 1.6	Conduct progress reviews
	SP 1.7	Conduct milestone reviews
SG 2		*Manage corrective action to closure*
	SP 2.1	Analyse issues
	SP 2.2	Take corrective action
	SP 2.3	Manage corrective action

Table. 16.4 CMMI requirements for supplier agreement management

Specific goal	Specific practice	Description of specific practice/goal
SG 1		*Establish supplier agreements*
	SP 1.1	Determine acquisition types
	SP 1.2	Select suppliers
	SP 1.3	Establish supplier agreements
SG 2		*Satisfy supplier agreements*
	SP 2.1	Execute the supplier agreement
	SP 2.2	Monitor selected supplier processes
	SP 2.3	Evaluate selected supplier work products
	SP 2.4	Accept the acquired product
	SP 2.5	Transition products

Table 16.2 specifies the CMMI requirements for the project planning process area, including requirements for estimation and requirements for developing and obtaining commitment to the project plan.

Table 16.3 specifies the CMMI requirements for project monitoring and control process area, and includes requirements for monitoring the project parameters, and managing corrective action.

The purpose of the supplier agreement management process area is to manage the acquisition of software from a supplier. It is concerned with best practice for establishing and satisfying supplier agreements, and includes practices to select suppliers; defining an agreement with the supplier; executing the agreement; and accepting the supplier product as discussed in Chap. 10. The specific goals and practices are stated in Table 16.4.

The implementation of these process areas involves implementing specific and generic goals and practices (up to the targeted capability level).

There is more detailed information on software process improvement and the implementation of the CMMI in [3].

16.4   Review Questions

1. What is a software process?
2. What is software process improvement?
3. What are the benefits of software process improvement?
4. Describe the various models available for software process improvement.
5. Draw the process map for the process of cooking your favourite meal.
6. Describe how a process improvement initiative may be run.
7. What are the main barriers to successful software process improvement?
8. Describe the three phases of an appraisal.

16.5   Summary

Software process improvement plays a key role in helping companies to improve their software engineering capability. It allows companies to focus on fire prevention rather than fire fighting and enables organizations to implement best practice in software engineering. It involves critically examining their processes to determine the extent to which they are fit for purpose, and in identifying improvements.

Software process improvement initiatives lead to a focus on the process, which leads to a culture of openness in discussing problems, and instils process ownership among the process practitioners. It has become an indispensable tool for software engineers and managers to achieve their goals, and it provides a return on investment to the organization.

Software process improvement may be limited to project management improvements, and this involves focusing on improvements to the CMMI processes related to project management or using best practice from methodologies such as Prince 2 or Project Manager Professional.

References

1. PRINCE2, *Managing Successful Projects with PRINCE2* (Office of Government Commerce, 2004)
2. PMBOK Guide, *A Guide to the Project Management Body of Knowledge*, 6th edn. (Project Management Institute, 2017)
3. G. O'Regan, *Introduction to Software Process Improvement* (Springer, London, 2010)

Epilogue   17

We embarked on a long journey in this book and set ourselves the objective of providing a concise introduction to the ethical software project management field to students and practitioners. The objective was to give the reader a grasp of the fundamentals of the software project management field, as well as guidance on how to apply the theory in an industrial environment.

Chapter 1 gave a broad overview of software engineering and discussed various software lifecycles and the phases in software development. We discussed requirements gathering and specification, software design, implementation, testing, and maintenance. The lightweight Agile methodology was discussed, and it has become mainstream in the industry.

Chapter 2 discussed professional responsibility and we discussed the code of ethics of various bodies such as the British Computer Society, the Institute of Electrical and Electronic Engineers, and the Association of Computing Machinery. Chapter 3 discussed ethical software engineering and we discussed notable failures such as the space shuttle disaster and the defective Therac-25 radiotherapy machine.

Chapter 4 was concerned with the ethical and professional responsibilities of project managers. Project managers have a professional responsibility and are required to behave ethically at all times with their clients.

Chapter 5 gave an introduction to project management for traditional software engineering, and we discussed project estimation, project planning and scheduling, project monitoring and control, risk management, managing communication and change, and managing project quality. We concluded with a discussion on the Prince 2 and Project Management Professional approaches to project management.

Chapter 6 discussed software project planning and discussed activities such as project initiation, effort estimation, project planning and scheduling, and risk identification. We discussed the preparation and evaluation of the business case to

G. O'Regan, *Guide to Software Project Management*, Undergraduate Topics in Computer Science, https://doi.org/10.1007/978-3-031-80578-3_17

determine if the project makes business sense, and we discussed the composition of the project board.

Chapter 7 discussed risk management activities such as risk identification, analysing and evaluating the risks, identifying responses to the risk, and selecting and implementing a response to risk. We concluded with a case study on risk management in dealing with COVID-19 that was prevalent throughout the world from early 2020 to early 2022.

Chapter 8 discussed software quality management for projects, and it is essential that the software is safe, reliable, and fit for purpose. We discussed software inspections, testing, audits, quality reviews, and frameworks such as the CMMI and ISO 9000 that play a useful role in improving effectiveness in quality management. We discussed various problem-solving tools to support quality management.

Chapter 9 discussed project monitoring and control and this involves monitoring project execution against the plan, and taking corrective action when progress deviates from expectations. It involves monitoring the project activities and checking that they are completed on schedule and with the required quality, and re-planning where appropriate.

Chapter 10 is concerned with the selection and management of a software supplier. It discussed how candidate suppliers are identified, and formally evaluated against defined selection criteria, and how the appropriate supplier is selected. We discussed how the selected supplier is managed during the project.

Chapter 11 is concerned with the activities during project closure, which include the successful completion of the customer acceptance testing, the handover of the software to the customer, and the preparation of the lessons learned report and the end project report.

Chapter 12 discussed software configuration management and discussed the fundamental concept of a baseline. Configuration management is concerned with identifying those deliverables that must be subject to change control and controlling changes to them.

Chapter 13 discussed the Agile methodology which is mainstream in software development. Agile provides opportunities to assess the direction of a project throughout the development lifecycle, and ongoing changes to requirements are considered normal in the Agile world. It has a strong collaborative style of working, and it advocates adaptive planning and evolutionary development.

Chapter 14 is concerned with metrics for project management, and we discussed the balanced scorecard which assists in identifying appropriate metrics for the organization. The Goal, Question, Metrics (GQM) approach was discussed, and this allows appropriate metrics related to the organization goals to be defined. A selection of sample metrics for an organization was presented.

Chapter 15 discussed various tools to support project management. We discussed the Cocomo estimating approach developed by Barry Boehm in the late 1970s. We discussed the ProjectLibre tool which is an alternative to Microsoft Project. We also discussed ProjectManager, Jira, and Planview.

Chapter 16 discussed process improvement of project management. We discussed the benefits of a software process improvement initiative and discussed best practice in project management from methodologies such as Prince2 and Project Management Professional (PMP). We discussed how the CMMI may be used to improve project management.

This chapter is the concluding chapter in which we summarize the journey travelled in this book.

17.1   The Future of Project Management

Software engineering has come a long way since the 1950s and 1960s, when it was accepted that the completed software would always contain lots of defects, and that the coding should be done as quickly as possible, to enable these defects to be quickly identified and corrected.

The software crisis in the late 1960s highlighted problems with budget and schedule overruns, as well as problems with the quality and reliability of the delivered software. This led to the birth of software engineering as a discipline in its own right, and the realization that programming is quite distinct from science and mathematics.

This led to a plethora of approaches to support software engineering such as waterfall and spiral models, structured methods, object-oriented design and programming, CASE tools, formal methods, and the process approach with frameworks such as the CMMI, and the Agile methodology.

There has been a growing trend of professionalism at all levels in the software sector, with professional qualifications for various roles in the software engineering field. Prince 2 and Project Management Professional are widely used project management standards with thousands of Prince 2 or PMP certified project managers around the world. The fact that these project managers are certified practitioners of leading project management methodologies provides additional confidence in their ability to deliver projects on time, on budget, and with the right quality.

There has been a move towards remote working and remote teams, and a hybrid model became popular during the COVID-19 pandemic with many companies adjusting their work practices accordingly. This trend is likely to continue in the coming years with remote project management becoming increasingly important.

Index

A
ACM Code of Ethics, 37
Agile development, 12, 13
Agile Test Principles, 229
Analogy method, 78
Appraisals, 278
Ariane 5 disaster, 8
Audits, 152

B
Balanced Scorecard, 236
Barriers to Success, 277
Baseline, 209
BCS Code of Conduct, 37
Bespoke software, 65
Breakthrough and Control, 139
Business case, 75, 99, 102

C
Celebrate Success, 202
Change Control, 214
Change control board, 85
Change request, 85
Clarity PPM, 267
Clearcase, 209
Clearquest, 209
CMMI Maturity Levels, 148
CMMI Maturity Model, 22
CMMI model, 146, 275
Cocomo, 262, 263
Codes of Conduct, 32
Communication Plan, 111
Complete Administration, 202
Computer Ethics, 31
Configuration Control, 210
Configuration Identification, 210

Configuration management, 207
Configuration management audits, 215
Configuration management plan, 117, 213
Configuration Management System, 211
Continuous Software Development, 14
Corporate social responsibility, 30
Cost of poor quality, 255
Cost predictor models, 78
COVID-19, 131
Customer Care Metrics, 251
Customer Satisfaction Metrics, 239

D
Data Gathering for Metrics, 257
David Lean, 49
Deployment Plan, 117
Development Quality Metrics, 245
Document Control Management, 212

E
Earned Value Analysis, 178
End Project Report, 202
Escrow agreement, 67, 190
Estimation, 76, 107
Estimation in Agile, 225
Estimation Techniques, 77, 108
Ethical Outsourcing, 192
Ethical Software Testing, 55
Ethics, 59
European Space Agency, 8
Evaluate Proposals, 189
Expert judgement, 78

F
Fagan inspections, 5, 21